The Solar Way
Nina Roudnikova

My mind is as bright as the sun. The heart is as pure as a crystal. The soul is as big as the universe. The Spirit is as powerful as God - and is one with Him.

D1730701

The Solar Way

Nina Roudnikova

English Translation of text, copyright © 2021 Shin Publications

First Edition

Published 2021 by Shin Publications, England

ISBN: 978-1-9163365-8-2

http://alchemical-weddings.com/

This new English translation of Nina Pavlovna Roudnikova's magical book, The
Solar Path – first published in the Russian language in 1936 - was completed
during the full harvest moon of September 2021, at the cusp of the fall equinox
and published on All Saint's Day of the same season.

On the front cover: Nicholas Roerich, Mother of the World / Матерь Мира
(Mater' Mira), 1924 {{PD-US-expired}}

Tarot Arcana images used throughout are from Papus, Le Tarot Divinatoire. They
are public domain images supplied by: https://insightfulvision.com. Whilst in a
similar tradition, these were not the images originally used by Nina Roudnikova,
which are likely to have been from the Schmakov or Mebes tarot books. As such,
some small but not especially signficant differences might be noted between her
descriptions of the symbolic images and the images themselves.

Dedicated to

Our Lady of Walsingham

&

Saint Seraphim of Sarov

Jesus said:

"I have cast fire upon the world, and look, I'm guarding it until it blazes."

(Gospel of St Thomas, 10)

Limbourg brothers, Les très riches heures du Duc de Berry,
Astrological Man

Contents

Ye are the light of the world.

A city that is set on a hill cannot be hid.

Neither do men light a candle,

and put it under a bushel,

but on a candlestick;

and it giveth light

unto all that

are in the

house.

Matthew 5:14

Introduction

Our joy in the acquaintance of Nina Roudnikova (1890-1940) is a reflection of the wonderful lightness in her work, which radiates with all the fullness of the Nineteenth Arcanum, traditionally called The Sun and also known as The Great Work, The Philosopher's Gold – or Stone – and Synthetic Philosophy.

The rays of this light illuminate some of the most heavily veiled aspects of earlier related works, including that of her initiatory master and Superior Incognuu of the legendary St Petersburg occult school of pre-Revolutionary Russia, headed by G.O. Mebes.

Born in St. Petersburg, Nina Roudnikova graduated from the Bestuzhev higher women's courses, where she received a doctor's degree. She was interested in the occult from an early age, especially the field of Egyptian Hermeticism – an inclination she shared with other Russian masters. She searched long for a master and it might be said that fate led her to the society for the study of Tarot Arcana that was headed by G.O.Mebes. She quickly became his first inner circle student.

Mebes was a true son of Holy Russia, which in those years produced hundreds of occult groups in St Petersburg alone, inspired by Titans such as Madame Blavatsky, 'Maharishi' Nikolai Roerich and Rasputin, conditioned by the Spiritist groups and empowered by the shamanistic Russian Folk Soul which enabled Russia to advance in the field of psychic spying long before the CIA picked up that baton during the Cold War. Even in early twentieth century Russia, where occultists flooded to the court of the last Czar, Nicholas II, like bees to honey, Mebes and his school were the flower of the intelligentsia, surpassing the knowledge attained by others who've long inhabited the realm of legends. G.O.M., as he is most usually known, was at the head of the three main branches of the Russian initiating movement – magi, Martinism and Rosicrucianism – with the mystery name 'Butator' (named for the angel of Mathematics) and a kabbalistic wisdom which far exceeds that of other leading lights of the Western Mystery Tradition.

The apartment Mebes shared with his wife, Maria Nesterova, in St Petersburg, was at the centre of magic circles which sincerely created blueprints for the governance of the World by occult means that were later adopted and subverted by other, darker orders, in the wake of the Bolshevik Revolution.

Nina Roudnikova went onto become a doctor by profession and ultimately one of the fabled 'White Russian Sisters', who worked in spiritual opposition to the dark occult forces unleashed by Bolshevism, Nina Roudnikova escaped the Red Terror in the early days of the Revolution and joined the Russian émigré community in Estonia. There she became highly regarded as a healer and teacher of spiritual work, maintaining contact with such illustrious figures as Nicholas and Helena Roerich, with whom she enjoyed a close relationship and fruitful correspondence.

She was twice married, first to Gavrila Yelachich, with whom she moved to Tallin, Estonia in 1919 alongside the retreating North-Western Army. She divorced him two years later and married Baron Andrey Vladimirovich Ikskul.

Though her official job was in the editorial office of the newspaper "Freedom of Russia", throughout the 1930s Roudnikova also worked in service of the white emigrant intelligence agencies, developing close ties with its head, Colonel Boris Engelhardt, a former member of the Russian State Duma and commandant of Petrograd during the February Revolution. In 1932 she was instructed by the ROVS (Russian General Military Union) to let herself be recruited by Soviet intelligence, which she was able to misinform for some time.

Already closely connected with the Tallinn society of metaphysical research, in 1937 Nina founded her spiritual society, 'Solar Way', for which she asked the Roerichs to send her blessings from the Great Teachers of the East, which they did by way of a letter that same year. Elena Ivanovna Roerich was highly appreciative of Nina Roudnikova, noting her exceptional intellectual level and deep knowledge. Nina, in turn, was sympathetic to the Roerichs' mission, contrary to the opinion of most of the leaders of the Theosophical society, who were jealous of the new teaching and its heralds.

A prolific lecturer and disseminator of knowledge, Nina was also a woman of letters, producing several dozen books and articles devoted to various issues of human development. Her most regular publishing channel was the journal "Occultism and Yoga", which was published for several decades, first in Europe and then South America. She was also a wonderful poet and writer of spiritual works, but the bulk of her huge manuscript heritage did not get into print and was lost during the Second World War. After the war, one of the issues of the collection "Occultism and Yoga" renewed in Asuncion (Paraguay) (1960, book. 23) saw the publication of her mystery poem, "Lazarus", written in Estonia in 1919-1921 in collaboration with her first husband G. Elachich.

A member of the Revel Literary Circle, her poems and articles about the occult were published in the Tallinn newspaper "Dawn", the magazines "Clouds" and "In a Foreign Land". Nina most frequently published her articles in the journal "Occultism and Yoga", published for several decades, first in Europe, then in South America by Dr. Aseev, a follower of the Teaching of Living Ethics. Extremely well connected with the leading occult circles of his day, Dr Aseev was also on friendly terms with the Roerichs, who were also published in this publication.

In 1936, Roudnikova gave a series of lectures at the Tallinn Society for Metapsychic Research, which later became the basis of her most famous book "Sacred Mysticism of Egypt. 22 steps of the initiatory path". The content of this work – and the present volume - is devoted to the presentation of 22 secrets of the universe, represented by 22 principles and laws, considered both from the macrocosmic, universal, and from the microcosmic, human point of view.

As a prominent Theosophist and one of the most favoured pupils of Mebes – himself at the pinnacle of Russian Freemasonry, Rosicrucian, Templar and Kabbalistic occult schools – Nina had left the motherland with more than a few worldly possessions and the will to survive. She also carried with her meticulous notes from the lectures Mebes gave to both his outer circle of initiates and the veiled inner circles to which she belonged, the only works of the master which would survive the ruthless intellectual purges of the OGPU, the secret police of the Bolshevik regime.

The OGPU caught up with Mebes himself in 1926, in what became known as the Case of the Leningrad Freemasons. The Master was arrested, accused of being a 'Black Magician' and sent to a gulag on the White Sea islands where he is believed to have died four years later.

Nina Roudnikova, therefore, helped ensure the survival of the greatest occult teachings of the modern era, which through her would find their way across Western Europe – where having escaped Lenin and Stalin they then survived Hitler – to England and then across the Atlantic to South America.

The Russian community in Estonia was the starting point for this activity and it is here that Nina – at the spiritual heart of the community - and others working with her encountered the young Christian Hermeticist, Valentin Tomberg and initiated him into all they knew of The Great Work. Tomberg had a long journey of his own to make but it would eventually bring him as a refugee to England. After spending several Cold War years working as a translator for the BBC, intercepting and interpreting messages from communist Russia, Tomberg took up the baton handed to him by Nina and completed one of the acknowledged spiritual classics of the 20th Century, Meditations on the Tarot, a masterpiece of the 'synthetic philosophy', which brought together the gold and silver threads of Russian occultism, Catholic theology and Hermetic lore.

This book would be given to John Paul II early in his papacy by the maverick theologican, Hans urs von Balthasar, who wrote in his foreword to the German and English editions that Meditations on the Tarot was written by "a thinking, praying Christian of unmistakable purity [who] reveals to us the symbols of Christian Hermeticism in its various levels of mysticism, gnosis and magic, taking in also the Cabbala and certain elements of astrology and alchemy."

John Paul II would make it his mission to bring down communism, not only in his Polish homeland but all across Europe – a mission he shared with the White Russian occultists who formed a spiritual core of resistance to the terrible egregore of Communism which afflicts the world to this day.

Whilst Tomberg, brought the Great Arcana of the Tarot to England and would become their most beloved exponent in the West, another friend of Nina – Catarina Sreznewska-Zelenzeff - was given a copy of her inner circle notes to take to South America, where they eventually took form as the Tarot Minors. Nina asked her friend to transfer the great legacy to 'someone dignified' who would be capable of preserving the lessons for humanity. On that continent and by a series of serendipitous events and acquaintances, they would eventually be taken up by another initiate of Mebes, the Martinist Nicholas Girs, but remained hidden from the English-speaking world until the publication of our translation in April 2020.

Thus it transpired that the primordial tree of knowledge and learning - always rare - was almost but never quite lost to the mists of time. Our task is to ensure the revival of this knowledge from the obscure annals of history and its continued evolution for present and future generations.

*

It is Titanic human personalities and public figures who are most often thought of as fashioning the grand art of History, conceived in the minds of gurus and genii, forged in the fires of war and revolution. Behind such Titans – the Kings, Queens, Popes, Emperors, Military Generals and cultural icons - are enigmatic 'hidden hands', the unknown masters whose words and deeds had a butterfly effect on the shaping of human culture, links in the chain of a more subtle and secret History. It is this, more secret history, that is revealed by the works of the White Russian School.

Nina Roudnikova's Solar Way treads a roughly middle path through the metaphysical and philosophic teachings of Vladimir Shmakov on the one hand and the astral occultism of G.O. Mebes on the other. Her text includes some rather surprising historical information and hitherto unknown details gleaned from mystical societies and secret orders, including the Templars. Like both Shmakov and Mebes she is a disciple of the wisdom of ancient Egypt, which she sets against a background of new spiritual revelations which came to the world through the Theosophy of HP Blavatsky and Agni Yoga of the Roerichs. Like all masterworks of this school her Solar Way has a decidedly 'synthetic' character, which sublimates and synthesises knowledge of key teachings from within the tradition and develops them further with her own unique insights.

The special value of this work is in its consideration of the hidden hermetic wisdom of ancient Egypt in the context of new spiritual revelations brought to humanity through the Theosophical impulse and Agni Yoga.

Nina Roudnikova died of liver cancer on July 15, 1940 in Konigsberg (Prussia).

Goddess Ma'at (or Maat) of Ancient Egypt, Tomb of Siptah, Valley of the Kings,

The Solar Way

N. P. Roudnikova

"The ways of God are as diverse as the breath of the sons of men."

The ways of God – the ways of ascent from the bondage of the material world to the freedom of the spirit - are innumerable, because they are deeply personal. There are as many paths as there are psychic complexes called personalities, and all of them are approaches to the great esoteric path of subjective fusion with the Essence of the Universe and to cosmic creativity. Ultimately, personality is the bridge between matter and spirit. The personality is formed from a combination of various vibrations, or tonalities, of the psychic energy of the environment, grouped around the nuclei of consciousness. Although there are an infinite number of combinations of psychic keys, there are as many basic keys in our system as there are resonators in it that transform synthetic Solar Energy – that is, as many as there are planetary orbits in it (plus the Moon for the Earth). And at all times, in their searches and individual approaches to spiritual manifestation, people are grouped according to these sectors – this is the reason and purpose of the existence of various initiatory schools, systems and cults.
Among them there has always been a synthetic, uniting sector, a way of direct application of the great Solar Energy in its pure untransformed form – the Middle Way, the Fiery Way, the Short Way – the Great Solar Way. And in moments of terrible danger, in moments of spiritual crises, everything positive and benign always rallied around him, everything sought support and support in him - whether it was the mysteries of Ra in Egypt, or Krishna in India, or the Delphic temple of Apollo in Greece, or the Pelican of the Rosicrucian brotherhood.
Because only the Solar Path, merging and transmitting the direct spiritual influx of the Sun, is truly synthetic, it alone is therefore able to maintain the mental balance of the Planet, it alone reconciles and coordinates all other paths, protecting them from hopeless differentiation. Only the Solar Path has the secret of the distribution of the solar influx in its aspects, only it has the key of centripetal and centrifugal orientation in our system, only it is

the direct transmitter of divine Love and Wisdom pouring to us through the prism of the Solar synthetic consciousness.

The study of cosmic mysteries and correspondences requires many incarnations of labour, search and tension. The knowledge of the synthetic essence of the world at three stages of its manifestation syntheses and replaces them all. Over many incarnations the soul can sweep from one sector to another, looking for additions and establishing balance, until it finds their one true, common deep essence. The Solar Path is just the direct unfolding of the core of all formal combinations and tonalities, and its stages correspond to the three stages of the Great Arcana of the Universe, i.e., the Solar Path expresses the three stages of the manifestation of the synthetic Essence of the world. This is the path commanded by Nature itself, which has placed on it the milestones of the natural symbolism of cosmic phenomena. Its light – the great Sun, the door to the world of divine Life, Wisdom and Love - is always with us, we ourselves and everything around us are filled with it; its descending and ascending stages are inscribed with the signs of planetary orbits. The synthetic Solar Path was announced by all the real Teachers of humanity, the embodiments of the spiritual flow of the light Centre. This is the Middle Path of the blessed Buddha; the path of Vedanta Advaita, which denies all form and confirms the Essence; Moses, who proclaims the Divinity of the eternal Subject ("I am the Lord Your God") and he who denies objective forms ("do not make yourself an idol"); these are the words of Christ: "Seek the Kingdom of God first of all, the rest will be added to you." They proclaimed about the shining Solar Path of non-identification with manifestations and creative domination, about the Path that runs over the paths. But people have distorted the meaning of their proclamation. They have turned the royally simple Middle Way into a church full of the most incredible superstitions; the spirit-making of Mosaism has degenerated into wild fanaticism about a materialised religion; the Christian churches do not seek the Kingdom of God, but long for everything that "will be added". The Teacher M. spoke about the Solar synthesis of religions and systems through H. P. Blavatsky, but the Theosophical Society turned into a narrow occult sect. This is the fate of the truths brought to people-truly similar to the fate of precious mechanisms that fall into the hands of children.

And the great Sun - the hearth of consciousness and life - burns in space and pours its love and its creativity into the planetary circles... And the Solar Path exists - close, natural, simple and clear – and is constantly being lost by human consciousness. The Solar Path is the path of the domination of consciousness over forms within itself and in the objective world. In the fiery laboratory of the Solar High consciousness, shining with creative lights, the great quaternary dynamic Law of differentiation of manifestations is transmuted in relation to the life of the Solar System into the "solar cross of elements". These four elements, or the four elements, are the foundation of the entire variety of forms of solar creativity, because the number of their proportional combinations is infinitely large. In the grossest aspect, these are the four states of matter, the combination of which creates bodies; in the mental world, there are four mental qualities that determine the evolution of a person – the boldness of search, the inquisitiveness of knowledge, the concentration of work and responsibility, and the ardent striving for the goal; the ratio between them is a measure of the quality and value of a person. Everywhere and in everything there are four mutually polar solar emanations; the objective world, woven by their innumerable combinations, closes the subjective psychic cross of the personality from all sides and carries it away in a stream of continuous changes, chaining it to the wheel of life by the great power of identifying consciousness with its manifestations.

The Solar Path – the path to subjective liberation - passes through the domination of the four main elements of the solar cross. Domination is acquired by the non-identification of consciousness with its four main manifestations. The non-identification of consciousness is achieved by fixing its spiritual core, its "I", which is always identical to itself, the subject of changes, by the sense of its unchangeable and unchangeable essence and its rooting in the Spiritual Essence of the Cosmos, in the cosmic Subject, in God. Self-consciousness is a synthesis of the four elements of the psychic cross and therefore its master. Self-consciousness combines them expediently, that is, according to the goal set by it, and snatches them out of the power of objective influences that make the personality a toy of causality – that is, it frees it.

"Conquer yourself, and you will be able to conquer the whole world", because a consciously harmonised in its elements, purposefully directed personality, owning its own composition, is a magnet of a powerful impact on the environment, its initiative centre, dominating and controlling the four elements of objectivity.

Domination over the elements of the world is the mainstay of knowledge, because knowledge is provided by domination, which turns it into direct knowledge, into clairvoyance of things, their internal and external regularities, into their infallible pricing, and the painstaking detours of the speculating mind become unnecessary.

Non-identification with manifestations gives the keys to solar creativity and to solar direct cognition.

The Solar Path is the path of Dominion. Dominion is the power over two mutually contradictory processes of solar creativity that intersect in each form and in each consciousness, the power to transmute forms – and responsibility for the fate of the transmuted processes.

Amon-Ra floats on two wings in boundless space, two world forces are the springs of his creativity. Two forces of the one Eternal Life gave birth to him and keep him in balance: centrifugal and centripetal - and these same two forces have coiled in his potential as the levers of his creativity: the differentiation of spiritual syntheses into innumerable forms of their objective manifestations and their integration through the spiritual self-creation of consciousnesses into the radiant synthesis of the centre. A ladder of progressive narrowing of consciousnesses, clothed in differentiating and coarsening energy shells – forms, leads from the centre to the periphery; from the periphery to the centre there are stages of expanding consciousnesses that refine and synthesise forms with their creativity and strive for great spiritual unification.

The mystery of evolution, involution, spiritualisation, and materialisation is contained in the solar creativity of the Universal Good and is expressed in the sphere of influence of its initiative - that is, in the planetary system – by the cooperation of two intertwining triangles of planets that materialise and spiritualise the life of our Solar world. The six Solar planets- Mercury, Venus, Earth, Mars, Jupiter and Saturn – are the stages of transmutation of the creativity of the great Solar synthetic consciousness.

Dominion – as part of one's personality over the two streams of Life and their sevenfold manifestation (including the shining Centre of the system itself) - is not only dominion over them, but also the power to replenish and correct them with appropriate energy vibrations from the solar environment. It is achieved by not identifying oneself either with the phenomena of a centrifugal flow controlled by the law of causality, or with a centripetal flow controlled by the law of expediency. This is possible only when one's consciousness is fixed in a fixed centre, in the Sun, which covers all the stages of the periphery and the entire energy cycle of the manifestation of Life in the system. The unification of one's personal consciousness with the synthetic consciousness of the Sun is the key to dominion, this is the second stage of the Solar Path, which always runs through the centres of the planes of consciousness along the elusive, but all-pervading Axis of the World. Dominion over the ways, i.e. above the crossing of two directions, is achieved most easily by solar non-attachment to the results of one's creativity, one's actions, because attachment to the results that are subject to the laws of one or another direction, draws consciousness after them into one of the streams and exposes it to the law of the reverse influence of consequences or the causes that gave rise to them, i.e. the law of Karma. Non-attachment to the results deprives the force of this reverse effect. A person becomes the master of Karma and the master not only of himself, but also of the surrounding world, because his actions create the Karma of the surrounding, where the power of the reverse effect of consequences is eliminated. Real creative dominion is reserved for the lights of self-control and self-creation, for whom "giving and waiting for nothing in return" has become a natural impulse of action. Such a consciousness is not afraid of darkness, because it itself glows with sunlight. For such a consciousness, evil is a superstition, and there are no enemies, because in the great creative Solar Path all possibilities are taken into account and all paths are measured.

The Solar Path is the path of Selflessness. Where there is a great flow of Divine Love and Life that generates cosmic creativity, there is no place for thoughts about oneself and self-perception-these thoughts have simply burned out of their insignificance, like moths on the fire of the altar.

The Great Flow of Divine Love and Life has generated in its tensions fiery centres of consciousness and creativity - the Suns of the Universe. Divine Love has confirmed in them the eternal omnipresence of Unity, Divine Life has breathed in the dynamics of boundless changes in their manifestations. The great consciousnesses, established in the Divine Unity, are identified in their action with the ever-flowing stream of Mother Life. The Great Solar consciousnesses form a magnetic centre in the environment - a kind of Divine Magnet - the central Consciousness of the Universe. They are entrusted with the realisation of Love and Life in the sphere of the Solar System. They are a creative prism that refracts, according to its potential, the radiation of divine Love and the flow of Cosmic Life. The great Solar consciousnesses transform the fire of divine Love and Life into the fires of countless creative combinations, into a stream of forms arranged along the steps of planetary orbits and expressing in their synthesis the specific potential of these high consciousnesses living among the fiery energies of our Centre. The representatives and collaborators of their spirit-making, the solvents of forms in the blessed synthesis of the Spirit are the consciousnesses of the three planets located beyond Saturn and each embodying one of the three principles of the spiritual world: All – being as its nature; Bliss as a result of freedom from dependence on forms-its state; and creative Omniscience as the principle of its manifestation.

The light-bearing Solar Souls communicate with the consciousnesses of other fraternal luminaries of the Cosmos by exchanging energies and opportunities, conducting and transforming countless cosmic radiations and emanations and imprinting their traces in the images of our solar-planetary world; they also send the emanations of their system to the distant worlds of space.

The Solar Path does not teach blind worship of these high consciousnesses, although a sense of reverence for ideals is, of course, a necessary companion and a sign of the expansion of consciousness. The Solar Path is the way to Them, to achieve their state of unity with the power of the Cosmic Spirit while preserving the individual potential of creative initiative. Selflessness leads to it, because only with its presence are the conductors of cosmic energy and the transformers of the divine flow of Love and Life forged – this is the only way to become one of the great creative Solar spirits, a true brother of Those Who came to us on Earth under the names of the Great Teachers of humanity.

The synthesis of the Solar Path does not recognise exclusivity. Therefore, the one who follows him embraces all of them with the same love and reverence – former, present and future, known and unknown Cosmic Solar Collaborators and Creators of the Universal Good – he always stands before Them all, knowing that someday he himself will join their ranks.

The Solar Path rejects time and unites all those who follow it into a single brotherhood.

The Solar Path, rejecting space, asserts an unbreakable fusion with the shining Centre of consciousness, which aspires to it from any point of the periphery.

The Solar Path denies form and transforms the Universe into a divine stream of One Life, the images of which are playing foam in the ocean of the radiance of the Spirit. The Solar Path, in its final stage, detaches consciousness from everything objective and plunges it into such a depth of the subjective Spirit, where there is not a shadow of forms, names or changes.

The Solar Path does not need a school. For those who follow Them, school is Life itself with its natural symbolism and occult schools are only one of the phenomena of Life. Like a bee, he collects his honey from everywhere and each flower is the best for him at the moment of collection.

The Solar Path does not need the milestones of artificial symbolism: The milestones along it are placed by God himself in the eternal symbolism of Nature, because the method of analogies reveals to him the secret cipher of the world.

The Solar Path knows no guidance, except for the inner leader – its divine Spirit: the principle of mutual assistance enriches those who follow it, and therefore everyone is provided with visible and invisible effective help of all.

The Solar Path does not know organisations and societies-because it lies above all forms and conventions, its measure is only personal consciousness, it invisibly unites all those who go by It into one real Brotherhood.

The Solar Path does not require exceptional conditions for its realisation: its realisation is the whole life, internal subjective transformation is the method of the Path.

The Solar Path does not require a change in external circumstances, it transforms them by itself, but its necessary condition is constant subjective tension and sensitive alertness, reforging of consciousness and unbreakable self – discipline of the spirit and body.

He or she who walks the Solar Path is outwardly lonely, but he or she is united with the Source and his brothers and sisters in that depth of the Heart where all facets disappear.

Scattered in space - sisters and brothers of the Solar Path, the Path that runs over the paths - is it not gratifying to exchange greetings on the pages of this book, provided for the development of the Solar synthesis of paths by the synthetic consciousness of the editorial office.

Revel, 1935

The Magician

The First Arcanum

Divine Essence

1. Divine Essence
2. The male principle
3. The nature that determines
Numeric designation: 1
Astrological correspondence: The sun

Hans Thoma, Sonne

In the symbolic picture of the great pyramid of Cheops, the first Arcanum is depicted as follows:

A human figure with his right hand raised and his left hand lowered stands in front of a cube; in his right hand he holds a rod; in front of him on a cubic stone stands a bowl, a sword and a coin. On his forehead is a gold hoop, around his waist a gold belt. This figure, symbolising the subjective consciousness, is crowned and girdled with the light of the One, the Source of Love and the Spirit that dominates the elements of the manifested world. The world in its essence represents unity: The inner essence of things is always the same and identical to itself. The One Spirit that pervades all forms and every phenomenon of the world is only the expression of this Spirit in form. Every phenomenon of the world is a manifestation of one of its creative possibilities, so The One Great Ocean of the unknowable Spirit is omnipresent, all-pervading, and underlies the whole world. It is the root of all things and, since our mind is one of the forms of its manifestation, it cannot know its own essence, which transcends the Spirit.

All forms and names are created by the Mind and define some form.

The same One, which fills all forms, has no form Itself, and therefore no name, no name can be applied to It. To somehow define It, formless and faceless, He is called the Absolute, the Deity, the Ain-Sof (the unattainable), or simply That (in Vedanta terminology).
It fills all the forms of the world, and at the same time It is infinitely greater than their totality. He knows Himself in all great and small creatures, and at the same time surpasses them all in His essence. He is everything in everything, and everything is in Him, and yet no infinity of worlds will exhaust His inner possibilities. He is manifested everywhere, and His inner essence moves Him.
the external entity move the Universe and It is everywhere manifested as a Single Force. The universe is Love. Love in its manifestation is the desire for unity.
Love is essentially the affirmation of a unity that does not exist anywhere in the manifestation. Everything in the world is born of Love, abides in Love, and expresses Love. But often, behind the endless, innumerable forms of Love, we do not see its single and all-encompassing essence. This Spirit Love is what expresses all

the infinite variety of worlds. But for its manifestation, Love splits the unity of the incomprehensible Ocean of Spirit into two parts - the Subject and the Object - which is expressed in their mutual desire for a radical unification with each other.

All the best aspirations are ways of acquiring this Love. Unselfishness, selflessness, self-detachment are only the affirmation of the Unity of Love, the blurring of the boundaries between "I" and " you " and the way to unite them. Therefore, one cannot speak of Love if one does not realise in the heart that these three messengers of God - unselfishness, selflessness, and self-denial - are to be found in the heart, and Love cannot be understood if there is self-restraint within the framework of egoism. The path to God, that is, to the Eternal Unity of All, to the Ocean of Love, lies through the stages of their manifestation.

Therefore, subjective development, which is so necessary for the acquisition of spiritual values and spiritual knowledge, is essentially a path from egoism to the ever-expanding stages of unselfishness, selflessness and self-denial, up to the accommodation in the spiritual world.

The subject of spiritual consciousness is in the heart of all beings and all the creatures of the manifested universe. This Subject, the bearer of Divine Love, who is everywhere, radiating from the centre to the periphery and embracing all Infinity, is expressed in the first symbolic card image.

The first Principle of the bestowal path is the recognition of the spiritual unity of the universe and the affirmation of the potential to create out of oneself a subject of radiating, all-encompassing, and creative Love.

The title of the Arcanum is "Divine Essence".

The masculine principle is a formative principle in nature, which in its essence is eternally creating itself. The subjective consciousness is merged with the Ocean of the Absolute Spirit, but in its manifestation it embraces a part of this boundless Ocean as the object of its self-manifestation - by putting the seal of the potential of the possibilities contained in it. This subjective consciousness carries in itself, in its potential, all the possibilities of the subsequently manifested Cosmos, the knowledge of all its forms, mastery of all laws and forces that unfold in its power spirals.

This subjective consciousness, all-encompassing and all-conscious in its depth, which is aware of everything and feels itself in everything, is the synthesis of all the manifestations of great and small consciousnesses. In the fullness of its potential, it carries within itself (as a possibility) the entire universe, and the potency of the affirmation of Being, which has been poured out of the Spirit by the conscious totality of the worlds, is self-consciousness, that is, a form of consciousness in which the subject is absorbed. It is recognised by the Divine Subject as a form of its manifestation. This consciousness, when applied to the Universe, is called God, that is, a Subject that carries within Itself and radiates from Its inner essence the great and small images and creatures of the world.

Self-consciousness, as applied to man, is that form of human consciousness in which everything that has a name or a form is rejected or dissolved in the eternal radiance of the Spirit, which is fundamentally one with God. This is the form of consciousness in which the boundaries between "I" and "you" are blurred and everything is absorbed by the self-radiating Love by the Spirit.

The first principle of manifestation in man is the very essence of our soul, our inner self, our subject, eternally immersed in itself, never changing in all the changes of its shells, the infinite Spirit, always remaining the same, regardless of any changes, no matter what the transformations of our consciousness. The consciousness of oneself in all its transformations, in all its states, in all the aspects of one's personality, in all the ideals of one's soul - here is self-consciousness. It never changes, it never acts, for its possibilities are effectively brought to life by the instruments of its manifestation through the Heart, Mind, and Pain

It is only a constant witness of the changes that are taking place in the spiritual, mental, psychic and physical shells that hide it. We are separated from it by all the stages of the planes of consciousness, that is, the knowledge and possession of all the manifestations of the ego in the Cosmos.

And at the same time, it is the inner being of our soul. But to achieve it, we must discard everything that is not it, we must know everything and own everything that we then have, then let us reject it, because ignorance and lack of mastery can make us accept some passing stage of consciousness as the reality of our inner self, and this mistake can have serious consequences. Although the truth lies in the realm of subjective consciousness, all the objectivity that lies between us and It must be known and transcended in order to reach It in all its purity.

In order to understand God in himself, there is a method of negating everything that He is not, but it must be emphasised that in order to really master negation, we must know what we reject. Only under these conditions can we merge the sensations of our "I" with our real spiritual essence. The method of negation is the method of not identifying consciousness with anything that is not essentially it. "Know thyself, and thou shalt know the whole world," says the ancient wisdom inscribed above the Temple of Initiation. Know thyself as all-present, all-knowing, all-blessed, all-holy. The eternal Unity of the Spirit and rule over all that is not your "I". Do not identify your consciousness with the changing objective forms in which it is constantly clothed, that is, perceive all its manifestations as roles played in the great Mystery of Life. It does not matter what this role is, because it manifests itself in it. One of the potentials of our great Spirit. What does it matter what the last role is?

It will also be a manifestation of the Divine self-realisation of self-consciousness.

At its root, our spiritual self, our inner essence, is eternally fused with the Divine Essence - the reality manifested in the universe. Therefore, all the beings of the world and all its phenomena are connected together by a common presence in the Divine Essence, which means that the real connection between us is actually the connection of the manifested spirit. Our mind tries to connect the phenomena of the world with the horizontal lines of the Law of Causality, but in reality, everything in the world is connected by radii going from the periphery to the centre, and from the centre to the next radius.

Through the Spirit, through God, there is a connection between the beings of the world. Therefore, the feeling of connection with the beings of the world, with those near and far, is actually there a sense of their own and their Divine Essence. And this connection, which exists through God, is called Love in the manifested world. Therefore, every manifestation of Love is Divine, because it establishes a connection that passes through God, and therefore it is impossible not to love your neighbour without Love for God, which can be expressed in the search for truth, the desire for the Spirit, for self-improvement, etc.

A single Spiritual Essence of the world is impossible, because when we break the connection with the Highest, that is, with the centre, we break the connection at the periphery, and then we are separated from each other. A friend with all the illusory shells that stand as an obstacle to mutual understanding and for Love. Theoretically, if a person denies God and the Spirit, but his heart is not dead for Love, then by this he shows that he is subconsciously affirms and recognises this Spirit; but of course, a theoretical negation, creating false ideas, in the end it can distort the consciousness in such a way that it will lose all connection with the Spiritual World and then it will dry up and die for the feeling of Love and will also lose connection with all its loved ones. Thus, the beings who have lost their "I" become shadows, bringing death and decay into everything.

The principle of Unity can be achieved only if the Unity of consciousness is realised in all life manifestations, that is, under the condition of the verticality of consciousness, when all the manifestations of the planes are grouped around the axis of the set ideal and are brought into hierarchical order. The nature of this order depends on the potential of self-consciousness, just as the established order of a person depends on the potential of the Divine Subject manifested in it.

The world is like this, because such are the potentials of the Spirit manifested in it, and such are the personal characteristics of people. This world must strictly correspond to the potential of our spiritual essence unfolding in it. It is impossible to deny the order of the universe.

The experience accumulated over thousands of years is constantly being filled with great consciousnesses, detached from their small personalities, who have firmly established in themselves the four planes through which the Divine Consciousness manifests in the Universe. According to this law of the four, which is the basis of every form, the inner potential of the Divine Spirit is developed.

In the symbolic picture, these four stages of the Spirit's manifestation are represented by the rod, the cup, the sword, and the moon. The rod is held by the Aleph itself, for it symbolises the principle of the spiritual manifestation itself, and on a cubic stone (again, the symbol of the four), three objects lie in front of him, as submissive instruments of his positive appearance. In man, in a small cosmos, these four planes of consciousness are poured out into forms:

- spiritual life and creation of spiritual syntheses;
- religious and mental searching for the path and building their ideals upon it, that is, the formulation of the world of ideas;
- psychic and energetic manifestations of the search for the ideal and service to it;
- physical actions that focus spiritual and ideological principles accordingly in the environment of our planet Earth.
[corresponding to the four kabbalistic worlds of Atziluth, Briah, Yetzirah and Assiah].

In short, in man, the Spirit manifests itself in four planes.

spiritual (soul)
mental (intelligence)
sense areas (astral)
physical (etheric body)

In the construction of inner unity, therefore, it is necessary to begin with the establishment of a subjective goal of the search, with a subjective living ideal corresponding to cosmic reality, and not to the fantastic ideas of an intellect detached from the Cosmos.

Secondly, it is necessary to develop a unitary worldview, which is reduced to a worldview based on the basic principle of this ideal, so that in all this worldview the knowledge was harmoniously merged with the spiritual axis but, at the same time, it is impossible to close the circle of the possibility of new acquisitions.

Thirdly, the growth of consciousness is directed towards infinity and, therefore, our ideological intellectual wealth should not be located in a closed circle, but in an upward spiral of all new self-disclosures and objective accumulations. Only the axis of the spiral, the spiritual backbone, must be worked out and remain unchanged and immobile, so as not to be destroyed. we are in a chaos of forms subject to all kinds of changes.

Fourthly, our worldview and world feeling, that is, the area of our psychic life, the area of feelings, must correspond to our worldview and we should not lock in any random likes and dislikes. All subconscious intense experiences must be illuminated by a ray of understanding: either introduced into the general worldview, or transformed accordingly. All our actions must be driven by the service of the ideal and guided by our worldview, -rather than being the result of random feelings, impulses, or a chaotic reaction to the impact of objectivity.

Only such a positive person is truly ready to manifest his or her Spiritual personality - an entity, a truly cosmic servant - who can develop his or her potential into blazing suns, into driving forces, into real achievements, through the continuous work of self-discovery in the four planes of their coordinated consciousness. Only such a person can really put the imprint of their spirit upon the environment and determine its order, just as God forms the cosmic environment and establishes its unshakable order. In nature on our planet, these four planes of manifestation of the Universal Spirit would have to manifest in the four realms of nature. Man is called to exist in the ideological and psychic forms of spiritual creation [Briah and Yetzirah], and the animal kingdom is called to realise it in the plane of the earthly intellect, which processes the matter of the Earth. The four realms of nature are the accumulators of psychic and physical solar energies. The mineral kingdom is intended to be a single cohesive foundation of all this creativity, fixing it in the realised material forms of the Earth. Therefore, every planet is such, down to its material forms, which are the tasks of the manifested potential of the spirit of its representatives.

But the human consciousness, called to the realisation of spiritual principles, has partially severed its connection with the Spirit that feeds it. It falsely realised the identification of its "I" with its earthly manifestation and earthly tasks and, therefore, the consciousness burned out and plunged into the flow of the earthly energy manifestation and self-consciousness was replaced by egoism.

The severing of the spiritual connection with the Cosmic Spirit caused the weakening of the ties between the immortal soul of man and his earthly personality. His earthly personality ceased to be plastic and flexible, obeying the dictates instead, it submitted to the material flow of the Earth. Its shells were roughened and its physical body was too dense and imperfect. The breaking of the line of consciousness between the immortal soul and its instrument, the personality, made the personality mortal and caused the need for the soul to manifest in many persons by the law of reincarnation.

The Great Creative Mind of humanity, which is a part of the Cosmic Mind, has been replaced in the severed earthly personality by the instrument of its partial manifestation - the earthly intellect or reason. The difference between the Mind and the Understanding is that the Mind is connected with the creative principle of the Universe and is the creative principle in man, giving rise to living effective ideas, living images, represented by such a complete reality as the forms generated by the Cosmic Spirit. The understanding is one of the organs of the Mind, created by it for understanding the earthly situation of its manifestation, the earthly facts. Detached from the [greater Cosmic] Mind, the [individual, human] mind is unable to truly assess the earthly situation and falls into numerous errors. [cannot see the wood for the trees].

The feeling in the detached personality of a human being, that is, the direct perception of the essence of things, has turned into impulses from unconscious instincts that are weakly aware of the principle of connection, and into an impulse of reactions to earthly objectivity, that is, passions.

The will of man is his constant striving toward the goal, that is, the Divine Essence. His intense creative impulse towards the realisation of spiritual values turned into his egoism, into broken chaotic desires for the possession of earthly objects and achievements. In fact, man, from his royal position as a companion of God, descended to the stage intended for the animals and, by this fall, caused the animals to fall. The decline of consciousness and the animal world, usurping its intellectual task and leaving it only a chaotic manifestation of distorted mental impulses, instincts and passions.

The vegetable kingdom was protected by the Higher Powers from the negative influence of the lower man and if this had not been done by the spirits, the leaders of creativity in the solar system, the Earthlings, would have ceased to exist long ago. The plant kingdom remained the only complete and conscious cosmic collaborator which did not break the connection with the world psychic energy and constantly transformed it into the generative flow of life force - in the juices that are nourishing and healing - thus taking care of people and animals even in their fall, healing them from the consequences of mental breakdowns and diseases. The growing vegetative kingdom produces fruits and grains in such abundance that they would be enough to feed all the creatures on Earth if they turned to this only legitimate way of maintaining their lives.

The mineral kingdom was thickened and coarsened by the breakdown of humanity and its material ceased to obey the direct formulation of thought. Instead, it requires the application of physical work for its transformation. Thought-creation, on the other hand, has an extremely weak effect on it and the identification of its results requires a long time and direct fixation of the thought in physical form, as well as a long effort and tension, which is necessary even for a disciplined person.

In order to achieve one's own spiritual essence and liberate consciousness from false self-identifications, the principle of unselfishness is recommended. To carry out self-denial and selflessness in your daily life, and to lead the I not to the self-worth that fills the consciousness but, to the way of solving the spiritual task in the work of each day and to perceive everything as a conscientious performance of the task: Whatever we do, we must remember that all our work is aimed at identifying one of the possibilities. The Universal Spirit from the realisation of the Universal Good to the extent that our personality deserves it. To develop such a life attitude it is recommended to take the following steps:

1. Separate your physical body from yourself, analyse this state and understand that the analyser and the analysed are not the same thing, and that the analyser in relation to the analysed is a Subject separate from the Object, independent of it, and do not identify your 'I' with your feelings. So you will master the secret of Self-control.
2. Concentrate on your thoughts, be able to analyse them, understand that again the Subject analyses them, dominating them. The mastery of thoughts leads to the possibility of conscious thought-creation.

3. Apply the same analysis to the area of your spiritual and religious life. Understand that the ideal you set is only the revelation of your higher self. By ceasing to identify yourself even with the spiritual ideal, you will achieve self-consciousness, self-immersion in the Immortal Ocean of your own Spirit, merged with the Spirit of the Universe and eternally affirming the Principle of Universal Unity.

The mantra for the first Arcanum is 'I am', which means 'I am eternal, immortal and free, nothing can destroy me, I can't disappear anywhere, nothing can harm me.' In all the changes of life, 'I am'. The I is the true cause and witness of all changes and all transformations of consciousness.

The High Priestess

The Second Arcanum

Primary energy

1. Life
2. The Divine substance
3. Nature defined by the Feminine Principle
Numeric designation: 2
Astrological correspondence: The Moon

Nicholas Roerich, The Mother of the World

The Primordial Matter, before it appears from there is only a "cold radiance, colourless, having neither form nor taste and devoid of any quality and aspect", which is awakened to the thrill of action under the impulse of Fohat. The aspects of the Eternal matter are:

The Mother of Mercy and Knowledge
The Mother, Wife and Daughter of the Logos
The Father, the Son and the Holy Spirit (refers to the feminine principle) - Shakti or Energy is the Nature of this Trinity.

E. P. Blavatsky writes: "In the Trans-Himalayan Teachings...this is the 'Mother' or abstract, ideal Matter, Mulaprakriti, the Root of Nature; from the metaphysical point of view, the correlate of Adi - Buddhi, manifested in the Logos – Avalokiteshvara – and, from the purely occult and cosmic point of view, Fohat, the 'Son of Sons', the two-pronged energy emanating from this Light of the Logos, manifesting on the planes of the objective Universe both the latent and the manifested Electricity, which is Life.".
The mantra for the first Arcanum [The Magician] is "I am", which means: I am eternal, immortal and free, nothing can destroy me, I can't disappear anywhere, nothing can harm me. In all the changes of life, "I am". "I" is the true cause and witness of all the changes and all the transformations of consciousness. Matter, Mulaprakriti, the Root of Everything, is indestructible and eternal.
If every manifestation of consciousness, whether reflexive or direct, or unconscious premeditation, belongs to Spirit, then Matter must be regarded as objectivity in its purest abstraction, as a self-existent basis, the sevenfold manvantaric differentiations of which constitute the objective reality behind the manifestations of all phases of consciousness and physical existence.
During the Pralaya period, the Cosmic Thought-Base did not seem to exist.
Under Manvantara, the Spirit is twofold and Nature is born - the second Arcanum - objectification, which contains the foundations of all forms, life-completeness, life-giving and affirming:
The Supreme Subject, the Self, the Spirit, the Principle of Love;
The Supreme Object, You, Matter, the Principle of wisdom. The subject is the centre, manifesting in the encompassed and the

periphery. Between this centre and the periphery, the relationship is expressed in mutual attraction:

The Subject is attracted to the Object by the thirst for manifestation, the Object is attracted to the Subject by the thirst for union with it. Love is eternally self-radiating, and the Life created by this radiation is eternally striving to reveal the hidden essence - Love. This is the basis of all forms of cosmic attraction, from the spiritual attraction of God to the spiritual attraction of God. The second Principle or Arcanum is the idea of polarising the cosmic environment. Once in the Cosmos, the principle is manifested. This Principle can only be based on the beginning of polarisation, that is, on the relationship of two essentially homogeneous principles; and if there is a polarisation, then there is a centre and a periphery.

The Principle of Life reveals a centrifugal orientation (that is, it proceeds from the centre), and the essence of the Principle of Love - always and everywhere striving for Unity - asserts ever more complete syntheses and is the manifestation of a centripetal force. The Principle of Life differentiates the Divine possibilities, the Principle of Love directs them back to the Divine essence. And like this fundamental force of polarisation, all the phenomena of life are polarised, as a consequence of the basic duality. The manifested world is based on the Principle of duality. There is no unity in it, but there is behind the screen of manifestation.

The philosophical Principle of the first Arcanum is the Principle of a single static space, the second Principle is the Principle of eternal, boundless movement, that is, time.

In the manifested world, each phenomenon must be considered as containing two poles. One, the positive pole, will be the moment of the centripetal direction of the phenomenon and the other, the negative pole, will be the moment of the centrifugal tendency and, since the centripetal direction depends on the tension and self-radiation of the inner subjective core, this pole is called active. The objective pole, that is, the centrifugal orientation, depends on the quality of the subject's environment of influence and is a passive pole in relation to the latter.

The goal of human life is liberation from duality through its cognition.

The second Arcanum contains both a single and a multiple principle of self-consciousness and the desire of self-consciousness for truth is the will to rise from a differentiated form to spiritual unity, that is, to the affirmation of true Love. But in his quest for liberation from differentiated forms, man must connect the poles of his spiritual attitude during his journey through the manifested world. Only by solving the problem of integrating the two into the common principle that unites this two can the correct path from form to Spirit be found. Otherwise, some of the forms, the counter-pole, which is not found, can be taken for the incomprehensible Divine Principle and this will close the only possibility of reaching the truth. At the same time, it must be remembered that the latter duality cannot be synthesised by anything that has a name, a form.

The problems of the human Spirit and its search are reduced to the correct setting of the poles. The poles that are correct in relation to each other are called binaries. Examples of correct binaries are as follows:

Unmanifest - manifest; infinite - finite; evolution - involution; impersonal - personal; centrifugal -centripetal; Spirit-form, etc.

Incorrect binaries lead to philosophical confusion and form a fantastic worldview that does not correspond to cosmic reality and therefore remains an empty abstraction.

Such are the theories constructed philosophically on the wrong opposition of "spirit - matter", for there is no real matter and material forms are one of the static forms in general. It is also impossible to contrast "absolute good" and "absolute evil", because both are relative and change depending on the level of consciousness and the stage of manifestation of Life.

It is similarly impossible to oppose the "principle of Life" and the "principle of Death", because death is not a principle, but only a transition from one stage of life to another, the opposite of which will be birth. The correct binary is: "birth - death".

Life on all the main four planes of its manifestation is always dual in its direction. On all the planes of its manifestation there are two of its currents: The first from the centre to the periphery and the second from the periphery to the centre. In the spiritual life of a person, these two directions are reflected: The first esoterically, by wisdom, the second exoterically, by Worship of God. At the heart of each religion is the centripetal force, the basis of the search for truth of a free and self-standing Spirit, but each religion is revealed by the cult Worship of God, materialising spiritual achievements with a physical symbol.

The intellectual life of man is also dual. The human mind, on the one hand, strives for the recognition and analysis of the objective world, thus creating science; on the other hand, man wants to know his own synthetic formula and, synthesising the acquired knowledge according to this aspiration, reshapes it into self-consciousness, that is, into philosophy. The duality of a person's psychic life is revealed in self-affirmation on the one hand and self-denial, on the other. The first is based on the search for truth, the second-on the service of the Common Good.

The environment, on the other hand, belongs to the fundamental ethical binary and, finally, the great duality of the embodied life is the division into two sexes. There is a binary "man - woman", which in its final form contains, symbolises, and embodies all the duality of the manifestation of the world.

The man - woman binary reflects the entire creative organisation of the Cosmos on our planet as a result of the interaction of polarity on different planes of Life manifestation. In many occult theories and books, the male principle is mistaken for an absolutely active, initiative radiating and the female principle is mistakenly drawn in relation to the male as passive, perceiving and bearing. In fact, both Principles, on different planes of manifestation, are active and passive, maintaining the correct polarisation in relation to each other.

The female principle in the spiritual world is active, proactive and radiating and the male principle in the spiritual world, in relation to the female, is passive, receptive and bearing. That is why, on the intellectual plane of consciousness, the male principle actively and creatively formulates the spiritual material received from the female Principle. The feminine principle, which is intellectually discerning, distinguishes the true from the false, the essential from the non-essential, in mental formations.

In the psychic world, both principles are passive and active, but the direction of their activity is mutually opposite. The masculine principle puts ideological formulations in images and representations and seeks to realise them with an energy flow on the physical plane, where it is the creative principle. The feminine is the great alchemist of the universe, sublimating, spiritualising and transforming the inner beauty and harmony of the forms of the World. It is the beginning that dissolves gross forms in subtle manifestations and subtle manifestations in the radiance of the Spirit.

In the physical world, the male principle is active and is its master, the female principle is passive, and its passivity is expressed in the art of adaptation.

From this polarisation follows the Universal Cooperation of both principles. A thoughtful mind can always draw consequences from the indicated opposites of male and female and will understand that no one phenomenon exists. The world cannot be created one-sidedly, by one of the principles. The secret of the stability of forms and the correspondence of their Cosmic reality lies in the harmonious cooperation of the two basic principles.

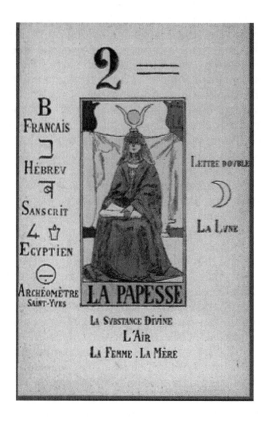

The Book of Nature, which the Woman of the second Arcanum holds on her lap, is opened before the eyes of everyone who sees the secret of mutual polarisations. All Nature is the result of harmonious creativity and mutual self-creation of the great principles and the narrative of the colour scheme of their identification.

On our Earth, man's thought-creation makes him the master of material life and the representative of Cosmic Intelligence on Earth. The directly perceiving heart of a woman opens up to the awareness of spiritual possibilities that seek to be realised on our Earth, puts spiritual guidance in her hands, makes her a representative of spirit-making, a carrier of the Heart.

We see from the comparison of different planes the polarisation of the feminine principle, the duality of its nature, while the man always adheres to the same orientation. The same duality is reflected in the two aspects of women on Earth: the woman-wife and the woman-mother; both of these aspects should be understood not in the zoological, but in the spiritual - in the psychic - sense. As a wife, a woman adapts to a man, being his assistant and obeying him in everything external. After all, the masculine principle determines the order of phenomena in the environment, it is the subject of external manifestations, putting its imprint on the environment. On the other hand, the feminine principle, as a spiritual leader, is the mother of a man and even of her own husband. After all, the medium of influence is as Divine as the subject of self-consciousness that manifests in it; when it has finished its manifestation, it dissolves in this medium, and the great waves of Life plunge the ego back into the unity of Love.

As a spiritual mother, a woman is an educator and a great alchemist, transforming the male consciousness, and thus all his creativity. The internal subjective domination of the feminine over the masculine provides the latter with the right direction and the possibility of returning to the bosom of the spiritual world. Therefore, women's love is most reflected in the essence of the very principle of Love, which is the affirmation of the unity of the Spirit.

The spiritually active feminine principle is the carrier of the pure principle of Love, the One Divine Power of the Universe.

Therefore, the concept of God in the image of the Mother of the World is the highest concept of man about God. After all, it is the Mother of the World, the Holy Spirit, who transforms all the forms of the world and its whole, "saves" it, that is, brings it to its original spiritual state. The Mother of the World lovingly carries all its forms and images, created by revealing the possibilities of the Father of Self-consciousness.

The Great One Life accumulated by Love, the stream of manifestation of Life inseparably merged with Love along the spirals of the Cosmos, transfers this Love from the great to the small, from the small again to the great, uniting the beings of the Universe in one Divine Brotherhood.

The covenant of the Mother of the World is self-abandonment both up and down, that is, complete non-identification with any manifestation. Self-abandonment downwards is the readiness of an unbiased, directly spiritual perception. This same self-abandonment in relation to the manifestations makes it possible to consciously perceive the Great Song of Life and identify with its flow as a whole. Thus, by renouncing the part, we get the whole; by renouncing a single gulp, we get the full cup of Life and this merging with the flow of Life opens up the possibility of subjective self-affirmation of consciousness at any stage of its manifestation, as a carrier and expression of Great Love.

The identification of consciousness with the whole stream of Life is the Cosmic Consciousness, which feels and experiences all the objects of the world and the whole object of manifestation as itself with a great and never-weary Sympathy. And finally, a whole rain of forms, facts and phenomena from it is radiated by these psychic formations that unite them. Schematically this can be represented as follows:

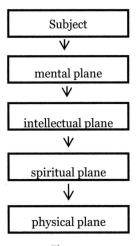

Figure 1

Life is boundless and infinite, for it manifests the boundlessness and infinity of possibilities contained in the ineffable Absolute. Dissolving some of the possibilities of self-consciousness, it causes him to thirst for new accumulations, makes him draw more and more new potentials from the Ocean of the Unmanifest and again realises them, carrying them through the infinity of spaces and times and again, synthesising them in the radiance of the Spirit, constantly manifesting in relation to the Aleph (the first The principle), as a submissive wife and as a protective mother. So, at the root of the manifested cosmic Nature lies the principle of duality, which means that for its manifestation, the unity of potential must always be polarised, split into plus (+) and minus (-), or into the Subject and Object of manifestation.

This polarisation passes through all the worlds, and as you move away from the centre to the periphery, that is, from the spiritual plane of manifestation to the physical, all diseases are differentiated. The great spiritual syntheses, the Principles of the manifested world, are each differentiated into whole systems of ideas; each idea is repeatedly polarised into images and representations, its energetic manifestations on the psychic plane.

And finally, a whole rain of forms, facts and phenomena. These differentiating polarisations form a whole network of manifestations of the world; the threads of the world are intertwined, and to find the corresponding pole in this network of polarisation is exactly what is called Wisdom.

The practice of the correct opposites – binaries - in one's activity and life is called the art of living. From the statements of poles which do not correspond to each other, all wrong and groundless worldviews follow and from the application of such worldviews in life, only an incorrect karmic confusion can result, burdening the individual paths of human evolution. Therefore, the content of the second Arcanum is Wisdom, just as the content of the first Arcanum is Love.

The root of Wisdom lies in the correct perception of cosmic correspondences, in the recognition of true and false, in the feeling of the universal principle of Love. Therefore, Wisdom is a manifestation of the Heart, a manifestation of the Feminine Principle.

In the centrifugal flow of manifestations from the radiations of the centre to the absorbing periphery, the primary radiation of Love is differentiated into increasingly partial and diverse condensed forms of manifestation.

In the opposite direction, from the periphery to the centre, in the flow of integration (that is, the connection of the main components into one whole) of disparate forms in the unifying flow of the Spirit, in the alchemical work of transforming the material, the female principle plays a leading role. It brings all created things back to their original Unity, awakening the EGO in the consciousness of each phenomenon and affirming it by the mutual connection of all that is manifested, its innermost essence. This consciousness of connection with all that exists is the form of consciousness called Cosmic Consciousness. As Vivekananda says:

To know God, we must all become women.

In every form, in every phenomenon, two streams of differentiation and integration cross. Where the centrifugal direction prevails, forms are in a state of involution, that is, in a state of expiring their creative potential. Where the centrifugal direction prevails, forms are in a state of evolution, that is, in a state of unfolding their Spiritual Essence.

This law is clearly manifested on Earth and in the life of nations. Peoples who are involutional, that is, aging, expiring of their creative possibilities and impoverished in spirit, live under the sign of the suppression of the feminine principle. Among such peoples, the woman plays a secondary role and is enslaved by the gradually coarsening male principle. Among the evolving peoples who follow the path of spiritualisation of their manifestations, that is, the path of cultural construction, the woman begins to play an increasingly important role.

Therefore, the cultural level of the people, that is, the level of their spirituality, can be assessed by their attitude to women and the degree of respect that they show for women's spirit-making. On this basis, you can find out which peoples are on the descending line of decreasing and narrowing consciousness and which are on the ascending line of increasing and expanding consciousness in their cultural development.

The harmonious cooperation of both sexes protects the people from becoming wild, since the feminine principle will always bring new spiritual possibilities into their psyche and give material to the male realisational creativity. Such peoples would be protected from spiritual impoverishment and therefore from death. The harmonious cooperation of the two principles would ensure the immortality of the peoples, that is, the possibility of unlimited cultural development.

Cosmic consciousness, that is, the knowledge or direct experience of deep connection between all forms of periphery and centre, is best expressed by the formula: "Not "I", but "You", for every "You" as "I" in any "You" felt "Me" without distinction of planes on which this You is manifest. This formula is the mantra of the second Arcanum.

The threads of the Mother of the World stretch from top to bottom, from the centre to every point of the periphery and, in this centre their unity is confirmed, which determines the connection between them. Therefore, you cannot love your neighbour without loving God.

Is it possible to assert a connection between the forms of the periphery and not establish the Principle of the Common Good, whilst rejecting their deep Unity, God? Only by seeking the

Truth, by striving for the centre, that is, by loving God, can we vividly and directly feel the connection with our neighbour and work for the Common Good.

The second Arcanum is the Principle that reveals to us the secret of the attraction of the periphery to the centre, established by the beginning of the Heart, the beginning of the female. Wisdom consists in a clear discernment between the Spirit and the Spirit and its manifestation, between the eternal Subject and the boundless objectivity of its self-revelation. Wisdom establishes the correct relationship between these basic polarities, which are reflected in the whole variety of cosmic inter-polarisations.

The Empress

The Third Arcanum

World Mind

Divine nature
The Principle of Birth
Separation of parts
Numeric designation: 3
Astrological correspondence: Venus

Venus, seated on a rainbow
from Christine de Pizan's Book of the Queen

The image of the third Arcanum: On a cubic stone standing on a segment of a spherical plane, the earth's surface, a woman is sitting, about to give birth. Her feet rest on the crescent Moon, ready to receive her child. Behind the woman's back are large wings. She is wearing a long robe, belted with a golden belt, and a golden hoop on her head. Twelve stars shine around the head like a crown. The whole figure is against the background of the rising Sun and is clothed in its rays. This is the wife clothed in the Sun, they wept and wrote (Apoc., CHI, 1-2).

The universe is the result of the interaction of two poles manifested on all planes. The very existence of the poles confirms the existence of that being, of that common source from which they have flowed, for both poles express this unity of two different aspects and two different directions of dynamic manifestation.

These two poles are attracted to each other: but by their very attraction, they are looking for the same point from which they have expired. This source of them is neutral or androgynous in relation to the poles of its manifestation. A constant force flow of the radiation of the Object and the attraction of the Object flows between the poles. And where these two forces are balanced, a spark of awareness of your being flares up. And once such awareness flares up, then it is located above both poles, and the principle that unites them has been found.

On the other hand, the same polarisations in the mutual search are connected by a common creative aspiration, as a result of which a single source is formed that constitutes their essence on a denser plane of their manifestation. Thus, the two poles create 'up' (find their synthesis) or 'down' (when they produce a synthetic but compacted and shaped imprint of their union).

Unity (synthesis)

Object (+)   Subject (-)

Result
(the imprint of your essence and your relationship)
Figure 2

Mutual attraction between the poles, reaching consciousness in harmonious cooperation, that is, the assertion of a common source, generates an image of this Unity - Love, and reflects this Unity in the environment of mutual manifestation by generating down, that is, creativity. Moreover, the female principle is proactive in the search for the source, the male principle is proactive in the creative representation of the source in the material of the medium of manifestation of both.

Love

The feminine   Masculine
principle   origin

Creation

Figure 3

The most general formula is the following.

Unity
Love

Principle   Self-awareness
of life   (aleph)

The World
Mind

Figure 4

Self-consciousness expresses a Subject, a principle Life is the
object of its manifestation. The relationship between the Subject
and the Object generates consciousness. The initial impulse to
manifest the self-absorbed cannot have consciousness, because
consciousness is not self-consciousness and always presupposes
the presence of two: a subject - immersed in its own Unity, an
all-encompassing, all-existent, all-blissful, all-free, but
unconscious impulse of Love, and the object - the flow of the
manifestation of Life, which by itself, without the presence of the
Love that fills its essence, is devoid of consciousness, and is
expressed in the mechanical principle of movement.
Consciousness flares up from the mutual penetration of two
principles, and its degree depends on the degree of the
phenomenon of the Subject and on the degree of absorption of its
Object. The more the Subject is absorbed by the Object, the more
conscious the form of its manifestation is, the more spiritualised
it is; the more the Subject is freed from the Object, the wider the
consciousness of the form of its manifestation is, and the more
spiritualised it is. But too close to the absorption of the Object by
the Subject causes an unwillingness to manifest, that is,
creativity, and leads out of the manifested world. The balance
between the Subject and the Object on the line of consciousness
generates a special kind of consciousness, best adapted for
creative manifestation, that is, for imprinting the original unity
of the Spirit and its possibilities in the forms.

In such a form of consciousness the Subject and the Object are equalised and therefore there is an outbreak of feeling; their mutual flow, is called the Mind, reflecting this single flow and embodying its spiritual potential in the manifested world.

On a cosmic scale, this form of consciousness is called the Universal Mind, the Creator of all Things, the Great Architect of the Universe, because it summarises and synthesises all creative manifestations, becoming a creative manifestation of the primary binary of Love and Life.

Reason, the child of Love and Life, cannot be dry and heartless, for it produces forms, creating all of them with the impulse of Universal Love. The mind cannot be static and rigid, since in the dynamics of creative forms it carries out the principle of the universal movement of a Single Life.

The True Mind is the only living, complete Love is the creative beginning of the world. And only its earthly degeneration - the shallow reason of people, thanks to the breakdown of human consciousness and the separation of the ego from the Cosmic Principle, often becomes a lifeless, loveless, drying, deadening principle.

Only if there is a balance between the Subject and an Object, that is, if the two main principles cooperate correctly, it is possible to correctly understand and truly evaluate phenomena. Only if this point of equilibrium is found, merging and reflecting the Subject and Object, in their fullness that is, in the presence of Reason, true creativity is possible - imprinting further in the forms and phenomena of the world the source of Love and Life.

The World Mind reflects in itself, uniting the poles that gave birth to it, the Unity of the Spirit. In the same way, in human cognition, the initiative must pass through the prism of Reason in order to acquire a truly creative power, but it is the Mind that reflects in itself the core of the Spirit, Love and plasticity of the image.

On the great principle of Love, manifested in the ever-flowing stream of Life and harmoniously shaped by the Universal Mind, the entire Cosmos is built in its entirety, in each separate part of it. Therefore, in Nothing is created in the Cosmos, but everything is born from an infinite number of reflections in the prism of the Creative Mind of the mutually polarising principles of Love and Life. And so since the Mind is the most perfect form and all phenomena produced in the Cosmos flow from it, everything in the world is conscious. There are no unconscious phenomena, no forms devoid of consciousness; the whole plan of the Cosmos, the construction is conscious and intelligent, and accidents are excluded in it.

The search for the source of the synthesis of polarities in the present on a higher plane of consciousness Unity is the birth up. When applied to a person, this is a process of cognition, and the synthetic forms found are again conscious, intelligent phenomena gifted with the mobility of Life and the self-manifestation of Love. This search for Unity in thinking and feeling is in itself a manifestation of Love and its source on an intellectual and psychic basis.

The creative thirst of the poles is a manifestation of their stream - They are related to each other, and if their union is reflected on the medium of manifestation, then this is a downward shift.

Earthly humanity is on our planet a representation of the World Mind, a guide to the specific forms of the Earth of the creative impulses of the Cosmos. It would have to transform the earthly intellectual, psychic and physical material embedded in his Mind and Spirit-making.

Such a process is a true Cultural Construction. But instead of applying cosmic Spirit-making to the earthly material, the mind of mankind's developing-I was afraid of this material, losing contact with the Cosmos, With his mind, he fulfiled his task only partially.

The generation of syntheses, the birth upwards, is often called in occult language "the neutralisation of binaries upwards".

The generation of polarities into the forms of their manifestation (and not into the more subtle world) is called in the occult language "neutralisation of the binaries downwards".

Schematically, both processes are expressed by triangles - hence the symbolic meaning of this geometric figure. A triangle with its vertex pointing upwards is called an evolutionary turner, or an evolution triangle. A triangle directed from the top down is called an involutional turner, or an involution triangle.

In Cosmic Construction, where there can be no breakdown of consciousness, as in human construction, both processes are performed simultaneously. The cosmic principle at each stage of its manifestation, generating its synthesis upwards, imprints it in a form that serves as a milestone for the consciousnesses following it.

Since all creativity is pulled out of an infinite series of polarisations, since it is all conscious and there is no randomness in it, then it is natural, and the subject of this law is the World Mind itself, which reflects everything subjective and absolute in itself. This regularity is an internal nature.

The mind and the method of its manifestation. Consequently, uniformity is a law, Turner's Law, and Turner is of dual generation: up is abstract in relation to the polarisation of synthesis, and down is concrete in relation to the form of manifestation.

The general formula of the Creative World Mind is also reflected in the human mind by the immutable law of logic.

Synthesis

Antithesis   Thesis

Figure 5

This is the conclusion on which the worldview is built. This law of logic, from time immemorial, is derived from - known to mankind, there is an internal law of intellect is in the search for its source and in the creative thirst for imprinting in forms. Once again, it is important to emphasise the ability to correctly distinguish the poles, because both the recognition and the creative process of the Mind is based on the correct polarisation, which protects against self - distortion, which is not able to reflect the truth of the world and creatively capture it in form. It is always necessary to correctly find the antithesis to the thesis and through the subjective transformation of consciousness to find their synthetic source. This process is called "synthetic thinking".

Life

Death   Birth

A living phenomenon, creature

Figure 6

Life in its transformations is polarised by the death of old forms and the birth of new ones from them. These two moments are constantly crossing in every living being, which simultaneously belongs to the stream of constant dying and the stream of constant birth: that is why it is alive, that is, eternally changing in its manifestations, it reflects the eternally mobile principle of Life.

The course of the life process is built between the time of death and birth. The equilibrium point of both processes is a necessary condition for the appearance of a living form. In the synthesis of consciousness of living humanity, the following turners of the Creative Mind can be cited.

1. The spiritual plane of consciousness and its three principles:

a) the creative principle
b) the solvent principle;
c) the preserving principle.

This gives the famous triangle of the Vedas, Trimurti, which expresses the principle of the three-face Deity and gives the fourth principle - Indra (personal God, divine form).

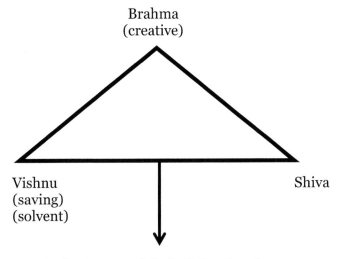

Figure 7

The famous triangle of Vedantism is based on the same principle, which generates a stale principle - the Universe of the Cosmos.

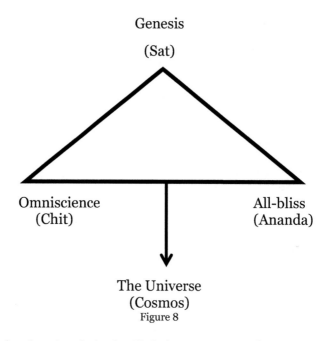

Genesis
(Sat)

Omniscience
(Chit)

All-bliss
(Ananda)

The Universe
(Cosmos)
Figure 8

And also the triangle in the Christian concept: Father, Son and
Holy Spirit. In Orthodoxy, this triangle is rotated by the vertex
up and in Catholicism-top down.

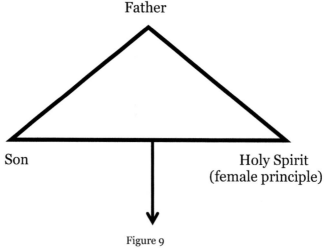

Father

Son

Holy Spirit
(female principle)

Figure 9

These triangles characterise the direction of both churches, the
principles of their separation and internal antagonism.

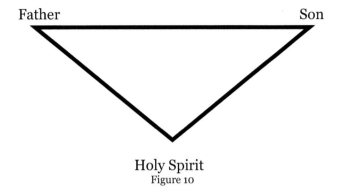

Father   Son

Holy Spirit
Figure 10

2. The mental plane

Each phenomenon belongs simultaneously to the differentiating law of causality and the integrating law of expediency. Each phenomenon in the Cosmos can be considered as the result of a differentiating manifestation or integrating striving for the primary source. Only with the participation of both directions, the true regularity of the phenomenon is revealed, its meaning and inner meaning are revealed.

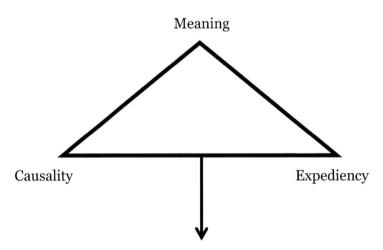

Meaning

Causality   Expediency

The Pattern
(the place in the cosmos of each phenomenon)

Figure 11

Knowledge is based on causality, Faith is based on purposefulness, in synthesis they give a true Religion, reveal the meaning of the Life of the Universe and generate a new form of manifestation of this religion -a cult.

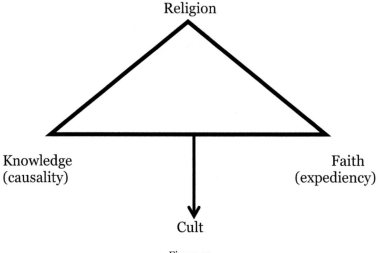

Figure 12

Causality will be reflected in our Responsibilities, expediency will give us Rights. Up they are synthesised into the principle of Duty, based on both polarities, down they generate a Set of laws that regulate-understanding their relationship.

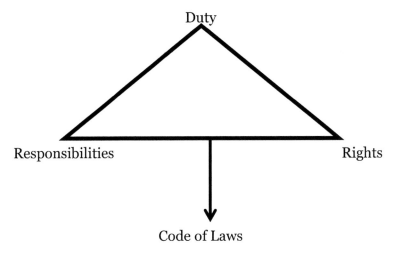

Figure 13

3. The psychic plane.

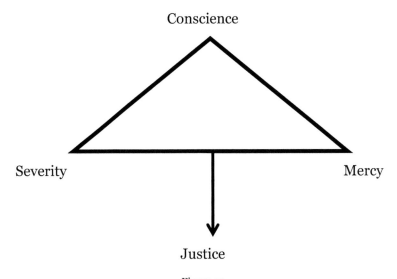

Figure 14

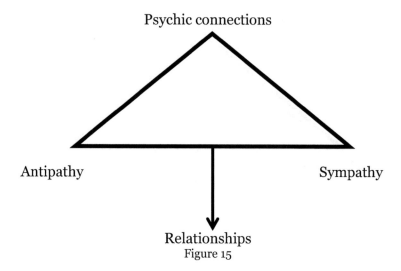

Psychic connections

Antipathy   Sympathy

Relationships
Figure 15

4. The physical plane. The love between a man and a woman, their attraction to each other, is a search for the Divine principle in a person of another polarisation. Marriage is their union, it is not an empty abstraction, but a living birth up of a person's synthesis. Therefore, in all religions, marriage is a sacrament, because the birth of a complete person in the Subtle world is the greatest desire available to earthly humanity. The physical child, the result of their union, captures the properties of the father and mother, and is, while he is a child, a reflection of the light synthetic essence that unites the parents.

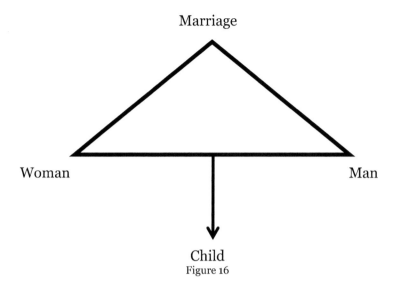

Figure 16

On the same plane, we will give an economic example.

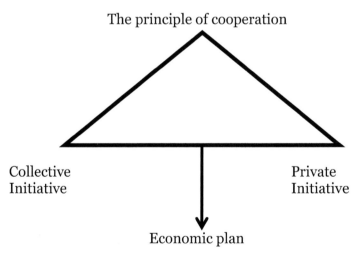

Figure 17

So it is necessary to make triangles relative to all life manifestations (that is, to find the antithesis), and, having found them, to synthesise them, because they imprint the correct relationship of factors and lead to a true knowledge of all kinds of small world phenomena.

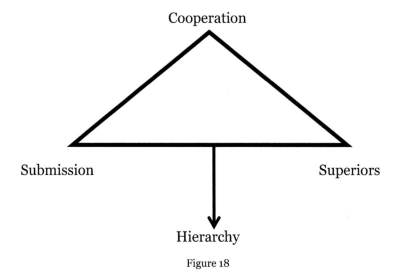

Figure 18

Identifying the triangle of synthetic thinking speeds up and facilitates the work of our intellect many times and protects it from unnecessary searches, wanderings and from creating false thought images.

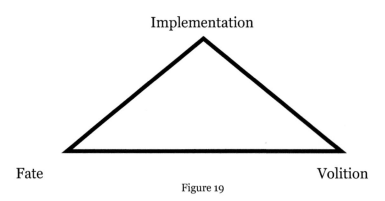

Figure 19

Here is another famous historical example - turner's measure of karma. Conducting is the general plan of cosmic evolution, reflecting the initiative of the Divine Creativity. Fate is the accumulated result of the past realisations that determine consequences and obey the law of causality. The will is an expedient determination for future achievements, for the realisation of ideas.

This triangle was composed by Fabre d'Olivet in the beginning of the XIX Century. The famous French occultist and historian explains the various periods of the creative development of mankind by the relationship between the vertices of the triangles.

If all three vertices of a triangle are in the Launceston consciousness of equilibrium, that is, throughout the past confess realisation of the Divine Pre-style, there comes a wise, bright period of cultural construction of the people, without shocks, wars and revolutions, with the correct hierarchical distribution - servants of the construction and illumination of the entire construction of the corresponding real space-values ideology.

If the human Will, in alliance with the Conduct, but ignoring the accumulation of the past, that is, Fate, seeks to build the future, then strong personalities arise in the people - the leaders who force the national consciousness to step through several stages of evolution. Such a combination is necessary if the accumulation of Fate is negative. The union of Will with Conduct is always victorious over Fate.

Sometimes it is associated with Fate against a distorted volitional initiative. This is done during periods when the presence of strong-willed individuals is characterised by incorrect concepts, false representations, and illegal motives for actions. In this case, the mass of the people, which is overcoming the accumulation of causalities, believes in the laws of Fate and its psyche. He sees the reflection of the Divine inscription, which is called to correct the mistakes of the leaders. The mass becomes superior to the advanced strong-willed personalities and, in alliance with the Production, defeats them. A period of psychological determinism and social collectivism comes.

Fate can unite with the Will and, in union with it, fight with the Conduct. Peoples, on the basis of the traditions of the past, decide through their initiative personalities to arrange themselves independently, regardless of the plan of universal human development. Their consciousness, detached from the spiritual influx (current, influence), falls into it, turns into ideological materialism and opposes everything to it, causes war, and forgetfulness of world laws plunges peoples into social chaos and anarchy. These are the saddest periods in the history of mankind.

In the individual life of mankind, the principles of this triangle are reflected by the following Turner.

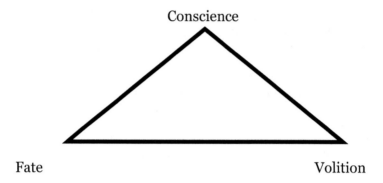

Conscience

Fate

Volition

Personal Karma

Figure 20

In a harmonious person who follows the path of wisdom, working for the Common Good, all three principles are balanced. His Will is directed to achieving the goals set by his Conscience, that is, by reflection of The Divine Principle in the personal consciousness. He illuminates his karma with the same Conscience and knows how to use its consequences to serve the Common Good.

If the Will is directed expediently, that is, in harmony with Conscience, but enters into a struggle with Fate, rejecting the results of accumulation, then a person becomes a person who does not take into account the foundation of the past, his activity loses its point of support and moves into the realm of mental deviations. Personal karma will not be transformed and there is a disharmony between reality and the chosen activity.

If Conscience unites with Fate, then a person becomes a fatalist and, believing in the inevitability of the law of causality, loses the initiative of creative power. If Fate and Will unite against Conscience, then initially a person is formed who defies God, a type of God-fighter, which then turns into a sceptic, an esoteric anarchist. If the Will breaks away from Conscience and fights Fate alone, challenging it, then we get a type of Byronist: a person who is unconditionally strong-willed, but without the necessary spiritual foundation that determines the purposefulness of the Will. In its extreme expression, this is hooliganism.

The will is always directed to the future, because it directs and determines the achievement of the goal. "Fate is the sum of the past", and both of them generate that invisible, but always present, which determines the penetration of the rays of the Divine Unity of Consciousness, which is the Conscience that has destined man to seek truth and serve the Common Good, as a reflection of the Divine Destiny.

The Fabre d'Olivet triangle, turned upside down, is the famous turner of Freemasons, referred to by the letters LDP, which for centuries has been the slogan of Freemasons in the fight against the Catholic Church and the French kings.

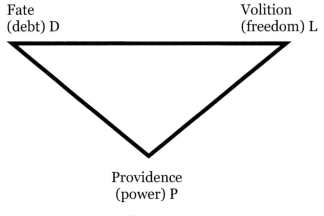

Figure 21

In this triangle Volition primarily reflects the property of Freedom (in French, 'liberte', 'L'); Fate reflects Debt, because the debt is the sum of the past (debt in French 'devoir', 'D'); and for both, Freedom and Duty, down pose Power (in French, 'pouvoir', 'P').

At the same time, do not forget the neutralisation of the upward triangle, Conscience, where Power is a necessary condition for the conduct of a pre-established Divine Plan and evolutionism. If this triangle is cut off from the top of the synthesis, as the Masons did, then this Power can degenerate into arbitrariness and act destructively.

Before briefly outlining the great action of masonry, LDP, let's briefly tell their story.

Since the formation of the Catholic Church, during the first Crusades, the later famous Order of Templars was formed, dedicated to the charitable centre of the Christian world, which has absorbed and synthesised in its Christian lodge all aspects of the initiatory Traditions and wisdom of the East. These mysteries were filtered through the Brotherhood of the Essenes, the foundations of the Pythagorean school, the traditions of the Mazdeists, Kabbalah, the alchemy of the Arabs, the magic of the Chaldeans, the high teachings of the dynastic Hindu philosophy (Raja-Yoga), intertwined and formed into one synthetic goal in the Degrees of Initiation of the Templar Order, which recognised the supreme leader of its Forefather Moria, whose deputy was the Great Hierophant.

This Order claimed to be part of the Archangel Mikhail's Lodge and called his mysterious egregore the essence of Elias the Artist, shining in the creation of beauty, clothed in silver light and radiating it on his companions.

Over time to the Templars, thanks to their improvements in magic (that is, the use of the laws and forces of the Subtle World) and skilful combinations, became unusually powerful, accumulated huge wealth. But the craving for material well-being and power distorted the consciousness of the Brothers themselves, whose primary goal was synthetic service. The truth and the establishment of a special world order on Earth.

In addition, the unrefined consciousness of the semi-savage and insufficiently cultured Europeans introduced a distortion of the understanding of the abuse of knowledge into the middle and higher part of the Order. And although the Highest degree tried to hold and held in its hands the banner of service to high ideals and the realisation of Cosmic Spirit-making, outwardly the Order began to lose its ethical beauty in some of its external phenomena.

At the beginning of the XIV century, the Pope and the French king found fault with these external distortions, finding in this a favourable pretext for the liquidation of the Order, whose power and wealth made it a dangerous rival to their power and influence. Both the Pope and the king were also interested in the appropriation of the land and property rights of the Order. Having used in 1307 the total by the assembly of the Highest degree of the Order in Paris, the King Philip IV of France with the blessing of Pope Boniface VIII arrested the entire high brotherhood of the Templars, led by their grandmaster Jacques de Molay. Almost all the brothers of the Middle Degree and many younger ones were captured. Only a few managed to escape:

three brothers of the Highest degree who did not appear at the general meeting due to illness, several of the Middle and about half of the Junior degree.

A gigantic trial against the Order was inspired, and its outcome was predetermined. The Order was charged with heresy, apostasy, black magic and devil worship. All the property of the Order was confiscated and divided between the Pope and the king, and the war for the Templar inheritance lasted between both for a very long time. So the Templar Order was destroyed, and all the arrested members were completely burned at the stake. The grandmaster, Jacques de Molay, was the last to be burned. As he ascended to his pyre, he invoked the justice of God on the Pope and the king, warning them that in forty days he would appear before the Lord together with the Pope and, a year later, with the French king. Ergo the prophecy has come true. The escaped brethren of the Templars disappeared in Italy, where, for their own safety, they asked to be taken to the masons' workshop, the only one that accepted members from the outside. Thus, the name "freemasons" or "Frank-masons" arose. The Masons swore to carry out the justice of God, to which they appealed to the Spirit of Jacques de Molay, to avenge the defeat of the Order on the Pope and the King of France. The sign of this Order - the triangle LDP - they turned into a formula for their revenge, giving the letters a new name, the meaning of which is "I will trample the lily" (lily is the coat of arms of the Bourbons) and "I will destroy the papal crown". Having founded their hierarchy, the Masons charged each of their members with this duty, to day and night repeat these formulas to themselves, write the letters LDP everywhere - on fences, houses, trees - carving them on stone and drawing them imperceptibly on all objects. This resulted in a powerful intellectual flow aimed at destroying the power of the Pope and the French king. And, of course, this intellectual stream found unconscious agents and guides in the masses of the people of that time.

On the other hand, the authorities who destroyed the Templars themselves created a heavy karma, because the retribution for the destruction of the spiritual core of the Templars caused the death of the Spirit in the Catholic Church, and in the French monarchies undermine the religious foundation.

The Masons celebrated their first revenge against the Catholic Church with a cannon shot of the Reformation in 1520. Luther's teacher and spiritual leader, Melanchthon, was one of the Masons of the Highest degree. Also, all the smaller reformers who preceded Luther, who prepared the ground for this explosion, were students and proteges of the Freemasons. Of course, along with negative motives, there was also a good impulse - the impulse to purify religion from distortions and spiritualise the newly expressed Christianity with a new impulse. The second cannon shot that shook the principle monarchies in general, but on the other hand, the creative initiative of the masses of the people, who had been inert up to that time, was given by the French monarchy. This cannon shot was the French Revolution of 1789. It was prepared by Masons who considered themselves tools of Divine justice, the guides of new ideals and new foundations of social construction.

Diderot, Montesquieu, the mysterious Cagliostro and many others, who so diligently prepared the overthrow of the monarchy and proclaimed democracy, were Freemasons. And it is impossible to call such facts as the names of the "Jacobins" club other than deliberate symbols".

The Mountain is a Temple, that is, an Order built on a Spiritual Mountain; the imprisonment of Louis XVI in the Gaitre castle, which belonged to the Templars from ancient times; his execution on the same day on which Jacques de Molay was convicted.

The Freemasons turned the LDP triangle upside down again, making it the slogan of a new social and state construction. This slogan is "Freedom, Equality and Fraternity".

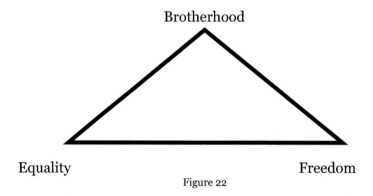

Brotherhood

Equality   Freedom

Figure 22

Freedom has remained, Duty has been replaced by Equality, and instead of the neutralising down-Power, the union of Freedom and Equality has been put up, reminding of the spiritual brotherhood of all things.

The only creative force of the universe is the Mind, which creates the world by the power of thought-creation. This creation is in fact a generation, that is, the identification of potential possibilities discovered in the inner nature of the Mind by polarising its thought-creation and generating the third element in a form that expresses the potential of the poles. And since everything is born out of Reason, everything is reasonable and conscious. The Mind, here, is a result of the interaction between the Object and the Subject, that is, a special point of creative consciousness.

The whole world is a ladder of consciousness, there is nothing unconscious and accidental in it. The more pronounced the Subject is, the brighter the flame of consciousness burns. All planes of consciousness located above the point of equilibrium, that is, above Mind, there are those planes where the Subject dominates the Object. Wisdom is born from such a relationship between them, and the stronger this Subject dominates the Object, the more this Wisdom is manifested and the more it controls the activity of the creative Mind, spiritualising it with new possibilities for the manifestation of spiritual impulses. Wisdom is the mother of Reason which constantly feeds his generative ability with the milk of the Spirit.

The more the Subject is absorbed by the Object at all the planes of consciousness that are below the point of equilibrium of the creative Mind, the more the possibilities of its manifestation are reduced, the variety of creative formulations decreases, and the involvement in so-called instinctive actions saturated with minimal creative potential is reduced.

Every being of the universe has one or another measure of consciousness, and it is at one or another stage of the manifestation of consciousness. Creatures in which the object absorbs the Subject, that is, those whose consciousness is flooded with the perception of the environment are the involuntary vehicles of the Creative Mind and are dependent on it for the expression of private possibilities.

Those consciousnesses in which the Object and the Subject are equalised are truly creative consciousnesses that generate forms of the objective world by their thought-creation. They, in turn, are controlled by those consciousnesses in which the Subject prevails over the Object, that is, wise consciousnesses that transmit to them the spiritual impulse of Creativity.

If many processes in nature seem meaningless or accidental to us, then we must attribute this idea to the low synthetism of our own consciousness and to the insufficient development of the recognition abilities of our mind, which does not grasp the entire chain of the World Mind. But we must once and for all banish this "randomness" from our worldview, as it does not correspond to reality.

The mind, in its essence, is the result of the Love that longs for its manifestation and the eternal dynamics of Life. The mind carries within itself the potential of the creative forces of the universe and the potential of the entire dynamics of its manifestation. Thus, the law of duality, which is already contained in the very nature of the Mind, polarises it into a plus and a minus. Its active side is the ability of creative formulation, and its passive side is the ability to recognise. Recognition expresses the possibility that is eager for manifestation completely. As result of this process a thought appears. Therefore, everything that lives and acts, thinks. According to this formula, the thoughts of God, the Holy Spirit and man are born. The mystery of Creativity is based on the polarisation of unity and the connection of these poles into a new creative combination with the following formula: first, polarise unity, and secondly, connect the poles into a new combination.

The mind

Recognition ability

The ability of creative formulation

Thought

Figure 23

The universe is the result of such a thought-creating process. Therefore, everything in it is not only reasonable and conscious, but also meaningful, that is, illuminated by creative thought, which, in turn, can manifest itself and generate according to the same thing that generated it the principle. Everything in the world has its place, its right to consciousness, existence and manifestation. Thought, being polarised and combining the poles into various combinations, generates ideas that are more formed than itself. By their internal polarisation and a new combination of their elements, ideas generate new representations and mental images. These ideas and mental images, again polarising, radiate from themselves forces and energies that clothe them in shells striving for realisation, which, in turn, generate facts and are embodied in them. This is how the idea is realised, so by it gives rise to phenomena. The process of such thought creation is called an ideomotor process and passes through all four glosses of consciousness.

The Manifest thought of consciousness

Development   Subject
Environment   Creative/Pulse

The idea, as a result of the reflection
of the idea and the environment

Figure 24

A plan is a means for the realisation of a thought manifested by consciousness. The thought is higher, the plan is lower down, into the outside world. The environment is the subject of the manifestation of the creative impulse.

Spark of thought

Causality   Expediency

Thought image

Stability   Energy sector
of the material   potential

The phenomenon
Figure 25

The central line, balancing all the time the subject and the Object are the line of consciousness, and each phenomenon is the completion of the previous stages of consciousness.

This ideomotor process is the occult, that is, forgotten by man, and the only spring of all creativity and the key to the realisation of power. The general mass of humanity has only a weak degree and unconsciously owns this process. And only those who are in his spiritual development, raised their consciousness above the plane of the bone of the earthly intellectual confusion and even above the plane of the creative Mind into the sphere of Wisdom, that is, into the sphere of subjective predominance, completely owns the keys of thought-creation; in the ideomotor process, they draw cosmic spiritual potentials and reveal them in the forms of visual thought images.

These mental images are carried in the waves of the intellectual sphere of the Earth and fall into consonant and therefore open to them consciousness. At the moment of the addition of the thought image, such a consciousness experiences an insight that passes into inspiration, that is, to encourage the creative potential to act. And the thought image is realised by such a consciousness in the development of thought images available to a person on the intellectual and psychic earth plane and is poured into a form corresponding to the specific abilities of the consciousness that captured it, and into the material that is needed for this. In most cases, this is how all great discoveries, inventions are made, works of art are created, the true author of which is not their realiser, but their anonymous inspirer, who created the thought image.

Sometimes such mental images are captured immediately they are formulated by several consciousnesses according to their potential. For example, Newton and Leibniz simultaneously discovered differential calculus, formulating it each in their own way: Newton-mathematically, Leibniz-philosophically. Of course, the main natural author of all human inventions are those greatest people about whom no one knows anything, because they are active in the field of only Subtle thought-creation.

The power of thought is great and the power of though creation is incomparably greater than any other power. Thought transforms, according to its specificity, the surrounding environment the energy environment generates in it living, conscious thought images, representations and formations. Therefore, each consciousness is always a focus and centre of radiation of the generated and formed mental energy, realising the inner essence of this consciousness; and the generated consciousness, in turn, acts on its originator, prompting it to new manifestations. The connection between the begotten and the begetter is unbreakable and through the perceptual ability of consciousness will always return to the Subject by the reverse radiation of the active medium transformed by him in one way or another.

This connection is the principle of the responsibility of the progenitor for what is generated: after all, with our thought-creation, we not only transform and formalise the environment of free energies, but also charge the knowledge that is consonant with us. The principle of the responsibility of the originator for the generated is at its root the law of the reverse effect of the generated on the originator, because we cannot break the connection with the generated and we cannot destroy the connection with the consciousnesses generated by us. And this connection keeps us in the circle of the generated until the thought-creating charge is completely exhausted, materialising and transforming the environment to the last possible opportunity.

People consider themselves responsible only for actions, that is, for visible and tangible manifestations. But a thought is the same act, although invisible. The effect of such a mental act is much stronger and longer. The postulate is performed once, causes a particular reaction of the environment and almost immediately affects the producer, thereby exhausting its energy potential. A more subtle action-thought-is reflected in many consciousnesses, transformed into them and flows further.

A thought that does not know physical time and space can act both in distant worlds and on distant worlds. Thought creates living mental images that are carried in the psychic atmosphere, experiencing the earthly life of its creator. Thought, charging and rebirthing many thoughts of consciousness, even unknown to the creator, is realised in phenomena, the existence of which he does not even assume. And therefore, the responsibility for thoughts is many times greater than the responsibility for actions. The range of the thought cannot be taken into account. The flow of intellectual energy is one in our solar system and therefore connects the inhabitants of all the planets.

People often think that not all thoughts are realised. They are mistaken: all thoughts generate something, but the time of their implementation, as well as their relief and adequacy of the plan depend on the degree of concentration invested in them. After all, the secret of a quick, accurate and clear implementation of the plan is the ability to gather all your thought flow into the focus of a certain idea, without allowing extraneous thoughts to change this focus. With such concentration, small thoughts, the so-called "invisible flies" that distract attention. It is easier to cope with a big thought than with small ones, which are the result of the fragmentation and identification of our consciousness with all sorts of trifles. Therefore, before starting to practice concentration, which gives the key to thought-creation, it is necessary to clear your consciousness of "small flies", and this means to educate your own thinking on great ideas and on striving for great ideals.

In some books that" teach " concentration, it is recommended at first to take some physical object or a memory from the past lives. But this is too difficult for a beginner, since there is usually no interest, that is, the tension of creative potential. Besides, what is the use of such concentration with an unclean consciousness: the result will be minimal, and the concentration itself is fragile and is subject to the danger of destruction by extraneous thoughts. It is at the very beginning that abstract concentrations on the ideal are necessary, capturing the entire subjective potential. In this case, the goal coincides with the means, because at the same time the enlightenment of consciousness by the ideal, the purification of consciousness and the ability to concentrate are achieved.

The ideal, and all our manifestations, large and small, must be comprehended by serving it. Therefore, it is necessary to avoid all unnecessary small thoughts that people are so willing to breed in salon affairs and conversations, in complaints and slander against their neighbour, in all sorts of everyday situations. Every little thing in life has its place as a partial expression of the realisation of the ideal, but there is no need to pay special attention to it. Such small thoughts fill up the consciousness with garbage, they generate astral "flies", which, according to the law of the reverse effect of the generated on the parent, break the integrity of consciousness and deprive it of the ability to concentrate.

We must not forget that all the great and pure thoughts, returning to us, help us with the force of a thousand angels, whilst our evil and petty thoughts return to us as small and evil demons, tearing at integrity, our personality, our thoughts. We enact the fate thereof, for, involving subjective consciousness, we change the object of its manifestation, i.e. the external conditions of our lives. Therefore, the mantras of the third Principle are:

"My destiny is my creation, and my creation is myself." "Fate is me, I carry it within me." So everyone can become the master of their own Destiny.

The third Arcanum has the astrological correspondence of Venus. It implements the creative principle of the Mind in our planetary system. The consciousnesses living on it generate forms exclusively by thought-creation, not needing, like earthly humanity, objective tools of realisation.

Venus is the next stage of human development: those who have completed their evolution on Earth, who have completed their task, move to Venus out of necessity. There, in easier conditions, they may continue the Path of Knowledge and Creativity for the sake of the Common Good.

In addition to this exercise, you should try not to clog up your thoughts and to clear them from the husk of vanity. After all, it is our everyday consciousness that must be transformed into the consciousness of service by all our actions.

The Emperor

The Fourth Arcanum

Cosmic Law

Form
Authority
Application
Numeric designation: 4
Astrological correspondence: Jupiter

Hans Thoma, Jupiter

The picture of the Arcanum depicts a standing male figure, with the left leg bent so that it forms a cross with the right. The figure's attire is also Egyptian. The man holds a rod in his right hand, ending with a sign of Jupiter. The figure leans slightly against the cube standing behind it and is crowned with a double crown of Egyptian pharaohs.

It follows from the previous principle that the creation of the world mind occurs randomly and chaotically, but it is guided by a certain regularity and its cycles follow one from another, not arbitrarily, but according to a strict and harmonious regularity of the sequence. This regularity is the inner nature of the Mind, which is imprinted on all its activities, as on each of its partial manifestations.
This internal regularity distinguishes the principle of the creative mind from the environment of free waves of the spirit into a

specific free formation, that is, into a form of manifestation of the spirit. Hence, the form is a consequence of the internal lawfulness of the phenomenon, which constitutes its nature and manifests itself outwardly in its action. Neither Love, nor Life - that is, the spiritual principles that generate the Mind - taken in pure form, have laws. They are free from all forms. Uniformity and forms manifest themselves only where the creative Mind manifests itself. This is the main secret of his work. Love and Life, the primordial parents of the Mind, voluntarily and consciously give.

The creative Mind creates itself and its freedom as a material for the formation of the creative Mind, and by transmitting a pattern, that is, imprinting its inner nature on the source of a Life saturated with Love, the creative Mind generates forms and beings in an impersonal form. Therefore, as a synthesis of all existing faces and forms, the Universal Mind is the personal God of the Universe, The Creator, Indra, Logos, etc., the One who is similar to the forms and therefore personal. This right to manifest the personality in an impersonal form creates the authority of creativity over the environment, as a result of a natural creative manifestation and its foundation.

The figure of a man in the picture rests on a cubic stone-a symbol of his manifestation. Without regularity, there can be no authority, because in chaos it is not known what manifests and what is the medium of manifestation. The whole world is the result of the manifestation of regularity, that is, the inner nature of the creative Mind, on the most different planes of its activity. And from the principle of this internal regularity of phenomena, forms that are limited from each other are born cycles of this manifestation.

The cosmos, the result of the thought-creation of the World Mind, is natural both in general and in all its parts, because the entire inner nature of the creative Mind is imprinted in it. Similarly, the human mind perceives the world according to its internal structure and imposes the seal of its internal regularity and form on this perception. That is why we cannot understand the essence of things by reason, because we are limited from it by the prism, the form of this knowing spirit.

So in creativity, the human mind always reflects its internal regularity and captures its own inner nature, creating mental images one by one and the same law. The human mind, being a partial expression of the World Mind, has the same regularity in its inner nature, and therefore human thought-creation cannot be random and chaotic: even in its unconscious processes, it bears the stamp of the same dynamic regularity and causes homogeneous results. To know and feel the freedom and direct perception of the essence is possible only by transcending your own mind, rejecting it as a cognitive tool and using it as an instrument of thought creation, a proactive and proactive element in relation to the environment related to the next cycle. A general example can be schematically depicted on the basis of already familiar principles.

Life   Love
(-)   (+)

The mind
Regularity

Figure 26

Thus, the cycle of the Quarternary Law is obtained in the given case - the general form of world construction.

Space Environment   Regularity
(-)   (+)

General plan
conscious cosmic manifestation

Plane of manifestation   Conscious cosmic
Conscious life   construction
(-)   (+)

Formation of the Four Worlds
The fundamental content of life

The spiritual Plane   World principles
(-)   (+)

Ideas
Intelligent plane

Figure 27

To explain the action of the dynamic law, we will give examples of earthly life. Let's take the appearance of the ideal of self-affirmation. This example of the manifestation of the dynamic law explains and personally proves how internal transformations affect the transformation of the environment and how subjective work on oneself bears fruit - the objective transformation of the environment.

Self-affirmation

Resistance of
the medium

The impulse
to show courage

Overcoming obstacles

Change of consciousness, gaining a spiritual victory

Subjective enemies
(obstacles)

Subjective victory

Internal struggle

Power as an influence

power as a factor

impact on the environment

Creativity (doing)

The transformation of the environment according to its masculinity

Figure 28

In parallel with this example, let us take a similar example from an objective manifestation: In this case, the desire for self-affirmation is manifested by active patriotism in the life of peoples.

Active patriotism

Resistance   The impulse to show
surrounding peoples   an active popular courage

The principle of conquest,
expansion of national borders

The readiness of other   Aggression, attack
peoples

War
Changing International conditions

Figure 29

The whole world is a manifestation of the Quarternary Law. Each phenomenon in it and each form captures one of its cycles and is in connection with the previous and subsequent cycles. Thus, the world of forms and phenomena is a continuous chain of the flow of life, conditioned by the Quarternary Law of Space Dynamics. This Quarternary Law, or rather, one of these cycles, is contained in each thing and groups the forms we perceive separately into a synthesis of phenomena connected with each other by a previous cycle that conceals the reason for their existence. Thus, the cause of phenomena is never on the same plane, but always higher. The causes of the physical world must, therefore, be sought in the psychological and astral world, and the causes of the phenomena of the astral world - in the ideological or mental plane. Ideological formations are rooted in the syntheses of the spiritual world, and this latter directly expresses the possibilities of the spiritual essence of everything that exists.

Ultimately, the phenomena of the world are connected with each other precisely through their common Spirit. This means that there is no direct connection between the parts of the periphery, that the connection between them always occurs through the centre, with which they are connected by their radii, that is, with the threads of the Mother of the World, or the continuous process of manifestation, The Dynamic Law. Therefore, the real grouping of things according to their essence is completely different from the one that we attach to them with our usual (detached from The Cosmic Law) thinking: after all, the material given by the Earth is transformed according to the idea that forms it. On this basis, the stones that served as the material for the walls of the temple and the stones that served for the walls of the prison belong to two completely different ideas, charged with a completely different energetic charge, and only our rough vision relates them to the same category of facts. So the general formula of any construction can be depicted as follows:

Idea

Material   Creative idea
(-)   (+)

Form

Figure 30

Therefore, the form depends on the creative idea and the material of the medium. The more perfect the design, the more stable the form. For an example of grouping phenomena in terms of the ideas embodied in them, depending on the plan and ideal, let's take the idea of mastering fire, which will look like this:

The idea of mastering fire

Material   Lamps, lighters
(wood)

Making Fire

Figure 31

Thus, all objects that serve as a means of producing fire are connected into one group of phenomena, regardless of the material, because in the Subtle World, the material is always subordinate to the plan, and only our isolation from the cycle of the laws of thinking separates these phenomena.

A vivid expression of the continuity of the cycles of the Cosmic Law is the system of twenty-two Arcana: The first Arcana (+), the second (-), the third (+ -), the fourth-closes the cycle. The fourth, in the future (+), the fifth (-), the sixth (+ -), the seventh closes again, and so on, and there are seven such cycles, because there are twenty-eight principles of the incarnate world.

Since each phenomenon of the world expresses the existence of spiritual possibility, it is also a symbol of this possibility. A symbol is not a conditional representation of an idea, the realisation of an idea in a form, and therefore has all the energy power of the idea's radiation, the dynamics of the ideomotor process embedded in it. Therefore, the physical phenomenon is the natural force of the ideomotor process. In its natural symbolism, the Great Dynamic Law is expressed by the most fundamental concept of Life, namely, the concept of 'family'.

A		B	
Person		Zoological View	
Mother	Father	Female	Male
Child		Cub	

Family

Figure 32

The difference between the human family and the animal family is that animals no longer have the possibility of a creative upper synthesis, that is, a spiritual androgen essence that unites the poles. For a stable and harmonious production of cycles, the positive pole must correspond to the negative pole, and the negative apply to the positive. The plus-minus element bears the imprint of the poles that gave rise to it and is associated with them by receiving an influx, that is, it is passive up, and it is a transmitter of an influx down, that is, it is active down. This is the basis of the law of heredity.

The fourth element, minus, which turns into a plus in the lower cycle, closes its circle, makes it a meaningful, integral phenomenon that has its place and meaning in the Cosmos, and serves as a passage to the next cycle of manifestation.

In Egypt, this Law was depicted in the image of a winged diskos, in the image of a sphinx and in the image of a pyramid.

Moses - Egyptian initiate, priest of Osiris - took it out of the temple and handed it over in the hieroglyphic script of the initiatory Hebrew alphabet, read esoterically as Yahweh or as the name given by the Israelites to God - Jehovah. Thus, The God of the Israelites is the Quaternary Law of Cosmic Dynamics, which expresses the nature of the divine:

-the tenth principle expresses the first.
- the fifth principle reflects the second
- the sixth principle reflects the third and close with the fifth principle, which is them main principle of the creative initiative of the manifested life.

Knowledge of the elements of the Dynamic Law and the ability to combine them gives great power. This power is both the power of the Ideological World over the Subtle World (energy, astral), and the power of the Subtle World over the world of physical phenomena. The use of power is based on authority, and authority arises due to reliance on previous implementation cycles (the figure of the fourth Arcane is based on a cube). And the previous cycle should, in turn, be a complete form that can give this point of support, because it is impossible to rely on chaos. The continuity of the cycles of the Dynamic Law is based on the continuity of the flow of life.

Life always flows continuously, but the break of cycles entails the capture of consciousness in the cell of a detached system of cycles. One cycle continuously and naturally it follows from the other, linking all the planes of manifestation into continuous conscious creativity. On this "continuity" and naturalness of cycles, the ideomotor process of thought-creation is built, which is mentioned in the third principle. To implement an idea in an earthly form (or the citizens of earthly phenomena and events), it is necessary to have the fulcrum of an auto-V pivot (that is, the force rolled up into power), the previous one cycle (that is, a conscious vision of the spiritual syntheses from which this idea has expired), as well as mentally rely on their previous realisations. Then concentration on the idea will give a relief plan, and it is necessary to take into account the energy composition of the medium. From this, a thought image is born, and he, imbued with concentrated thought, feeling and will, already receives the necessary energies himself, finds the appropriate vehicles and implements the plan.

Thus, after the thought image is created, there is further volitional intervention of the creator of the thought image only would have prevented the realisation, for it would introduce new energy and ideas into the thought image - you, who, in turn, would make it chaotic and erase its relief. Therefore, when creating thoughts, the moment of "letting go" of the thought image and abstinence from attachment to it, which causes confusion, is very important.

Therefore, people's desires are usually fulfilled when the desire is extinguished, that is, when the thought image is released and non-interference gives it the opportunity to really come true. Once realised, the ideomotor process will collapse, and the realised phenomenon, which in turn the queue begins to emit an energy charge, partly transmitting it further, and partly striving back to its original source along the same continuity of cycles, but only in the opposite order, causes by its reverse effect the further evolution of the consciousness of its originator. Thus, the inner karma of an active thought-creator and his responsibility for the work is born.

The whole Cosmos lives, develops and breathes this Quaternary Law, and it will appear everywhere and in the phenomena of earthly nature. For example, the four seasons of the year: spring is an active and proactive element according to its earthly nature; summer is a passive, bearing a conceived fruit; autumn is the birth of fruits; and winter is summing up the results of the previous cycle and gathering forces for a new cycle. Also the four stages of the day, and the effects of solar radiation on the earth nature is: Morning gives initiative, creative activity; Day – the carrying of this creative initiative, calm maturation; evening – liberation, the result of the earthly work; and the night is rest, the creation of a general formulation in the Subtle World, made during the day, and gathering strength for a new cycle.

In this way, the cycles of the Dynamic Law continuously flow in the earth's nature, bearing an infinite variety of manifestations in their apparent monotony, because no day and no year is like another. But they are all cycles of the Earth's evolutionary development. And it is only in the human consciousness that these cycles are broken, and the continuity of their expiration of one from the other is not perceived, and therefore, cannot used. Human consciousness - a special expression of cosmic consciousness - is eternally connected with the latter in the roots, but in its manifestation it has identified with the earthly personality, that is, with the instrument of its manifestation, and thus has fallen out of the continuity of cosmic consciousness. Man closed his " I "into the narrow framework of the earthly personality and therefore lost his spiritual" I " and the possibility of continuous and conscious expression of its forms. Therefore, when the evil personality becomes obsolete and exhausts the energy reserve inherent in it, when the tool wears out and the need for its alteration and transformation is revealed, then the human consciousness, identified with this tool, perceives the transformation of forms as death, as the end, as a tragedy.

And if the human "I" had not enclosed itself in this cage, had not limited its consciousness to an earthly personality, then there would have been no death, even physical, because the physical body would then have connected with the psychic energies of the Subtle World and the transition to them would have been gradual, and not sudden, associated with separation consciousness from the Higher sphere. As a result of the rupture of consciousness, the limitation of the sphere of the "I" by the earthly personality, humanity has distorted its nature, lost the correct perception of cosmic relations and possession of the ideomotor process based on the continuity of the cycles of the Dynamic Law. This also distorted the plane of the manifestation of human creativity, the sense of cosmic realities, that is, faith turned into superstition - frivolous and easily expressed postulates of other people's superstitions. The mind was replaced by the mind, that is, one of its parts, created by it to assess the specific earthly situation of its manifestation. And therefore, human creativity, called culture, is constantly being disrupted and distorted.

It is being transformed into a surface civilisation, that is, simply into the coordination and formulation of earthly material and earthly relations. The feeling, that is, the affirmation of the connection of Love and real relationships, was replaced by the instinct of likes and dislikes, the chaos of passions; the will, that is, the continuous striving for the realisation of the ideal, turned into broken desires caused by the desire to possess objective objects. Accordingly, degeneration occurs, the earthly shell of people has become coarsened to the density of the physical body with its coarse sense organs and uncouth perception. (Mind turned into reason, faith into superstitions, culture into civilisation).

This is the so-called cosmos, the fall of humanity, that is, the fall of consciousness from the chain of cosmic cooperation. The task of those who follow the esoteric path is not to identify their " I " with the earthly personality and its hypertrophied requests. Therefore, the principles of subjective development and self-liberation from the framework of a small personality are the fundamental principles of the esoteric path, without acquiring which no real achievements are possible on it. And, bearing in mind the importance and power of thought-creation, this work should begin with the purification of our thoughts and with the construction of a new dynamic worldview to replace the usual static worldview for people. Any static worldview based on taking into account the facts as they are perceived by the human consciousness, and denying the possibility of boundless transformations of consciousness, the boundless arrival of new spiritual possibilities, is a worldview that closes both God, man, and Nature in a narrow circle of the framework of its private life, taking it for the absolute truth, acts corruptively on human consciousness, because it stops its evolution. And since there are no stops in the continuous running of life, the impossibility of progressive development will cause a reverse movement of regression and decomposition.

Only a dynamic worldview based on the broadest syntheses, recognising the possibility of infinite transformations of the prism of human consciousness and affirming the incomprehensibility of the Absolute, is a worldview that corresponds to cosmic realities and serves the evolution of human consciousness. Since in human thinking, the individual cycles of human manifestations are disconnected from each other, then it cannot logically build an upward spiral of its awareness of the truth.

It can create upward syntheses only by jumping, called Insights of consciousness. These moments are the most valuable in the history of the development of human consciousness, because they create a bridge between the worlds, make it possible to ascend to these worlds and from there, that is, identifying your consciousness with a more subtle and higher cycle of life, restore a logical and forceful connection with the Dense world and master the continuity of the Dynamic Law, gain dominance over his earthly personality and over the material of the Earth.

Just one utterance of the Dynamic formula by a person who has risen to the next stage of consciousness will cause an energy process that can be used to carry out a plan and implement it in an earthly environment. The cycles of the Great Quaternary Law are reflected in all the stages of cosmic formations - both themselves and life on them.

Passing through the circle of the visible Cosmos, designated by the constellations of the Zodiac, and being formed by the great consciousnesses of these luminaries, the Quaternary Law takes the form of the elements-Fire, Water, Earth and Air that is, the four formative principles that make up the inner nature of the vital luminary of the universe is the Sun. Like everything else in the Cosmos, the Sun, being the hearth of creative life, is spiritualised by the syntactic consciousness, which includes in its spiritual state those possibilities that are then realised in the circles or orbits of the generated planets. The Great Quaternary Law enters into nature.

The sun is the so-called cross of elements or elements. The nature of these elements corresponded to the original elements expressed by the Quaternary Law of Cosmic Creativity. The initiative process of Love and its objective reality – Life - is the contrast that the Sun will radiate in the forms of its creativity. Love is reflected by the element of Fire, and Life is reflected by the Love-fixing element of the Earth. The World Mind, which plastically forms this flow, is reflected by the principle of Water, and the created syntheses are reflected by the principle of Air. But since the Sun itself is already a co-created synthetic form that carries whole cycles of previous formulations, its creativity is an expression of this cosmic potential inherent in it. Therefore, Fire, that is, an initiative push to creativity, is a transition from a higher cycle to a specific cycle and brings to its special creativity the principle of mobility and spirituality of cycles.

The principle of solar creativity, expressing its potential, is Air. The principle of objectification of possibilities is the Earth. Solar creativity creates prototypes of what is then realised by the manifested principle of Love, Fire. It will contain in itself the secret of the transition from one cycle to another, from one planetary orbit to another, from one form of manifestation of life to the next, both in the differentiated order of creativity, and in the reverse striving of everything existing towards its primary source - the Sun.

Thus, the element of Air expresses the process of synthesising the possibilities of creativity of the general plan of manifestation, the domination of the Spirit over the form and the beginning of a free creative game. The Earth is a fixing element, which builds the separation of forms from each other, creates the Spirit's cells in order to prevent it from previously going back into Space, and guarantees the possibility of the existence of the form, that is, of wounding forms from decay and premature dissolution. This is the principle of work, responsibility and implementation.

Water is the result of the interaction of both. As a part of the Universal Mind, a specific solar Mind reflects cosmic phenomena in itself, has the same plasticity and fluidity of its own material, formed by cycles of Dynamic Law. This is the principle of transferring Love and Life from one form to another.

Fire transmits the actual spiritual potential of the evolutionary orientation from one stage to another, it is the principle of the sublimation of forms, the spiritualisation of matter, the liberation of Spirit from form, the expedient aspiration of all phenomena of the world into their original unity

- Love. That's why fire is the open essence of all phenomena - both our system and the earth's nature. It is "Yod" and He", that is, the First and Fourth of each cycle, he is an initiative spiritual influx, and he also appears as a result of each process.

In the creative work of the solar system, everything is built on the principle of the cross of the elements. To find the right combination of them in each phenomenon and in each form means to reveal the secret of solar creativity. To find them in oneself, to distribute them in the right combination on all planes of manifestation of consciousness and in the totality of one's personality means to find the key to domination over oneself and over the world of earthly forms.

The vehicles of our consciousness, that is, the planes on which it manifests, already reflect one of the elements by themselves:

- spiritual plane - the plane of Fire
- mental plane - the plane of Air
- psychic (astral) plane - the plane of water
- physical - the plane of Earth.

From such a distribution by elements follows the mechanism of creativity of the plane of consciousness in general. The Spiritual plane is the plane of Fire, being both an initiative type (aspect) of the manifestation of consciousness, and the medium of manifestation. This is the physical plane of the Earth principle, that is, Fire and Earth are polar to each other. From this, the psychic plane of Water is born, which then creates a general synthetic conclusion of the mental plane, that is, Air. This explains the mysterious saying of Egyptian wisdom: "Man himself must create a soul on Earth", and that is why our earthly life is so important.

For only by coming into contact with the fixing element of the Earth, that is, having a firm foothold in the objective world, can the subjective spirit transform its spiritual manifestations and build its ideals. Having lost a fulcrum, that is, a state between in two incarnations, the spirit is immersed in the subjective depth of itself on the plane of psychic consciousness that it has reached in this incarnation.

Every solar system, like everything in the Cosmos, is gifted with consciousness. The spirits of the elements are the carriers of this consciousness. Their body, or rather their form, is identical with the element in which they are located, and therefore the consciousness that wants to enter into communication with them must create and give them the form that it is capable of itself. The spirits of the elements are embodied in this the form. That is why they appear in human representation either in beautiful, or in ugly and frightening images.

Air

Water   Fire

Earth

Figure 33

Air is the beginning of the expansion of consciousness, the synthesis of everything, the comprehensiveness of contemplation.

Earth - absorption, differentiation, concentration of consciousness.

Water is the principle of transmutation, the fluidity of consciousness (conclusion, meditation, formulation).

Fire - the principle of self-emission, the assertion of self-liberation, subjectivised consciousness, the non-continuity of consciousness (illumination).

Figure 33 shows the cross of elements in the refraction of the evolution of consciousness. On the spiritual plane of human manifestation, the cross of elements is symbolised by four sacred animals.

Eagle

Man   Leo

Taurus

Figure 34

Eagle-symbolises the spiritual quality of life
Taurus is the quality of silence.
Man is the quality of knowledge.
Leo is the continuity of the aspiration of the will.

A person in his spiritual aspiration is looking for the truth, but
for this he needs, first of all, to have the quality of daring,
because it is impossible to go to the truth without courage. After
that, a person must develop in himself the quality of silence, that
is, to close your soul for self-processing on the basis of the set
ideal, to fall into the period of gestation, because excessive
expansiveness prevents the realisation of power. The quality of
cognition is generated from the set ideal and its inner bearing,
because we know only what we have managed to perceive, that is,
completely pass through the prism of consciousness; and only
then there is the ability to continuously strive along the spiritual
path, the transformation of consciousness, that is, the transition
to the next cycle of spiritual self-manifestation.
The movement along the cross of the elements in human
consciousness goes counter-clockwise, that is, against the activity
of nature in the direction of the synthetic collection of forms and
their spiritualisation in the direction of evolution, while the
activity of nature goes clockwise in the expression of the spirit in
forms. There is a differentiation of synthesis in the
manifestation. This is how you can create a cross of elements in
the mental plane.

Eagle
(deductive thinking)

Man   Leo
Analytical   synthetic
thinking   thinking

Taurus
(inductive thinking)

Figure 35

Deductive thinking is thinking from the general to the particular,
from the principle to the law, from the law to the fact, and it is

necessary to be able to cover the ideological concepts from which the process follows.

Inductive thinking is the reverse process of thinking, going from the particular to the general, from facts to laws and from laws to principles, and for its correctness, a concentrated immersion in objective facts is necessary.

Analytical thinking is a mental process of turning phenomena on the same plane, that is, horizontal thinking, as opposed to deductive and inductive thinking, which are vertical thinking.

Synthetic thinking is a process described in the third principle.
The cross of elements on the psychic plane.

Eagle
(expansiveness)

Man   Leo
(consciousness)   (tension)

Taurus
closeness

Figure 36

The cross of the elements on the physical plane.

Eagle
(sanguinity)

Man   Leo
(phlegmatic)   (choleric)

Taurus
(melancholy)

Figure 37

In the refraction of human activity that goes against nature, the elements of the cross are rearranged, that is, the initiative elements of the cross are rearranged, that is, the initiative element is the Lion or Fire, and the polar element is the Earth or Taurus element.

A cross symbolically expressing a person's tasks, looks like this.

Eagle

Man   Leo

Taurus

Figure 38

Eagle - daring, expansiveness, deductiveness thinking,
sanguinity
Taurus - silence, isolation, inductive thinking, melancholy
Man - cognition, consciousness, analytical thinking,
phlegmatism
Leo - aspiration of the will, tension, synthetic thinking, choleric.
The Eagle and the Taurus are on vertical line, the man and the
Lion are on a horizontal line, and the Eagle and Taurus are
polarised in relation to Leo and Man. In nature, the cross of the
elements is reflected by four states of matter, with Air
corresponding to a gaseous state, Earth to solid, Water to liquid
and Fire to radioactive.

Air

Earth   Fire

Water
Figure 39

In alchemy, this cross corresponds to the alchemists'
physical elements.

Air
(azoth of the sages, a rod with a snake and wings)

Earth   Fire
(salt of the sages)   (sulphur of the wise men)

Mercury
(mercury of the sages)
Figure 40

81

The four main qualities of a person on all the planes of his manifestation are symbolised by the four sides of the cross.

Eagle
(the predominance of activity over passivity)

Taurus   Leo
(closed perception   (everything is open)
passivity)

Person
(activity is closed, perception of cognition is open).

Figure 41

These are elements expressed in nature and humanity. The human consciousness should stand in the centre of the cross, not being identified with any of its branches. Usually a person has one or two branches developed at the expense of others, so his manifestation is not harmonious, knowledge is wrong and construction is one-sided. For correct cognition and commensurability in construction, it is necessary first of all to establish the harmony of the person's personality itself.
People are divided according to the elements, depending on the predominance in one or another person of one of the branches of the cross, that is, one of the main qualities.
So, people of the element of Air will be inclined to abstract thinking, audacity in their pursuit of truth, they are expansive and sanguine. A person belonging to the element of Fire will differ in synthetic thinking, mental orientation and choleric temperament. The people of the Earth are silent, prone to inductive thinking, closed and melancholic. The personalities embodying the Water principle are distinguished by clarity of recognition, analytical thinking, consciousness and phlegmatic temperament.
Having determined the main element in yourself, it is easiest to engage in the development of the opposite element, that is, complementary. So, a groundlessly distracted Eagle should develop a Taurus in itself, and one who does not know how to fly - Taurus - will acquire eagle wings, and then develop the polar elements and complement the lines of the cross. Such work on oneself will achieve a balance of manifestations and basic

qualities, domination over oneself. What prevails? - Yes, those basic three principles that make up the human individual soul, that is:

a) the spiritual core;
b) manifested Love - individual consciousness
in its eternal transformations, the self is identical to itself;
b) the Creative Mind.

These three principles should rule over the four cross of earthly qualities that make up a person's personality. The manifestation and self-affirmation in the cross of the immortal personality belonging to the Cosmos of the individual soul is what we call will. Thus, the will-the active self-affirmation of the soul in its form - stands in the centre of the cross of personality, but the cross of elements in its four planes of manifestation creates the shell-form of the immortal soul.

The more human consciousness resides in the soul and the more stable it is rooted there, the more a person has power over himself, and therefore over the earthly environment that he is called to transform. But in the chaos with which modern human personalities are overflowing, the individual immortal soul is not able to find itself and assert itself without clearing the "Augean stables" of thoughts and without restoring order in mutually repelling phenomena. To understand the methods of "clearing the stables" and "taming the animals", it is necessary to first understand the negative manifestations of the four main psychological types:

The eagle breeds frivolity.
Taurus - inertia and laziness.
Man is egotistical.
Leo - fanaticism and short temper.

Therefore, the Eagle, as a rule, becomes a groundless philosopher; Man-a sceptical, prone to the vice of self-conceit, a suspicious grouch; Taurus-an indecisive and cowardly moralist who denies everything that is beyond his own nose; Leo becomes an obsessive and impatient, even cruel, a fanatic who does not consider anything. Thus, the treatment of a sick animal occurs by instilling the personality of the positive qualities of the opposite animal.

The frivolity of the Eagle is treated by acquiring a sense of responsibility and introspection of the Taurus, who always considers objective facts. Thus, the Eagle is attached to the Earth and its groundless philosophy turns into a synthetic worldview. It turns out, the so-called winged Taurus, capable of flight and concentrated work. The Winged Taurus cures a Person from self-conceit, doubt and scepticism.

The lion is treated by itself, by changing its orientation. As an example, we can cite the Apostle Paul, a representative of the element of Fire. A fanatical and cruel persecutor of Christianity, after changing his orientation, turned into an apostle, bringing a synthesis of all ancient wisdom to the teaching.

After such taming of animals, it is necessary to jealously distribute them along the poles, that is, it is necessary to make sure that their manifestations in different planes of consciousness correspond to each other. It is necessary that all of them are organised by the principle of commensurate proportionality of manifestations, that is, to establish mutual stability in the direction of the cross. The whole of this work is based on the education of the will, on the ability to fearlessly discipline their astral manifestations and control their relationships. And only after the establishment of such an objective order is it possible to transform the personality, that is, its transition to the next cycle with the acquisition of existing qualities. This transformation is achieved by the so-called "rotation of the wheel of animals", that is, the ability to take turns, according to the elements Of the Dynamic Law, to awaken to expedient activity every branch of the cross. Moreover, the daring audacity of the Eagle should pass into the concentrated objectivity of the Taurus consciousness, the results of processing should they should be evaluated by a Person, and this evaluation should find the resultant, according to which a Lion could hide in his eternal aspiration and spirituality.

Astrologically, the Fourth Arcana corresponds to Jupiter. The synthetic consciousness of this planet is The Father and the Ruler of the law and order of the whole of the solar system.

The Pope

The Fifth Arcanum

Manifestation of life or
World Magnetism

1. Natural Religion
2. Individual initiative
3. Worldwide communication
Numeric designation: 5
Astrological correspondence: Aries

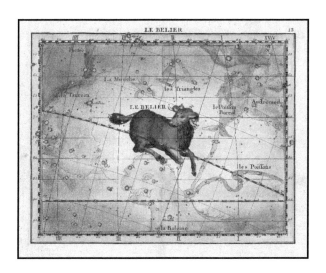

John Flamsteed, Le Belier (Aries), 1776

The painting depicts a seated hierophant. On his head is a disk with horns (just like in the second arcana on the head of a woman). In his hand is the staff of the hierophant, that is, a cross with two crossbars - a sign of power over three worlds of manifestation of conscious creative will. The Hierophant sits between two columns symbolising the principle of polarisation. Two figures are kneeling in front of him. The Hierophant blesses both with a triple finger.

The Fourth Principle has revealed to us that in every form there is a cycle of the manifested Great Quaternary Law and the application of the same law to each plane of co-knowledge and to each stage of life manifestation. The Fourth Principle showed us that each form belongs to two sources of the creative manifestation of the Mind - the centrifugal and centripetal and, finally, the Fourth Principle revealed to us the presence in the centre of such a quarternary form.

The Fifth Principle reveals to us the essence and manifestation of the centre of the cross, this fifth element of the quintessence, which is located in the centre of each form and, at the same time, above it. The manifestation of the spirit in forms is the generation of form, the process of manifestation of the creative initiative of the World Mind occurs in the Cosmos not by a mechanical outflow of one cycle from another, but each time it is individualised into a conscious creative impulse. Creative initiative of the Ecumenical.

The mind is granulated into foci of its manifestation. In this way, great consciousnesses are created, clothed in the forms of luminaries, who, in turn, granulate the spiritual impulse of their creativity into the following, differentiated in relation to them, creative centres of individual initiative.

The law of individualisation of initiative makes a single great organism out of the Universe, each organ and each cell of which is a focus of self-emission that generates further forms. Thus, in each Quaternary form, wherever it is manifested, there is an individual core that controls this form as an instrument for the realisation of the manifestation of its self-government, that is, the realisation in the world of those possibilities that are contained in this core.

This core is the immortal soul-individuality and is always the same in all the objective forms of its self-manifestation. She is the immortal soul that, when incarnating on Earth, consistently creates for herself a necklace of individual personalities in the chain of her incarnations, each time showing one of the sides of her potential in their activities.

Thus, this inner essence is that monad (individuality) that always exists and is identical with itself, which in man is a cosmic citizen, unchangeable and independent - it depends on the place and form of its manifestation. The instrument of manifestation, the energy form in which it is clothed, always corresponds in its structure to the task of the next manifestation, and in its material to the hearth, the cosmic place of consciousness development, where this monad manifests. This shell plus the monad is the person's focus for the manifestation of individual creative initiative. Individuality, as we have already noted, is threefold:

1. Its core is the immortal All-Blessed Spirit, the Divine spark, eternally merged with its source, as a wave is merged with the ocean.

2. Its objective manifestation, Consciousness, is a direct reflection of the flow of life in this essence, which manifests itself in it and which is akin to its own essence. This is the principle of feeling or what is called the organ of cognition of the Spirit or the Heart, which unites us with the entire Cosmos.

3. The third component corresponds to the principle of the generative and cognising Mind, as the source of the only self-manifesting creative thought.

The Creative Mind and the Heart are polarised in relation to each other. The Great Mother-Life-becomes his (Spirit's) spouse, that is, the sphere of his manifestation inside our soul, and both of them are fed by the emanation of the spiritual core. And in their outward manifestation, they manifest the Creative Will, and in their striving for the primary source - the Spirit - the Will to liberation. Thus, the Will is the organ of the manifestation of our demi-mortal Soul. It is impossible to talk about Free Will, because these two terms are contradictory to each other. The will is a constant intense striving towards a goal, with a twofold goal:

- finding the source;
- capturing the search for the source in the objective world.

Therefore, the very existence of the Will shows the absence of Freedom, but at the same time points the way to it: the way to Freedom lies through the Will, because without the Will there can be no movement either forward or backward. It is itself, as it were, the result of the application of the principle of individualisation of initiative, which is the basis of all Cosmic creativity and dissolution. Freedom is where there is no form, because form is a limitation, it is subject to the law, subject to change and the double direction of the life source, subject to the general plan of the World Mind. Where there is no form, there is no law, there is no general plan, but there is only the Radiance of the Spirit - free play and unbreakable Unity, the fusion of all possibilities. There is Freedom, but the Will is no longer there. But despite this, the Will is the only lever for the manifestation of individual initiative, the only spring of the entire World Construction. Therefore, it is so necessary to protect the integrity of the Will and the purity of its manifestation. It is a reflection of the spiritual force in the form - of the "I" - the quintessence in relation to the quaternary substance. The domination of the Spirit over the form is the domination of the Will, controlled by the Spirit or Spiritual ideal, over personal manifestations.

By controlling each form, the individual will also controls us, that is, the two streams of manifestation of the Cosmic Law of Dynamics, which intersect in each form, individualising their cycles.

An individualised manifestation of the will, these two currents, Freedom and Will, are formed into the law of causality and the law of expediency. Both of them are manifestations of the same Law of Dynamics in two directions.

The law of causality is the law that objectifies the individual creative potential, that is, manifesting it in objective phenomena and transmits the initiative impulse further along the differentiating cycles of manifestations. The law of causality governs the creative involution of the Spirit into forms, the imprinting of its capabilities in the flow of objective phenomena. The law of expediency is the subjective law of self-development of consciousness in the form, it is the law of striving for a subjective ideal, for its realisation in consciousness.

This is the law governing the figurative movement of the form towards the Spirit. The law of expediency governs the self-creative evolution of the development of consciousness, that is, the development of the subjective core of each form, and, consequently, the refinement of the ideal. In each focus of manifestation the conscious creative initiative is polarised in relation to the environment that this focus affects, transforming it according to its specific potential, which means that each such focus is a centre of magnetic radiation that polarises the environment according to the law of momentum transfer and excites it to further creativity, to realise the potential of its centre. And on the other hand, each such initiative centre is a magnet of attraction for the environment, prompting it to concentrate everything around itself and synthesise its energy manifestations, in accordance with its central inner essence. Each such centre is the reason for the transformation of the environment and the goal. Like the cosmic establishment of a Spiritual Centre that resides everywhere and a periphery that goes into infinity, each part of the Cosmos is also the centre of the manifestation of Spiritual Creative Consciousness and the periphery - the forms of its influence and reflects in its construction the construction of the Cosmic Spirit. That is why man is the image and likeness of God, a microcosm in relation to the Macrocosm (the big Cosmos).

Synthetic foci of conscious creative initiative attract more private foci to themselves and influence them. Great Consciousnesses in the environment of their spiritual influence group smaller consciousnesses around themselves, attract them to the environment of their consciousness and influence them. Large charges are differentiated into smaller charges, which, in turn, create forms of their manifestation, and encompass these forms with their more synthetic broad and subtle form. Thus, systems of worlds are formed in the physical, mental, ideological and spiritual aspects.

These worlds are again attracted to each other, mutually coordinated, creating more and more complete synthetic and large systems. This is how the Harmony of the World is created, based on the principle of attraction of polarities, this is how the universal gravitation is created along the steps of small manifestations of initiative to the circles of a more extensive and intense manifestations of creative initiative, up to the Universal Hearth of Divine Creativity. This is the Universal magnetism of attraction of the periphery to the centre, realised in all circles of radiation by the centres of consciousness of their creative potential in particular and in the whole comprehensive scale of the Divine Revelation as a whole.

Every manifestation of creative initiative is a Will. The will has its roots in the innermost essence of the spiritual core of consciousness. It feeds on the radiations of the Heart and is guided by the Mind. It dominates the medium of its manifestation and the instrument of its manifestation, and consequently, the Great Dynamic Law. This domination of the Will over the Quaternary Law of Dynamics is graphically symbolised by the Pentagram, which is a commonly used sign of magical influence and the domination of the disciplined Will over the phenomena of the world.

The will that has found its source and is strengthened in it is the Will about which Christ said: "The will of the will and of my Father is one." Such a Will is based on Faith, that is, on unification with the Spiritual Core and dominates the world: both over the centrifugal orientation of the law of causes, and over the centripegal direction of the law of expediency.

In the state in which a person is, that is, if there is a possibility of a breakdown of consciousness and the last fall from the Spiritual Flow of the Universe, the pentagram symbol has another meaning. The human Will should be directed to reconnect consciousness with its own spiritual core. This is its goal, for the achievement of which the Will must coordinate all the elements of the human personality on the three planes of its manifestation.

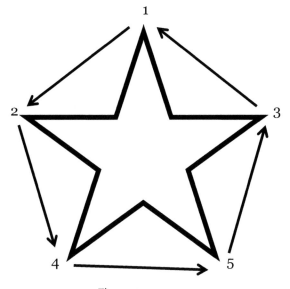

Figure 42

This is the Pentagram of the White Magician, directed upwards, to search for its source and to recreate the human being as it should be. The will, directed to the realisation of its spiritual task, subordinates to this task the cross of the elements from which the personality is created. The fifth ray is the centre of the cross, brought up, that is, cleared of stupid self-identification with the material of the personality and dominating in this personality. If this domination of the Will over the personality is realised and its spiritualisation is achieved, then the external world also obeys it. Then and only then is she the ruler over the cycles of the Dynamic Law manifested in nature and man.
Both the spirits of nature, and angels, and archangels, that is, the psychic forces of consciousness that weave the Fate of humanity, obey and are guided by a spiritualised initiative in the name of realising the truth and building All the common Good.
Since the Sign of the pentagram is a sign of human influence on the Earth in general, the inscription itself, mental or graphic, already makes an impression or impact on the beings of the Subtle World, as a symbolic statement of the domination of the human Will. Therefore, the Sign of the pentagram is always used as a protective weapon against the attack of hostile forces of the Subtle World and a weapon of their submission. And since the pentagram is a symbol of the expression of the Will in general,

when applied to humanity, it is called the Law of the Microcosm, which means that ultimately the conscious volitional manifestation similar to the manifestation of the Divine Spirit and the Cosmos.

In our humanity, there is another direction of the Will, namely, the direction to destruction, the will to refuse to fulfil the Spiritual Task of humanity. This is the Will of the Black Magician, which is graphically symbolised by an inverted pentagram, in which the initiative manifestation of the Will is detached from the Spiritual core and consciously subordinated to the differentiating cycles of the Great Law. In this case, we are not dealing with a will divided into desires, which has lost its unifying axis of spiritual self-emission, but with a constant volitional orientation towards the destruction of all intellectual, psychic and spiritual unity, to the coarsening of forms and the narrowing of consciousness. Of course, in the end, such a will loses its own unity and, subject to the dynamics of the differentiating centrifugal flow, breaks up in it, and the consciousness of its carrier, narrowing, gradually fades and dissolves in the general material.

In any case, the engine of the Black and White Path is the same principle of Will, but in its two different directions. The methods of external influence of the Black and White Path are often similar to each other, but the internal motives of actions, as well as the methods of educating the will, are different. Both White and Black magicians must possess the material of their personality, that is, the cross of elements, both must establish the domination of the will over the manifestation of the personality, that is, discipline their will. Ordinary people live by impulses born in them under the influence of objective facts, phenomena, events, and their actions are reactions to incidents in the objective world.

The first task of a magician, that is, a person with a disciplined will, is self-awareness of the attitude to objective incidents: not to allow oneself to be involved in their flow, but to extract from them those elements that are necessary for conscious construction. This self-awareness can be cultivated in yourself. The discipline of the will is the easiest way to start training with control over your physical manifestations. Any involuntary movement, such as drawing stupid figures during a conversation, twisting a moustache, etc, should be eliminated and replaced either by complete calmness or conscious work. The disorderly movement of our body parts must be overcome and brought into harmony. All unnecessary physical fussiness and anxiety should give way to reasonable self-control. Excessive appetites must be tempered, the enjoyment of food must be overcome - after all, food is a way to maintain the vitality of the body, and not an object of pleasure. The sensations of cold and heat, pain and illness, fatigue and drowsiness must be overcome by the will so as not to interfere with the fulfilment of the tasks set.

Psychically, the will must control and overcome the impulsive immediate reactions of our feelings, and objective reactions to incidents: expressions of joy, grief, anger, annoyance, irritation and sensuality should be moderated, coordinated and ordered by the will. Self-control is the key to the psychic domination over oneself and the world.

Intellectual impulses should also be tempered by the will, that is, hobbies with theories, teachings, and all sorts of intellectual streams. This does not mean that we should treat everything coldly, but this means that we must have our own ideal, which has grown out of the innermost recesses of our subjective Spirit, and that this ideal, supported by the will, must stand unshakably, and the will, which has roots in it, must lead us to complete self-control, that is, to the complete domination of the subjective Spirit over the objective instrument of its manifestation.

The great calmness of the magician is the result of his self-control and the source of his strength. This great calmness of a disciplined will and a disciplined personality carries within it the secret of influencing the environment, the natural world and the invisible world. This discipline of the will or discipline of the Spirit is reflected in well-known tests of students, and the tests of white and black magicians are almost the same. These are tests for fear, for passion and for conscience, and the tests for fear and for passion are the same for students of both paths, but the goals of domination are different.

The disciple of the white path must be fearless and dispassionate in order to successfully fight the enemies of human evolution; the disciple of the black path must be fearless and dispassionate in order to enter into an alliance with the ugly psychic formations of human involution without disgust and fright. The white student must dominate the passions so that they cannot distract him from the fulfilment of the tasks of the Common Good, so that all his passions can be sublimated and extracted from them the black student must be dispassionate, so that some passion does not awaken in him an echo of a human positive feeling or his conscience.

The test of conscience is available only for a White magician, for Black it is replaced by a test of commitment to evil. The White

Path begins with the requirement of strict discipline. This path does not require complete submission to the will of others, but requires independence and self-activity, because its goal is to educate a dominant person, an servant of the construction of the Common Good. The Black Path requires strict external discipline. He removes all responsibility from the student, shifting it to the leader or organisation, because his goal is to create an obedient and submissive tool for carrying out destructive actions.

The white path is difficult and thorny at the beginning, because the burden of responsibility is not easy, but it leads to peace, bliss, knowledge and power. The black path is easy and convenient, because it removes responsibility from the shoulders of the person walking, but this mental comfort leads to the enslavement of the will and the narrowing of consciousness, to the oblivion of cosmic relations, to the extinction of individualisation and initiative.

In the above white pentagram, the elements of the Dynamic Law are arranged in such a way that the element of will (tire) with its three lights, denoting the triplicity of our individuality, dominates the cycles of the Dynamic Law. The direct pentagram expresses the law of individual collectivity, which gives meaning and value to each individual existence, the potentiation of his creative initiative.

In the inverted black pentagram, the lights are overturned, that is, the individuality of the Dynamic Law is suppressed. The inverted pentagram expresses the law of collective individuality, that is, the suppression of individual initiative by the collective principle.

Therefore, the will can be brought up both for domination and for submission: on the white path, it is brought up for domination by self-subordination of the individual to its ideal; on the black path, it is brought up for submission, here a lawless obedience is imposed that does not explain anything to someone else's will which, in exchange for this, promises to achieve a state of personal immortality.

What ideals should the Will serve? It must act for the sake of developing its strength, for the sake of dominating the hobbies, passions and impulses of the individual. After all, humanity, which has fallen out of Cosmic cooperation, has lost the threads of natural relationships and the knowledge of its role and its significance.

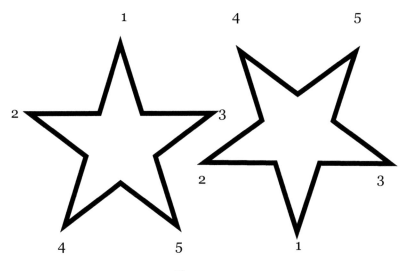

Figure 43

In the process of building the Kingdom of God, that is, it has lost its natural connection, the direct awareness of the Divine Unity, what we call Religion. Direct knowledge of God, a sense of oneself as one with the Divine Spirit, was erased in the human consciousness and it ceased to use an inexhaustible source of spiritual possibilities, doomed itself to spiritual impoverishment, crushing of creative potential, decomposition. Humanity lives according to an inverted pentagram, which condemns to death in the sense of individual existence and the manifestation of creative initiative. This condemns the entire planet to destruction and threatens to bring chaos to the Overall Creativity of the Solar System.

In this trouble, the powerful Consciousnesses of the fraternal planets came to the aid of humanity, who, under the guidance of the Solar Spirits who control the Life and Creativity of the system, undertook to restore the connection between the blinded servant - humanity - and the Spiritual Flow of the Cosmos. These Brothers of humanity took upon themselves the immense burden of incarnation in the environment of fallen humanity in order to grasp the threads of his consciousness and attach them to the Common Chain of World Cooperation They formed light bridges between the fallen humanity, human consciousness and the Cosmic Spirit, which people call God. They built a whole Spiritual World of ideals for humanity and set milestones on the way to restoring the connection of human consciousness with the

Divine Cosmic consciousness, outlined the ways of subjective search for people in the name of birth and entry into the lost Kingdom of God.

This Spiritual World that they brought to people is the world of ideals and spiritual tasks of humanity itself. The fulfilment of the Precepts of the Great Teachers is the fulfilment by humanity of its own tasks. In this newly built World, the great Brothers of humanity have breathed their own strength, the life of their soul. And as long as the Ideals set by them exist, as long as earthly humanity has not passed through the milestones of the Path indicated by them, as long as it has not reached the spiritual growth that would allow it to master the Creative Mission assigned to it again, the Great Brothers of humanity remain connected with the Earth and with humanity and cannot free themselves from the task they have assumed and go further along the path of Cosmic Evolution.

Truly, humanity must help its saviours and redeemers by subjectively transforming its consciousness, after taking on its shoulders the burden of saving earthly humanity, redeeming its karma - this is the Great Sacrifice of the Brothers of Humanity: The Great Brothers of humanity, in their desire to help people, gave their Spiritual potential to the Earth, filling them with the creative shells of the cross of elements.

In the process of their descent from the Spiritual World to the earthly World, the Brothers of humanity are an inverted pentagram of the so-called Great Redemptive Cliche, in contrast to the illegally inverted pentagram of the black magician. They carry in the depths of their consciousness the Spiritual Cross that people have lost Elements of, and by this cross they establish the existence of the spiritual earthly world.

These Brothers of humanity are the great founders of Religions, which all come down to the only Natural Religion that has been lost by human consciousness. Humanity can come to this Divine Religion only through the bridges laid by its saviours, and these bridges are the spiritual self-emission of their own consciousness, in the form of teachings adapted to human consciousness. At the heart of every religion The Great Redemptive Cliche of the spiritual path of man, awakened by contact with the Saviour, is once again established in the Spiritual World of the Earth created for man and dominates the elements of his earthly personality and earthly environment.

Fallen humanity could not produce a single value, in the sense of spiritual achievements, from the potential of its consciousness. All great cultural values, all cultural construction, are based on religious provisions brought by the Brothers of humanity. The Words of Christ: "I am a stone - the cornerstone of the building being erected " - these words refer only to Christ, but are applicable to all the Teachers of humanity, because all the others are his servants who help to establish all that Christ has contributed to the evolution of humanity. Therefore, the Christian truly belongs to Christ, the Buddhist to Buddha, the Mohammedan to Mahomet, the Hermetic to Hermes, etc.

The more complete the spiritual dedication of human consciousnesses to their Leaders, the closer the connection, the more powerfully a person's potential is imbued with a spiritual impulse, the greater his creativity, its significance and influence on the environment. Through many incarnations, the human consciousness is fed alternately with the spiritual influxes of all the Brothers of humanity and thus acquires its synthetics, that is, the ability to fully master its task, restore its natural connection with the Cosmos and, already standing on its own feet, not relying on saviours, fulfil its Creative Mission.

Then, saved by the great Brothers (there is only one Saviour, Christ, and the others are the Brothers of humanity), humanity itself, in turn, will become a shining bridge of hope between the Kingdom of God and the Earth. Thus, everyone is called and everyone can save his Saviour and free Him from the difficult task of being a bridge between heaven and Earth by walking on this bridge with his own feet, replacing a Great Brother.

In essence, all the Teachers of Humanity spoke about the same thing: about the Love of God and the Love of one's neighbour, and the Love of God is our natural connection with the Cosmic Spirit, and the Love of one's neighbour is the same with each other, restored by the affirmation of the Universal Unity in God. All the Laws, all the Covenants and all the advice given by the Teachers of Humanity are methods of restoring spiritual connection with the Kingdom of God and ways of establishing universal cooperation. They are all formulations of the Creative Mind, various aspects of Love and Life. The difference in the methods and methods of establishing the lost connection is a specific difference between one religion and another. The difference between these methods depends on the spiritual and energetic tonality of those peoples whose turn in cultural construction has come. In general, every religion bears the stamp of a Redemptive Cliche and consists of five elements:

1. A specific spiritual impulse.
2. The environment in which this impulse will manifest itself.

3. The magnet of religion, corresponding to the specific consciousness of its founder.
4. A cult that depends on the magnet's environment.
5. The politics of religion, that is, the ways of influencing and spreading influence, as well as cultural construction in all areas.
By the presence of these elements, you can make out any religion, understand its spiritual essence and determine its cultural construction.

Buddhism

The Doctrine of independent self-improvement. A person, an example of which was the Buddha himself, by means of selfless self–sacrifice and self-denial, with the correct recognition and coordination of all his manifestations around the ideal of spiritual perfection.
Environment: meek, passive-minded people, prone to contemplation, in need of potential active support.
Magnet: the illusory nature of the world of phenomena, from which one should be freed by its sublimation.
Cult: the conquest of natural forces by personal influence and self-determination of the individual.
Politics: a personal example.

Christianity

The doctrine of restoring the connection with the Kingdom of God through the manifestation of Love. The inner perfection of a person by combating the consequences of a fall.
Environment: the cultural decomposition of the feral and the gross: a system of initiatory secrets, open to such peoples of mixed eastern races. They are formed as the degrees of Initiation increase.
Magnet: the personality of Christ as the Incarnator of the Redemptive Cliche.
Cult: unification by the principle of deification of the personal
Politics: missionary work and recruitment by persuasion.

Mohammedanism

The doctrine of the all-pervading Will of God, connecting the human will with the Cosmos.
Environment - primitive honest warlike peoples with a materialistic worldview.
Magnet: permeating everyday life with religious foundations, turning life into a battle.
Cult: worship of the Prophet and sacred places.
Politics: conquest and strict hierarchy.

Judaism

The doctrine of obedience to the Will of the One God through strict observance of the religious law. Awareness of the symbolism of life phenomena.
Environment: persistent, true to themselves, but not knowing spiritual subordination and leadership.
Magnet: the ideal of being chosen and Messianic.
Cult: Worship and Bringing to Life the Great Dynamic Law that restores the connection between Heaven and Earth (Jehovah).
Politics: the mental and intellectual domination of the chosen people over the rest.

Freemasonry

The doctrine of the Fall, the reintegration of humanity with the recognition of all the methods of the latter, that is, a synthetic knowledge of the common spiritual tradition of humanity.
Environment: psychic selection of incarnationally developed personalities without distinction of nationalities.
Magnet - the system of initiatory secrets, openly formed as the degrees of initiation increase.
Cult: performing secret rituals that allow one to master the world astral, symbolised by the image of Baphomet.
Politics: the imperceptible implementation of one's ideals by revealing them, as needed, to the initiates.

Truly, humanity is rich. Indeed, if it had accepted all that was brought to it by the Brothers of humanity, it would have long ago erased all signs of its fall and returned to the Kingdom of God. But the great vice of humanity-self-conceit-and its great weakness-doubt-these two shallow children of the human mind, claiming an independent, leading, creative role, prevent them from accepting spiritual riches and all the time expose him, the mind, to the most unexpected distortions. If we look at the human Pantheon of various ideas about God, we will find there such unexpected images that we will truly doubt the cognitive abilities of people. We will see that the concept of " God " serves to cover up human weaknesses, vices and stupidities.

Everyone puts God in an image that is convenient for him, in an image that serves to justify his shortcomings and his vices. So, a weak person sees God as a kind guardian of himself, who at the right moment, without effort, will give him everything that is needed; a vicious person blames God for his vices; a person seeking rewards for his actions imagines God as a cornucopia, etc. But let us remember that the ideomotor process of such thought-creation creates corresponding images in the Subtle World, which, thus, is filled with all sorts of "ideals" of human self-justifications and weaknesses.

The Fifth Principle, revealing to us the essence of religion as a cosmic connection, commands us to clear our consciousness of these false ideas by giving ourselves and following one or all of the Redeemers of Humanity, by working out karma and strictly fulfilling Covenants in our lives. We must tread the paths laid by them firmly and dispassionately, accepting the Sacrifice of the Redeemers and freeing them by this acceptance.

This should be the direction of our constantly and gradually growing willpower, the main spring of our spiritual growth. From an impulsive person who has lost the unifying Thread of the Spirit, unworthy and shameful in his manifestations, each of us must become a real Person, a Pentagram, that is, a conscious spiritually-strong-willed person, or, as it is customary to call in occultism, a "magician", an adept of Initiation.

"The Magician with Heaven, and hell is subject to him." The adept has entered the Chain of World Cooperation and has the right to use the Cosmic Spiritual Stream to fulfil his task of serving the Universal, The good. But even from the forces of the Earth, powerful, although fallen tools for the implementation of their tasks, he should not, has no right to refuse, bearing in mind that he is connected with the Earth and humanity by an immutable common karma. He must put these artificial forces of the Earth in order and spiritualise them, using them for his construction.

All the power of hell can be sublimated and forced to serve the Cosmic Construction. Wisely using the most negative features of the human psyche in the name of Building a New Humanity means conquering hell and forcing the transformed evil to serve the Common Good.

Therefore, the hierophant from the symbolic picture of the fifth principle blesses both white and black, for both are his servants; and the" brother of the left hand " - the black-finds his redemption in his all-transforming activity.

Saint Lawrence Church (Lawrenceburg, Indiana),
Offering of Melchizedek window

The Lovers

The Sixth Arcanum

Choice of paths

The method of analogy
Pentagrammic freedom
Space environment
Numeric designation: 6
Astrological correspondence: Taurus

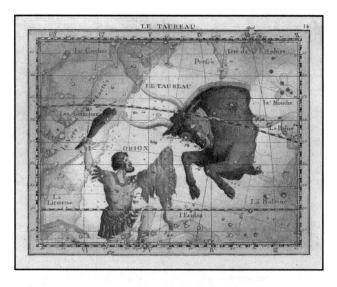

John Flamsteed, Le Taureau (Taurus) 1776

The symbolic picture depicts a young man standing at a cross-roads. To his left is a wide path leading down, and from there a smartly dressed woman beckons him. On the right is a narrow mountain path that winds uphill and points the way to the top. Above - a light genius aims an arrow from a bow at a woman on the left path.

"Everything that is above is like what is below, and what is below is like what is above, in the name of affirming the wonderful Unity of the Universes." The Sixth Principle reveals and explains these mysterious words of the great sage of antiquity - Hermes Trismegistus - the words inscribed on the famous Emerald Tablet found by Egyptian priests in the temple of the Great Sphinx half-buried in the sands about two thousand years before the Birth of Christ.

The one hidden essence of the manifested world, the Cosmic Spirit, is expressed by universal Love. Life is one - the energy of the world is the process of manifestation of Cosmic Love. The Mind of the universe is one, for its nature is everywhere identical with itself. There Is One Great Quaternary Law - The Law of Cosmic Dynamics. There is a single principle of individualisation of Creative Initiative. These five principles are valid in all worlds, they form the Life and phenomena of all planes of Consciousness manifestation.

The Cosmic Spirit is manifested by the energy of Life. This energy is all formed by the Mind in vibrations that differ from each other in the strength and frequency of their vibrations. The law of Cosmic Dynamics distributes these vibrations according to the cycles that follow from each other, forming the spiral of cosmic Life and the principle of individualisation groups, concentrating these vibrations into foci of individual conscious life, that is, creates living conscious beings who, through the manifestation of their initiative-will, deploy their spiritual potentials in the construction of objective phenomena.

The dynamic Law differentiates a single energy, that is, the substance of the world, depending on the quality of its vibration. This means that the planes of consciousness differ from each other not in kind, but in the degree of intensity and frequency of vibrations and in the intensity of the mutually polarised magnets that create its images, conscious centres of Creative Initiative. This means that the spiritual world differs from the mental world only in the quality of the vibrations of its energy material, and the mental world differs from the psychic world and the psychic world from the physical world in the same way.

This creates a scale of thickening vibrations from matter to Spirit. The higher the world is, the finer, purer and more intense its vibrations are, the more plastic the shapes are, and the more powerful and intense the magnets, that is, the consciousness of the beings inhabiting it. The world principles with the laws that follow from them penetrate into the Universe through all the planes of their vibrations. Thus, wisely revealing the essence of the phenomena of the physical world according to the principles operating in it and, therefore, we can draw a conclusion about the principles and laws operating in the following planes of the Universe. The great natural symbolism of nature is built on this. The facts of the physical world are symbols, imprinted images of the phenomena of the mental world. In turn, the phenomena of the psychic world are pictures of the unfolding ideas of the mental plane, and the ideas of the mental plane are framed symbols of spiritual possibilities.

Consequently, all these worlds are governed by the same principles that formalise them and are different from each other's materials, that is, the degree of condensation of a single energy, are similar to each other and represent a chain of analogies, a chain of different energy potentials with uniformity of the forming principles. And it is only thanks to this actual similarity of the worlds to each other that the only real method of world recognition is brought to life - the method of analogies, which is denied by academic science, which, as a result of this denial of the method of cognition given by nature and God, has reached a dead end of its false understanding and cannot know the essence of things.

According to the method of analogies, consciousnesses located in one of the four worlds can cognise the planes above and below themselves. Cognising the phenomena of the physical world, consciousness can, by the method of analogies, draw a conclusion about the facts of the Mental World, about the laws of the Ideological World and the great principles of Spirit-making. The method of analogies makes it impossible to fundamentally ignore areas that lie outside of his usual experience. In addition, thinking and cognition by the method of analogies transforms consciousness, introducing other vibrations into it, opens up the possibility of an inaccessible experience.

If we look at the entire Universe as a great symbol of peace-making and see the laws governing the Universe in every fact of the most private manifestation of the physical world, then we will truly be able to read the book of Nature, see its laws, as well as all the mistakes made against this law and all the consequences that follow from them. After all, the worlds transferred to the next stages of consciousness form subtle phenomena that reveal the deep meaning and meaning of physical phenomena. Thus, physical sensual love between the two sexes by the method of analogies means:

1. In the spiritual world - eternal mutual understanding and interpenetration of the great principles of Love and Life;
2. In the mental world - the mutual attraction of two generally creative elements, passive and active, that is, the principle of teaching;
3. In the psychic world - the unbreakable spiritual closeness of the non-polarised souls.

The fact of procreation is a symbol of the creation of a new life from two mutually contradictory principles and a symbol of the science of spirit-making.

The presence of the four states of matter is a sign of the existence of the four main spiritual forces that weave the veils of Life. And even non-aesthetic manifestations of nature often symbolise positive and beneficial facts in other worlds. With this disclosure of the symbolism of nature, we comprehend and spiritualise our earthly nature. The vegetable kingdom by its desire for the Sun and its calm rootedness in the earth is similar, but not equal in its potential to the ability of the human spirit to grow from a state of absorption in form into a state of freedom and radiant essence. The animal kingdom in its different breeds embodies different impulses of the human psyche. Almost all the definite forms of the mineral kingdom symbolise different degrees of crystallisation of the human personality. The entire Universe and everything on Earth is built according to the method of analogies. Therefore, the method of analogies applied to thinking is the only real method of cognition that expresses synthetic thought-creation.

The whole process of the Spirit's striving to manifest itself in form is like an all-encompassing triangle with the vertex facing down, expressing the other two angles of the two great world principles. And the reverse aspiration of the Spirit to its source is symbolised by a triangle with the top turned up, in the corners of the base of which lie again two great world principles of the Universe: the subjective Spiritual core and the shell of the objective form. These two triangles are intertwined in every phenomenon, in every living being, as well as in the entire totality of the Universe, forming themselves everywhere two intersecting streams of involution and evolution. Involution is the flow of karma of the manifesting Spirit, formed by the law of Causality. Evolution is the same flow of karma of the liberating Spirit, determined by the law of Expediency. These triangles are also similar, but not identical to each other, because the stages traversed in involution are the same as those traversed in evolution, but the forms expressing them are different.

These two triangles, intertwined in a hexagram, form a sign of the all-encompassing Macrocosm, in contrast to the pentagram, which symbolises the microcosm, that is, the individualised world of creative centres of consciousness reflecting the laws of the Macrocosm, with the difference that in the great Cosmos both flows are balanced. In the small world, in the individual, one or another orientation always prevails, which causes its activity and constant radiation from creative initiative.

The triangle facing upwards is called the triangle of Fire as an element that translates forms into a more subtle state, as a sign of the ascending Spirit. The triangle facing downwards is called the triangle of Water, symbolising the plastic and regular continuous outflow of the Spirit into the form.

The triangle of Fire in its ascent prevails over the triangle of Water, therefore, on the active right side, its line overlaps the line of the latter from above, but the obstacles of the involutive current in the first steps are symbolised by its overlapping with the involutive triangle at the bottom. Similarly, the opposite is true: The further the involution goes, the less resistance there is from the evolutionary orientation. But in the beginning, it has to overcome the suffering of the Spirit, which does not want to withdraw from its source.

Consciousness in the Cosmos is an intersections of these two sources and, according to their tasks, uses one or the other of them. Their pentagrams freely turn over either in the direction of self-destruction or in the direction of the realisation of the chosen spiritual opportunities.

In the World of the Kingdom of God the inverted Pentagram does not bear a black magic seal, it is only a symbol of the initiative of the individual condensation of the Spirit in one of the stages of manifestation and, therefore, while maintaining the continuity of consciousness, the journey along the triangle of Water (Knowledge) can at any moment be turned into flight (Will) along the triangle of Fire (Action).

Consciousness, thickening to the extreme in the name of performing a particular task and symbolically being in the lower corner of the triangle of Water, has all the wide possibilities of the base of the triangle of Fire above it, to whom these threads are stretched. The triangle of Fire is golden, the triangle of Water is silver, their nature reveals the nature of gold and silver as metals in their occult meaning (occult because the coarsened perception of the human psyche does not catch the vibrations of the Subtle World).

When humanity fell, it broke away in its consciousness from the macrocosmic hexagram of the whole world of its ideas about the Cosmos. Therefore, it has lost the knowledge and possession of the process of condensation of the Spirit, that is, the secret of involution. His consciousness, passive to this involution, obeyed and coarsened beyond measure to the material boundaries set by the intervening Spirits of the Solar System, with which it was identified. The further manifestation of involution has become an illegal phenomenon for humanity, decomposing material forms created by Higher Forces in the name of preserving it from destruction. Further involution would lead to the death of the human soul, to its decomposition into its constituent elements. Therefore, the involutive triangle (top down) in application to human activity is a black magic triangle, symbolising a set of illegally materialising, decomposing, destroying, deadening and ossifying forces.

The triangle of evolution (with its top up) is the expression of the human soul, striving to escape from self-law, from the earthly kingdom, from the material world that enslaves it by realising in itself and in its creativity the ideals of the Spiritual World set by the Brothers of Humanity. In the earthly world, these triangles are called good and evil, because evolution and involution in the fallen world of humanity have taken on an ethical colouring. Ethics arise only where there is an antagonism of the two principles. But where there is their cooperation, the place of ethics is only an immutable Service for the Good. The great Brothers of Humanity, the saviours of the earthly world, have built a triangle of Spirit, intertwining with the triangle of the coarsened matter of the earthly spheres, which refines this matter on all planes of existence. But at the same time, they left people the freedom of personal choice between these two directions, as a reflection of the pentagram freedom existing in Space.

Only free choice really decides the path of the human soul. Any compulsion, however subtle, may at first lead to an evolutionary path, but then the more painful will be the breakdown of consciousness caused by the protest of the suppressed will. Having chosen the path of involution, the will obeys either the objective laws of causality, that is, it falls into a passive state, and the personality rolls along a convenient path of self-indulgence until the moment when she gets into the black small triangle, where she becomes an exhibit and an agent of destructive forces. Having chosen the path of evolution, the personality overcomes the materialising involutive flow in itself, as well as the temptations of the external world, until it falls into the upper small triangle, where the struggle stops, where the breakdown of consciousness is impossible and where it is carried out into the Kingdom of God by a powerful spiritual flow created by the Brothers of Humanity.

The hexagram of the earthly world is a symbol of the great journey of earthly souls during numerous incarnations.

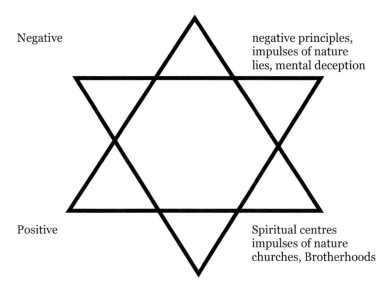

Paradise
The Spiritual World

Negative

negative principles,
impulses of nature
lies, mental deception

Positive

Spiritual centres
impulses of nature
churches, Brotherhoods

The Physical World

Figure 44

Two small black triangles symbolise human consciousnesses that
have chosen an environment corresponding to the average level
of human development. But at the same time they also border on
great Truths of The Spiritual World. The lower part - the psychic
world - is strongly influenced by the activities of the White
Brothers of Humanity, who first of all try to transform human
feelings as instruments of perception but, at the same time, this
same part borders on the strong materialising influence of the
black triangle. In the middle part, the whole pathos of the
struggle between the black and white armies is manifested, the
battlefield of which is every human person.
The middle line, the line of balance of black and white forces,
symbolises the moment of a person's conscious choice between
both paths, because ethical consciousness is born only at the
moment of balance in the person of good and evil motives, just as
consciousness in general is born from the interaction of subject
and object. Before the achievement and after the transition, this
line of choice, even if it is conscious, is devoid of the element of
Will, because it is determined either by causality or expediency.

But at the moment of ethical balance, a conscious Will breaks out, put before the pathetic dilemma of a decisive choice of its orientation, which will determine the fate of the individual for many incarnations.

The soul that is below this line rushes between both streams and, descending into the involutive streams, it meets numerous warnings from the Adherents of the White Doctrine and even from the earthly nature itself. Souls that have already finally embarked on the path of involution lose their human appearance, the spiritual core of consciousness and become conductors of destructive, corrupting forces of evil, mental-conscious larvae that create coarse and subtle temptations that can drag souls, unnoticed by themselves, into the fatal stream of service to evil and spiritual destruction.

The lower black small triangle symbolises what is called Hell in religion, that is, a state of consciousness devoid of influence, the impulse of love and life, a state of deadness of the heart and decomposition of the mind. This is the state to which souls who listen to the temptations of spiritless beings before they themselves join their black ranks strictly come.

The small white upper triangle symbolises the Kingdom of Pure Spirit, on which earthly matter and earthly involutive currents can no longer have any effect. This is a subjective state of consciousness, immersed in its shining possibilities. This is what is called Paradise in religion.

The upper mental part of the hexagram is under the strong influence of decomposing black mental currents, which manifest themselves both in nature and on the borders of Hell.

Thousands of hands are stretched out to the human soul to keep it from finally falling into the lower black triangle, and all the Laws and Forces of Nature rise threateningly against the soul, trying to establish boundaries and obstacles in the essence of the personality itself to its decomposition. Therefore, it is not so easy to finally die and become a black larva, because the very nature of a person can stop him if he is still able to heed psychic warnings. To such souls, who have felt a great longing and spiritual thirst at the limits of their destruction and have therefore agreed to evolution, are widely opened the ways of this evolution, all the possibilities of ascending along the base line of the white triangle, which glows with thousands of lights. But the further up, the greater the objectively provided opportunities, the less help, the firmer the personality. Based on everything previously received, she must stand on her own feet and, keeping in mind all the White Ways and Covenants, be able to recognise the white and black path.

The higher the path, the more temptations, because the triangle of involution expands its plane upwards, and when subjective aspiration and objective temptations balance each other, the soul again faces a choice. Every Adept of the White Way, every Saint of any church knows this hard work and this fate-deciding choice, which can take on an extremely subtle character, such as the temptation of Christ by the devil in the desert.

The two white triangles at the base of the hexagram denote people for whom, in the left triangle, the Brothers of Humanity filled the nature of the Earth with natural symbols, and in the right triangle-all the Bright Organisations and Spiritual Streams lit by the Centres of the Spirit of the embodied life of humanity, which draw the rays of ascension for human souls.

The higher path is the path of fighting the black forces that have attacked the white fighter from all sides. Here, a breakdown of consciousness is still possible, because even an Adept is in danger of falling if he abuses the power obtained after choosing the path. The higher, the narrower the white path becomes, the more lonely and abandoned its Adept feels.

Those who have renounced all external help and support and are guided only by the holy thread connecting their consciousness with the consciousness of the Great Brothers are no longer looking for anything in the external world, only they are able to see the whole light of the Spiritual World in themselves. Despite all the karmic hardships and blows raining down on him, he can enter the bliss of the Spiritual World with all his consciousness, but just before entering it, the shower of misfortunes, sufferings, sorrows becomes the strongest, because here the widest band of evil possibilities of this world intersects.

Once in the Spiritual World, the soul is no longer subject to these influences, because it reaches what the Buddha calls Nirvana. Arriving in this spiritual state, the Adept, even in the embodied state, affects human consciousness with his radiations, in religion this is called "prayer for peace". But the grief for the world, caused by great compassion for him, does not pass away, and all the experience taken out of earthly incarnations is summed up in it. This is the dark spot in the World of Light, which connects the soul of the Adept with humanity and does not allow it to leave it. On the other hand, these souls who care about humanity, who have become, on a par with the Brothers of humanity, its connection with the Kingdom of God, have set a limit to the involution of human consciousness.

The involuting consciousness, passing into the lower black triangle, breaks away from the Spirit, loses its own Spiritual Core, which can no longer manifest itself in the narrowed framework of its egoistic, persistent, downward-directed perception and distorted thinking, and returns as a disembodied spark to the white, bright triangle, where it is in an unconscious state of passivity and unmanifest, guarded by Older Brothers. The personality abandoned by the Spiritual Core is embodied in the lower realms of nature, where the materialisation of consciousness protects it from being dispersed, it is purified there by spirits and forces of nature from their depravity, passing through all sorts of planes of suffering and self-purification. In other words, nature reforges and melts material unsuitable for human evolution. And there, at the very bottom of its involution, in this consciousness, narrowed and crushed by objectivity, but purified and put in order by the spirits of nature, the possibility of evolution awakens again. It is into the very depths of Hell that the ray from the top of the light triangle falls, that is, the most powerful tension of the spirit Cosmic Love - lowers its ray into the very depth of the fall.

In the apocryphal Gospels, this Sacrament is symbolised by the descent of Christ into Hell. This ray of Divine Love awakens in the object, that is, in the material, longing for its pole, that is, the subject of its essence, and a thin thread is again stretched between the spiritual core that has fallen asleep and the psychic material that has begun its evolution. This connection grows stronger as the material evolves and the spiritual core awakens. Through all the Kingdoms of Nature, their convergence takes place, until they are reunited again in a human personality. Truly, Hell has been conquered by the Brothers of Humanity and in the darkest part of it the white ray of their influence shines. Materialistic teachings, despite all their negative aspects and deadening influence, save consciousness from its final decomposition by the black sorceries of spiritualism, mediumship and all sorts of obsessions. Thus, "evil serves the good" due to the intervention of the Brothers of Humanity in its mechanism. This is the genius of the symbolic picture of the sixth Arcanum, striking a woman of the left path with an arrow. Every soul rushing around in the closed plane of the hexagram must eventually choose one or another path to get out of this state of flux. All humanity must pass through this conscious choice of paths and consciously, with all its will, with all its being, strive along one of them. The moment of separation of black sheep from white ones is predicted by all prophecies. The great apocalyptic battle between black and white sheep for the future fate of humanity and the existence of the planet is constantly happening, but it will reach the predicted apogee by the end of the existence of the fifth race, because the sixth should already eliminate the breakdown of consciousness and enter the Kingdom of God of Cosmic Cooperation.

In this Great Battle, everyone must take one side or another, be it white or black, or hot or cold. Hesitant, forced to abandon the expensive habits of their petty, torn personality, those who do not dare to openly turn their backs on the ideals of the Spiritual World built by the Brothers of Humanity, according to the law of Karma and Causality, will either be attracted to the white path by all the sufferings of the individual, or used by the black path as traitors and provocateurs, discrediting the path of spiritual ascent and weakening its achievements.

Black and cold in relation to the Spirit, as open enemies, consciously struggle against the influence of the Great Redeemers, consciously desire further separation from cooperation in the Kingdom of God, consciously strive to erect their own little world of malice and self-destruction against him. In this great battle, the victory of the white forces is predetermined. Black sheep, however, are the obstacle with all their activities, when overcoming which the strength of white warriors grows, and when recognising them, their self-consciousness is confirmed. So, black is a blessing for the whites, because they accelerate their spiritual growth in this struggle, just as misfortunes and sufferings accelerate the soul's impulses to seek spiritual joys.

But the "grey", "lukewarm", theoretically recognising high ideals, but practically living in the swamp of their small interests, passions and lusts, refuse to make efforts, to undertake the great struggle of self-purification, fearing its difficulties and pain. The lukewarm ones who try to somehow reconcile personal passions with spiritual aspirations; who talk about the golden mean and moderation; who accept only what is convenient for them from spiritual values and what justifies their psychological swamp, mental stagnation-in the end, they always become agents of the black sheep. After all, if they accept the spiritual path only to the extent that it is convenient for them, thereby belittling and profaning its immutable and absolute value as the only possibility of entering the Kingdom of God, then all the principles of the Kingdom of God that first awaken the muffled conscience, in the end, causes irritation in such people. At this moment, the black sheep attract them to their side, revealing and inflating their impure passions, cherished by their self-justifications, and this increases their irritation against the servants of the White Brotherhood, whose spiritual advantage they unconsciously and resentfully feel.

All the betrayals of the white way, its Teachers and servants, all the profanations and all the perfidies are committed not by the blacks, but by these "grey" and "those " lukewarm" who refused to follow the Higher Precepts with their whole being, who did not want to sublimate and transform their entire nature in the crucible of their wisdom. After all, Judas, one of the closest disciples of Christ, listened to his Teacher with delight but, at the decisive moment, an unclean review prevailed, a conscience distorted by self-justifications aroused anger and hatred, and he betrayed the One Whom he followed out of good will and love. And when the Buddha proposed to one of his closest disciples, Devadatta, to enter the written path with all his being, with all his nature, Devadatta became sad and withdrew, and then even tried to discredit his Teacher in the eyes of the Brahmins.

"I will spew the lukewarm ones out of my mouth," John said in the Apocalypse. At the victory festival, his warriors will say his ways: "Great Lords, have mercy on our brothers of the left hand, for they also served our victory and the establishment of the Kingdom of God on Earth." And the Lords will find this struggle just and will find an opportunity for spiritual awakening and evolution of the left-hand brothers.

But everyone will turn away from the betrayal of the lukewarm ones. After all, even the blacks despise them for their half-heartedness and, using them as an instrument of their struggle against the whites, leave them to their fate. The whites will say, repeating the words of Christ: "And they saw me and did not recognise me, and they were called to the feast and did not come, pleading personal matters." All the opportunities were given to them and were not used by them, all the help was extended to them, and they responded to it with treachery, and the white warriors will not stand up for them. These lukewarm ones, who do not have a spiritual axis of consciousness and a psychic backbone of the will, who are "neither a candle to God, nor a poker to hell", will be scattered. Their consciousnesses will be melted down, into the furnace of common material, the material of psychic energy, where the processed psychic and astral elements will be used as material for new formations.

Freedom of choice is given to a person and obliges him to really choose and go with all his being along the chosen path. It obliges us to undertake a great work of subjective self-purification and a feat subjective self-development without trembling before suffering, without thirst for fleeting earthly joys.

Hilma af Klint: Svanen, 1914
PD-US-expired

The Chariot

The Seventh Arcanum

Chariot of the Victor

The domination of the Spirit over the form
The victory of the Thin over the Dense
Ownership rights
Numeric designation: 7
Astrological correspondence: Gemini

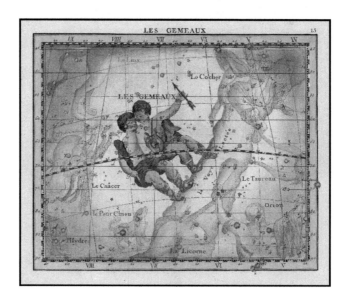

John Flamsteed, Les Gemeaux (Gemini), 1776

The right choice of ways, the choice of affirming subjectivity and self-affirmation in the Spirit leads not only to the domination of form, that is, the subjective nature of freedom from the world of forms and the possibility of redistributing elements both in one's personality and in the environment, but also the possibility of creating new formations, new objective forms for the manifestation of the possibilities of the Cosmic Spirit. This is no longer a simple domination, but a dominion over two streams of Life in the Universe. This dominion over the spirals of evolution and involution is destined to the one who correctly chose the path of the domination of the Spirit over the form, that is, the subject over the object. This state of consciousness with all the hidden knowledge of the ways and creative power over the elements of the world is symbolically depicted in the picture of the seventh Arcanum.

On a chariot under a canopy in the shape of a Pentagram stands the Victor, dressed in armour made of fish scales. On his head is a seven-pointed crown with three pentagrams. The chariot is harnessed to two sphinxes, black and white, with human faces facing each other. In the rims of the chariot, instead of nails, there are eyes looking in all directions. The victor holds the reins in his left hand, and raises a trident with his right hand, symbolising the three fires of the mysterious sign (Shin).
The domination of the Spirit over the form, that is, the affirmation of one's "I" in the Spiritual core, is actually an aspiration by one's consciousness to the eternal, unchangeable subject, to the Inexpressible, to the Deity, to the Source of Love, which fills the entire Cosmos with its Creativity. And since the possibilities of the subject, the Divine principle of the cosmic Essence, are inexhaustible, the assertion of its dominance over the objective expression in the form establishes the principle of the Infinity of evolution. The world is not a closed system, as it would be if there was a balance of subjective and objective principles.
The spiritual possibilities of the world are inexhaustible, and therefore there is no repetition in it. The energy flow that comes from the Spirit, creating the forms of the world in an inverted triangle, returning to its source in a straight triangle, does not bring the process of the Universe to rest, but excites the radiation of new possibilities in it. And since this return of the worlds to a new state and the expiration of new opportunities lasts continuously and occurs constantly in the Cosmos, new worlds,

new systems always arise in it, embodying more and more new self-emanations of the Deity.

It can be stated that there is no return to the past, but there is no repeatability of the process anywhere. The worlds that have completed their evolution do not return again, but new carriers of unprecedented self-disclosures of the Spirit appear instead of them. Therefore, the creativity of the Cosmos is never finished and strives forward in eternal evolution, into the Infinity of creative possibilities.

Therefore, the triangles are not really equal, but only similar, because the creative potential is exhausted and exhausted by the flow of evolution, but the flow of evolution is never exhausted, awakening to self-manifestation more and more new emanations of the subjective Spirit.

Similarly to this cosmic process, the Boundlessness of evolution and the human Spirit is affirmed. Rooted in the eternal and unchangeable, he draws ever new opportunities from its boundless treasury, creates ever new opportunities for self-manifestation, finds ever new tasks and, accordingly, consciously creates new and new personalities for himself.

Six days of creation, six zones or six Elohim, symbolised by the hexagram of the sixth principle, never lead to peace, because the seventh day - the day of rest, the day of self-immersion in its spiritual source - again enriches it with creative possibilities. That is why this day is so important for an earthly person, dedicated to rest from objective activity, dedicated to prayer, which in fact should be a deep self-immersion of the subjective consciousness into its spiritual source.

In the cosmic cooperation of the Kingdom of God, the consciousness of every servant, of every Great Radiating Spirit, is always strengthened in the eternal subject. This is the immutable and true equality of all the sons of God, the Creators of world systems, the helpers of the One Creator of the Universal Mind. At the same time, each of them is at his special post and performs his special task according to the specific colouring of his initiative potential, that is, the embodied aspect of the Creative Mind. The rooting of consciousness in the eternal will reveal the possibility of boundless creativity and the infusion of new possibilities into the worlds and systems controlled and created by them. Therefore, just like the entire Cosmos, each part is in a state of boundless evolution in it, joyfully and freely expressing all new spiritual outflows in its specific prism.

The Cosmic Hierarchy is not a ladder of subordination and domination, but an equal cooperation of creative consciousnesses occupying different positions and places, and the fulfilment of their specific tasks. It does not interfere, but only helps the constant and boundless subjective self-disclosure, their enrichment and affirmation.

The emergence of world systems with all the forms of consciousness inhabiting them depends on the initiative of these consciousnesses, these Great White Cosmic Brothers of Humanity. The terms of the existence of these worlds depend on them, they hold the threads of their destinies in their hands, from the order and all forms of space construction depend on them. The subjective rooting of consciousness in the Eternal gives them power over the involutive and evolutionary flows, that is, power over innumerable self-transformations and the power of new formations in the environment. According to the

Quaternary Law of World Dynamics, they can create for themselves any personalities and even several, acting in different places, to carry out the tasks set by themselves.

Owning the continuous flow of cycles of World energy according to the same Quaternary Law, they, these Great Cosmic Brothers, by their thought-creation realise all new pictures of conscious worlds in the flow of life. For the sake of the Common Good, having the possibility of a comprehensive creative manifestation of the Spiritual Precepts of Love and Life, they hold the reins of involution and evolution in their hands. The consciousnesses moving in this stream, that is, the Spirits of cosmic nature, thickening and discharging its energy flow in different degrees of vibrations, are not in a struggle, but in the cooperation of these two world principles, reflected on all planes of Creative manifestation and always looking into each other's eyes with understanding and awareness, like two sphinxes in front of a chariot in the picture of the seventh Arcanum.

The victor is dressed in a shell made of fish scales, that is, he is dressed in all the creative forces of space. The fish in the symbols of all peoples is a sign of a citizen of the cosmos, so it was the symbol of the ancient Christian, for Christ introduced his followers into the Kingdom of God and confirmed them as citizens of the cosmos. And the earthly man, who has chosen the path of spiritual evolution of the white triangle of Fire, Spirit and Good, thereby chooses the path of his boundless evolution, solemnly dragging him on the chariot of a re-created personality along the paths of the World Infinity.

The path of the soul along the white triangle, that is, the final choice of Good over evil is actually the choice of cleansing the immortal and infinite in its possibilities spiritual core of consciousness from its small and narrow self-identification with the imposed objectivity, that is, freeing oneself from passions, whims, egoism, impulsive reactions aroused by this egoism, which entails an ever deeper understanding, perception, expands the range of connections, the personality itself, and makes it possible for the Eternal, All-encompassing and All-knowing Spirit to shine in it. But having overcome the involutive current in itself in its earthly aspect of "illegal confluence", which has acquired the form of evil, the next task of man is to dominate the evolutionary current, the so-called Good, which in fact is only a method and a way of returning to the Kingdom of God.

Therefore, a person does not have to be proud of his goodness and to boast of his good thoughts, feelings and actions. After all, by the manifestation of their positive qualities, which in their synthesis are reduced to the principle of selflessness in its various manifestations, a person only helps himself, and it is unfair to expect a reward for this. On the contrary, one should be grateful to those towards whom one is able to show one's good qualities or overcome evil ones, because only in this way can one turn one's personality into a pure vessel for the Spirit, free one's consciousness from the bondage of earthly nature and enter the Kingdom of God Victoriously.

Unselfishness is not a merit, but only the right path, which itself carries a reward, and therefore does not need any reward. Overcoming evil and dominating the involutive current is the first stage, the second stage is the overcoming of good and dominating it, which is even more difficult in the conditions of human development. This means not to surrender to the evolutionary flow, not to identify with the joy of its achievements, but to consciously apply it in the name of fulfilling duty. The conscious application of good is the knowledge of the moments and circumstances in which one or another facet of good should be applied in action, and the power over one's personal psychological composition in the application of a particular ethical principle of good. Not to be carried away by virtue, not to seek it not only for the sake of rewards, but even for its own sake, means to rule over good, and to consciously apply virtues in the name of fulfilling duty means to rule over them. The consciousness rooted in its eternal essence is not connected with what we usually understand by the word "duty", that is, unconditional submission to a circumstance imposed by objective conditions. The victor over evil and good, who himself has rooted his consciousness in the spiritual core, is free. Guided only by his conscience and the immutable knowledge of his next task, he creates a form of fulfilment of this task, creates a plan of his duty to realise the Universal Good, the deployment of Spirit-making. And by doing this, he is the winner over his karma, that is, over the objectivity that binds his activities, over the environment.

He carries all his karma within himself, since its inner spring is the axis of the fulfilment of his spiritual tasks. The new cosmic currents created by him overcome the old, inveterate ones, refining and dissolving them and making them tools for the expedient construction of spiritual tasks. The winner over himself, the master over the subjective streams of good and evil, subordinates both these streams to himself and in the surrounding world, harnesses them to the chariot of his boundless evolution and forces them to cooperate to fulfil their tasks, owning all the secrets of their relationships and interactions.

Truly, only the victor over both directions, who equally owns the secrets of both, sees the innermost springs of both, understands how both of them serve to build the Common Good, how joyfully they affirm the Good, the rule of the Spirit, and how evil, through suffering and the possibility of self-determination, contributes to the growth of the human soul. For the Victor, good and evil lose their earthly ethical colouring, because the seal of the fall has been erased from his soul, and he sees only two similar creative currents justified by life, causality and expediency. Involution and evolution are equally necessary for the approval of Cosmic Construction, and their existence in terrestrial conditions is just as legitimate as in other parts of the Cosmos.

The victor over karma has the power of conscious incarnations and consciously creates his personalities from earthly material in the name of realising his spiritual tasks. The winner of karma feels just as good on Earth as in any other part of the Cosmos. Having rooted his consciousness in the Eternal, he cannot be identified with anything transitory and, therefore, with the instrument of his manifestation - a person - and therefore he stands above joys and sorrows, not renouncing them, but accepting them figuratively as tools for carrying out spiritual tasks. In addition, being the master of all transitory things, he can constantly renew and regenerate the material of his personality, which ensures its immortality and the continuation of life in one body for as long as it is necessary, without changes in the incarnation.

The mystery of eternal life and eternal youth belongs to the Victor over the transitory. The Victor has an immortal soul that dominates and dominates his changing part. Three permanent subjective principles constitute the immortal principle of the earthly man, and only this Immortal Soul is preserved after the death of the body, as if it returns to itself from the earthly journey and reincarnates into the next person in the body. These are the three components of the Immortal Soul:

1. The spiritual core, immersed in its roots in the unchangeable Cosmic Spirit, in the Absolute, in Bliss. In Vedanta this principle is called Atman. This Spark of Divinity, inseparable from the entire Fiery Ocean, sparkles in the individual human consciousness. The Atman or Spiritual core is Omniscient, and all cognition is only a self-purification and self-expansion of consciousness so that it can manifest itself in the omniscience of

the spirit eternally established in it and eternally residing in it. Because everything that we are on we know that it actually opens a valve for what is always present in us, and we value the information we have acquired only insofar as this valve opens. This Spirit is All-blissful, and what we call Happiness and Joy is only the creation of conditions in which the screen that covers it opens, and its rays penetrate through all the vehicles, activating their activity, that is, creating what we call cheerfulness. The reality of such perceptions creates for us the true Knowledge contained in the Spirit.

This Spirit is All-free, and all our longing for freedom and all our sensations of it are only vague presentiments of our creative self-disclosure. In the Spiritual Core of consciousness, all the possibilities of spiritual radiation are stored, which are expressed by Creative impulses.

2. The heart is what is called Buddhi in Vedanta - the root of our Soul. This is our Consciousness, which is possible only if there is a perception of objectivity. Our Soul is eternally connected and united with the Souls of all beings of the Cosmos, constantly ready for self-forgetful help.

Our Soul or our Consciousness has the constant property of recognising between truth and falsehood, between the eternal and the transitory, and in transitory forms they seek Life. Our Soul is a reflection of the Spiritual Core in an ever-changing Life, which makes all our manifestations plastic, changeable, always striving forward. Our Soul is a vessel with a Spiritual core, a Cup filled with the Spirit and pouring out its light on all the phenomena of the world.

All our unselfish feelings and the best impulses of the heart are the voice of the speaking Soul, our conscience is a reflection of its discerning ability, and the whole world of our attachments, sympathies and mutual understanding is only a partial statement of its connection with everything that exists, of its Love, directed at everything. Each illumination of consciousness is the radiation of its direct perception of the Spirit, and is directly the reality of such perceptions, creating for us the true Knowledge contained in the Spirit.

3. The mind, the Big Manas in the terminology of Vedanta, is the Creative intellect with its ability to abstract thinking, and the creation of concentrated thought images from thought waves; the creativity of ideas that control the life of peoples and the planet-

all this is the nature of the creative part of our Soul, the individual prism of the Universal Creative Mind.

Every true Creativity is actually an expression of the Mind's thought-creation. Only ideological creativity can be called real creativity, everything else is not creativity, but only the application of created ideas to different materials. Every abstract idea, every synthetic mental education that arises in the waves of our thinking, is an expression of the activity of the Mind. Every influence that we exert on the people around us and on nature is an influence on Creative Mind. Every idea saturated with life, which directs both its own and someone else's thinking in a different direction, is an echo of the activity of the Creative Mind. His influence is so great, his creativity is so diverse, and the possibilities for the realisation of this creativity are so numerous and unexpected that we cannot take into account our consciousness, narrowed by earthly karma, on which our creative thoughts are realised to the star, if the earthly conditions are not suitable for their implementation. We cannot take into account where the created representation will find a consonantly reacting receiver, and a person of another race in a completely different part of the world can realise the idea that we carry unfulfilled in ourselves.

These three great principles, the top three-eternally divine and immortal, always radiantly proactive-are the individual spiritual part of man and every other being in the Cosmos.

Its purity from everything extraneous, stuck from the outside world, guarantees as a result of its purity phenomena are the continuity of consciousness and dominion over all laws and all processes of the world. These are the three flames of the mysterious sign (shin), whose symbol in the form of a trident was raised in his hand by the Winner. Everything else is just the shells of the form created by these three principles for the sake of resistance. Only these three are not subject to karma, because the Dynamic Law that creates the Karma of the world flows from the Mind as an expression of its inner nature.

He is the Lord of the world who recognises himself as the carrier of the Karma of the worlds, because his consciousness recognises and asserts all responsibility. The one who has contained not only his karma, but also the Karma of the Cosmos, is its master, the master of absolutely every form, who is not afraid of anything and does not rejoice in anything.

These three principles form three planes of manifestation of consciousness in the Universe: the Spiritual world, the Spiritual

124

world and the Intellectual world with the corresponding energy formations, with the consciousnesses inhabiting them and working in them.

The following four principles are the instruments of the manifestation of the three higher ones through the third principle of the Creative Mind. These four lower principles formalise the creativity of the Higher Worlds and unfold the forming activity of the Mind according to the Great Quaternary Law of World Dynamics, the general formula of which they express. When applied to a person, these four principles are embodied in his earthly personality, which is an instrument of the manifestation of his individuality on Earth, that is, the totality of the three higher principles.

The first of these four principles of personality is the so-called small Manas, the earthly intellect or reason, the organ of recognising the earthly situation, the "speculative mind", combining earthly elements and combinations suitable for the embodiment in the thought-creation of the Great Mind. Of course, these vessels of earthly intellectual formulations created by a small mind only partially fit the great ideas and thought-creation of a large Intellect associated with all Cosmic Creativity. That is why no earthly thought satisfies, that is why the longing of creators who are not able to express their creative potential entirely in one formula. A tool of small intelligence - language, expressing thoughts in its own words, always reduces their range and reduces the depth of their content. And only gradually developing over time, the thought-creation of a large mind can be embodied in numerous mental combinations of a small intellect.

From the energy thought waves of small intelligence that form the intellectual sphere of the Earth, the mental shells or the mental body of the earthly human personality are born. The more the earthly reason is subordinated to our Great Reason, the more it expresses the ideals stored in the latter, the more clearly, vividly and powerfully the mental body of the individual and the more powerfully it fertilises its earthly thought-creation.

A truly intelligent person is not the one who has accumulated information about earthly relations in the mental body of his personality, but the one who has sanctified these earthly cliches with the influence of the creativity of the Higher Mind.

Therefore, idealists, even if they take very little account of earthly conditions, are always smarter than practical materialists who are able to combine earthly relations and are devoid of thought-creating abilities. The latter do not see either the past or the future of ideological creativity and are limited only to an arbitrarily captured narrow link of the current moment.

Of course, a harmonious combination of large and small Reason is correct, and every idealism should be, at the same time, practical, that is, take into account the conditions of its manifestation, but not reconcile with these conditions, but on the contrary, process the conditions according to its goals. The Great Manas must always assert its dominance over the earthly reason and use it as its tool and analyser, without at all reducing the requirements of its ideals in favour of so-called practicality.

The mental sphere of the Earth is inhabited by intellectual pictures of the creativity of the human Mind. The streams of his energy in various teachings flow through the receivers of personalities and are formed by the mental bodies of the latter into new theoretical formations, the value of which depends on the quality of the mental body, that is, ultimately, on its connection with the intellectual creativity of the big Mind. The small mental body is a reflection of our large mental essence, which always remains the organ of the manifestation of our Soul, in whatever part of the Cosmos this Soul is embodied.

The second principle of personality, the psychic principle, reflects the life and activity of the Heart principle, applying it to the earthly situation. In our personality, he creates an astral body-a carrier of feelings responsible for the direct perception of the energies of earthly objectivity. This astral energy builds the Psychic World of the Earth, in which all the flows of its specific impulses flow around the axis of individual consciousness, and highlights them with the life of the heart, thus building in this way, the earthly relations between themselves and between the earthly nature and themselves. The astral world is inhabited by energy formations created and imbued with the psychic power of our personalities, pictures and representations of our perception are carried in its atmosphere, personified images live, that is, formed by the feelings and passions of our hearts clothed in earthly shells. By the power of a small intellect, all these mental images receive formulations or bodies, and live their own lives, affecting in turn the psyche of our personalities.

The more our earthly feeling is illuminated by the life of our conscious Soul, our great Heart connected with the entire Cosmos, the greater the psychic energy of our astral, the purer and more beautiful the astral body of the personality that reflects the soul: its direct perception, intuitive realisation, self-control, a sense of connection and empathy for everything that exists. In the shells of earthly feelings, our soul is expressed in all forms of earthly love, in sympathy for everything that exists on Earth, in compassion and readiness to help. But if the perception of earthly objectivity prevails over the reflection of the soul, then the earthly feeling is expressed in passion, instincts and unconscious psychic impulses that bring the personality closer to the animal state, creating a corresponding form created by people in the earth's atmosphere.

all external events are reflected in the astral atmosphere of the Earth. It is like a cinematographic tape that captures every manifestation of earthly life. There we will find the true reflection of all the impulses of our personalities; there our true psychic faces are outlined with immutable clarity, for even the suppressed and hidden feelings and impulses of the earthly astral bodies create their vibrations there.

The third principle - the principle of Prana or Life Force-is the principle of the creative form, the tangible and visible form of earthly life, that is, it is the principle that finally objectifies the creative impulses of the personality, in which our senses of external perception are potentially collapsed and develop in time - the five sense organs that then act in the physical body, and other organs of perception of specific earthly conditions that are not developed in it.

The etheric body determines the reserve of the vital force of our personality, and thus - the term of its earthly existence. The etheric body of the personality is fed from the reserves of prana of the Earth, forming an etheric environment of his vital force around a person, which determines the duration of his existence and the stages of his physical development.

The etheric body of the Earth contains all the stages of its evolution, all the characteristic differences of its nature and the timing of its changes. Similarly, the etheric body of a human being expresses all the stages of his physical development from birth to death. The situation is recorded there the whole picture of his physical existence, due to his karma, the full potential of his health, as well as the beginnings of his diseases.

The fourth principle of the personality - its physical body - is the final stage of the materialisation and objectification of everything previous. In the material plane, the general form of life of the planet with all the possibilities contained in this form is turned over in time. Thus, this physical form unfolds in the objective world all the subjective spiritual potential expressed by this Divine Possibility. The physical world is an objective mirror that reflects the spiritual principle and unfolds the spiritual creativity that has passed through all the previous stages into a complete picture of the potential possibilities realised in space and time. Thus, the physical Cosmos is a reflection of God, a mirror in which He looks. The physical body of the Earth, our planet, in the totality of its historical and geological development, is a reflection and expression of the spiritual essence of the Earth, that is, the individual potential of its spiritual representative - humanity. The physical body of a person bears the seal of the fulfilment of a spiritual task and the imprints of all his other bodies. That is why the facial features and the structure of the body can be concluded about the character and level of consciousness of a person.

"The body is the temple of the Spirit", namely the body, because it should be the final expression or vessel of our divine essence, its carrier and manifestation.

A sin against the body is, strictly speaking, a sin against the Soul, the Spirit, because it interferes with its manifestation. Therefore, we are obliged to protect our body, its health, its balance, its beauty and its longevity, because in it we can work for the Common Good of Earthly Construction, only in it we can fulfil our earthly tasks. The sin against the body is threefold:

1. The body often comes out of the subordination of the Spirit, with the help of guides, but as an independent formation it does not matter and loses the meaning of its existence.

Excessive pampering of the body coarsens the organs of its perception and makes it unable to perform spiritual tasks. Therefore, the discipline of the body is necessary.

2. People with a distorted lower mental and promiscuity of the astral body exhaust the physical body with passions and lusts, exhaust the reserve of its vital force, that is, its etheric sub -base, instead of using these forces for the creation of spiritual values.

The earthly force is gathered in the etheric body, with which the physical body is closely connected and of which it is the expression. And we are obliged to use this earthly power, which is received only in the incarnate state, for the creation of earthly spiritual values, and not at all for the egoistic experiences of a perverted astral conductor. By this sin of wasting the life force accumulated in the body, we deprive ourselves of the opportunity to fulfil our task and stretch its fulfilment by many incarnations. The meaning of taking care of the constant replenishment of the physical body with the earthly life force is that, given a larger supply of it and a longer duration of physical life, we will be able to perform several tasks in the second incarnation.

3. Another sin is asceticism, which is an exaggeration of the expedient and rational discipline of the body. Asceticism is based on hatred and contempt for the body, but since the body is the temple of the Spirit, asceticism shows a deep misunderstanding of the task of earthly incarnation, Asceticism forces a person to prematurely break away from the forces of the Earth, not using them thereby for the implementation of earthly tasks, but forcibly suppressing and destroying this earthly natural potential. Moderation, reasonable discipline and respect for the earthly forces accumulated in the body, according to our own pure and legitimate way, that's what we should do in relation to our body.

The seven principles, reflected in each cycle of the manifestation of the Quarternary Law of Dynamics, are called secondary principles that form, that is, create the forms that inhabit these cycles, and are opposed to the primary causalities, that is, the triangle of the Upper Principles, which in their unreflected form are the primary causes of every quarternary manifestation.
The four is the number of the form, but this form also reflects the three, and together with it creates seven forms of manifestation of consciousness in every cycle of creation. That is why the seven determines every objective manifestation and underlies it.
In all cosmic systems, there are these seven forms of consciousness that manifest in the four worlds, that is, on the four planes of consciousness. Similarly, the creative seven is manifested in the solar system in the form of seven creative planets, including the radiant centre of the System. Each of the planets is one of the representatives of the seven principles and builds its own part of the system's organ. And, in turn, these seven principles of the body of the system weave the body and all the shells of the earth person.
The sun is in our Solar system the representative of the spiritual divine core of consciousness, which self-radiates potential opportunities rolled up in it. In its potential, the entire Cosmic Flow of Love and Life, refracted in a special prism of synthetic Solar Co-knowledge and then realised in the life of the entire system, starting from the planetary orbits and ending with the smallest beings located on the planets. Everything that lives within the system is the embodiment and diversity of the refraction of solar possibilities, is the realisation and unfolding to

the smallest detail of it, the Sun, the reserve of love and Life in a specific (through the prism of his Intelligent Creativity.

The sun is the constant presence of God in our system. All formations of the Spiritual World, all spirits, all ideas and all forms are radiations of solar possibilities on the four planes of manifestation of his creativity, the carrier of which are the consciousnesses inhabiting these worlds. Just like the great Divine The potential of the second principle radiates from itself the periphery of its influence, forming the common space of the system, the extreme boundary of which is the orbit of Saturn. Thus, the orbit of Saturn, in contrast to the radiating centre, is a sphere of extreme absorption, that is, the ultimate objectification of subjective self-emission. Since the solar consciousness with the spiritual poison shining brightly in it is subjective, the consciousness that is locked in the orbit of Saturn is also subjective, and to the extent that it expresses the subjective possibilities of the Sun in the most differentiated and condensed objective forms.

Saturn is a representative of the material principle, is the limit of the narrowing and differentiation of consciousness in space and time, and the particular forms in which consciousness is broken are so tightly enclosed in the framework of materialisation, so separated from each other that communication between them is impossible.

The consciousnesses living on Saturn are doomed to constant loneliness. The range of their perception and activity is extremely limited, and each of them completely and in concrete materialised form expresses one particular of solar possibilities, but the expression of this particular in the objective world is brought to perfection. The iron law of causality floods these consciousnesses, which are completely identified with it and do not dream of any aspirations, goals and opportunities, except for the realisation of that particular link in the chain of causality that each of them represents.

The creative potentials on Saturn are narrow and small, there is no self-consciousness in its forms, and therefore the element of personality, as a microcosm, is not expressed. Jupiter is a representative of the etheric principle, the prana principle. He manages the order and regularity of the distribution of life force in all its aspects throughout the Solar system. Jupiter, therefore, is the creator-sculptor of life forms in our system, and all the planets are covered by this influence of his.

The consciousnesses living on Jupiter are strongly identified with the form of their manifestation, but this form is not as narrow as on Saturn and does not represent a particular link in the chain of causality. Consciousness living on Jupiter have knowledge and power over the Cosmic Quaternary Law in both its manifestations, but only in the sphere of their special task. As a representative of the order of distribution of life force, Jupiter coordinates the hierarchical structure of the Solar system and builds a hierarchical ladder for the consciousnesses developing in it. Therefore, Jupiter patronises the establishment of a hierarchical order and regularity in the distribution of accumulated vital forces in any expression, that is, from spiritual to material wealth, on all the planets of the system.

Mars is a representative of the impulsive hierarchical life. In the orbit of Mars, the psychic energy of the Solar System is concentrated into foci of differently coloured psychic impulses, called feelings on Earth. The consciousnesses on Mars are identified with these psychic impulses and are their representatives. All the forces of individualised spiritual, mental and etheric-vital energy are concentrated in these psychic foci. Therefore, the feelings in which these consciousnesses are embodied, neither in strength, nor in intensity, nor in range, can be compared with earthly feelings.

Mars is a concentrator of all psychic energy on all planes of its manifestation into psychic multi-coloured conscious foci. And Mars, therefore, is a representative of the power of concentration, that is, establishing the centre of personal consciousnesses with the help of a sense of self-perception in the environment. Mars at the same time has a capacitor of psychic energy into powerful psychic charges of high energy.

The Earth, or rather the Moon, is a representative of the lower Manas, a small intellect or reason. The Earth is only the centre of a sphere, the periphery of which is the lunar orbit. Ethically-psychically and intellectually the Earth is a product of the lunar sphere, it is a material condensation, which means that the Moon should not mean a small lunar ball describing only the outer orbit of the lunar sphere, but the entire sphere enclosed between the Earth and the material Moon, since etherically, psychically and mentally this sphere represents one whole. Therefore, the influence of the Moon on the Earth is so powerful, and the Earth is only a special case of the manifestation of the Lunar sphere, condensing and concretely expressing all the possibilities contained in this area. And since the Moon is a representative of the lower manas, the influence of the Lunar sphere on the Earth is mainly destructive. But under certain aspects of the material moon, the phenomena of intuitive power increase wonderfully, because new psychic pictures and forces located in the Lunar sphere materialise.

The Earth and the Moon for the first time ignite a ray of self-consciousness of individual psychic cosmoses formed by Mars, that is, a personality appears on Earth for the first time as a microcosm reflecting the Cosmic thought-creation, feelings and will, expressed completely in the form of the spiritual core of consciousness and therefore being an instrument of spiritualisation and individualisation of materiality, that is, the state of absorption of the subject by the object.

On Earth, the Subject and the Object are at the stage of equilibrium, therefore, the personal consciousness of the spiritual representative of humanity is manifested here for the first time, and this is associated with the manifestation of self-activity and responsibility, which must be developed it is the earthly humanity. Not blind submission to the law of authority, no matter how beautiful it may be and no matter how natural such subordination may be, but a conscious attitude to the whole regularity, creative mastery of the process of realisation and conscious cooperation with the cosmic regularity- this is what earthly creatures are called upon to accomplish. Therefore, the Earth is a turning point from the irresponsible and blissfully lawful transmission of orders and impulses through the hierarchy, from top to bottom, to independent creative work associated with a constant struggle in the name of establishing and approving conscious personal focuses. Therefore, the direction of earthly creativity is not a top-down transfer for those who are on Earth, but the growth of consciousness from the bottom up, from the personal focus to the spiritual core, which should be embodied in the personality. Venus embodies the great Manas, that is, the principle of the Creative Mind. The creative force of the Solar System is the radiation of Venus, the thought images are created in it by the work of the consciousnesses embodied on Venus, of course, taking into account the nature of the environment into which the thought images fall. The consciousnesses on Venus are quite individual, and the process of thought creation is the only, but also quite sufficient tool for their manifestation.

At the same time, being a representative of the Mind, Venus manages the dynamics of polarisation and the relationship of the poles in the Solar system. That is why the manifestations of the polarisation of Love on Earth belong to Venus. The creativity of the Mind reflects the truth of spiritual unity in an objective form.

Therefore, the creativity of Venus establishes beauty and harmony of manifestations everywhere.

The consciousnesses of beings on Venus relate to human consciousnesses in the same way that human consciousnesses relate to the consciousnesses of animals on Earth. However, in essence, Venus and Earth are very related to each other, since both are representatives of the same principle of intelligence in its two different aspects - higher and lower, creative and implementing. The humanity of Venus and the Earth should have been the closest collaborators, older and younger brothers, but the breakdown of the consciousness of earthly humanity made the task of the humanity of Venus difficult.

To help the earthly humanity, in the name of fulfilling its tasks, seven Great Venus Consciousnesses were incarnated on Earth, who found their servants among the earthly humanity. These seven "Kumaras" are the elder Brothers of Humanity who have overcome the breakdown of consciousness, that is, the fall, and constitute the true White Brotherhood on Earth.

Mercury is a representative of Buddhi, the principle of the Soul, which directly perceives the Spirit and reflects it in the game of its transformations. The consciousnesses living on Mercury live in a whole, unbreakable connection with all cosmic consciousnesses and therefore have God-Knowledge. They know the plasticity of all objective material and own it, reflecting the Sparks of the Spirit in it. They establish in the system the Continuity of consciousness through all its transformations, that is, the true principle of immortality for all beings.

They also establish the principle of Brotherhood, that is, the deep connection of all souls and the unity of the Spirit. They affirm the relativity of manifestations that have value only as expressions of the radiance of the spirit in the flow of life. These consciousnesses also establish the order of the flow of life and the sequence of its changes in the Solar system.

Managing each special stage of the manifestation of the flow of Love and Life creatively radiated by the Sun, all these consciousnesses build the building of the Solar System both in its general features and in its smallest details.

According to the form of their consciousness and their task, the Spirits of the great planets influence the life and construction of the worlds they create, the life and character of the beings inhabiting them, creating a connection of mutual understanding and cooperation in the entire planetary chain by such interpenetration.

The signs of the fraternal planets are imprinted on each planet. They are also recorded on our Land. The flow of the undifferentiated consciousness of the carrier of Love and Life, pouring out from the Sun to the orbit of Saturn, then returns with already formed individual consciousnesses along the ascent steps, tablet along the way, organising all the objective material of the Solar System, that is, its life, according to the Precepts of Love according to the laws of thought-creation.

The signs of the previous stages are fixed on each planet in concrete or material forms. The signs of the subsequent stages are reflected in the particular cases of these forms and in the psychic possibilities realised by the humanity of this planet. Thus, on our Earth, the achievements of the previous stages of its development - the stages of Saturn, Jupiter and Mars - are recorded as follows: Saturn created a material stronghold - the Mineral kingdom; Jupiter created the guardians and converters of prana - the Vegetable kingdom; Mars embodied psychic impulses in the Animal kingdom. Humanity itself, in its form of existence, is under the influence of Venus, while its spiritual materials are created by Mercury, and the creative initiative in its general construction and in the manifestations of individual personalities belongs to the Sun.

Already by this characteristic of the planets, their influence on the characters of their prints, the signs of their influence on humanity are also outlined. Human personalities are the developers of the details of the general human task, they are the performers of that filigree work of particular general construction, which is necessary for the harmony and completeness of the implementation of the entire general plan of the task to the smallest detail.

Human personalities, as such, are created in harmony with their particular tasks and take from the material of the Solar System what they need to fulfil such, that is, they draw those planetary influences that are suitable for their special work. Therefore, psychic personalities, despite their microscopicity, bear the signs of the predominant tonality of a particular planetary influence. The sun in human personalities gives a strongly expressed initiative, self-radiance and non-need awareness with manifestations, that is, manifested mental domination over oneself, or self-control and natural domination over others. The sun is imprinted in the spiritual life of a person by natural and joyful religiosity, in the mental life - by synthetic thinking, in the psychic life-by the mentioned self-affirmation, in the etheric-psychic life-by cheerfulness, which no one can ever break. The sun gives a sense of self and self-awareness of the individual. Mercury instils understanding in the human heart and makes consciousness plastic, easily adaptable to other consciousnesses, a natural recognition of the unity of life. Spiritually, Mercury is reflected by the desire for self-transformation, that is, with a natural recognition of evolution. Mentally, Mercury gives recognition and combinatorial thinking, that is, the ability to create new syntheses from recognised parts. Psychically, Mercury helps in recognition and adaptability, which is expressed in shifting consciousness from one form to another, gives independence from conventions and prejudices, and also, the management of patterns. Therefore, in the highest atmosphere of humanity, applied to the planes of lower manifestations, Mercury is often expressed in adventurism and cheating, but with a major shade, which can be sublimated by translation to higher planes. Etheric-physical Mercury gives mobility, adaptability and ease of life.

Venus gives souls creativity, consciousness of beauty and the intensity of striving for each other harmonic poles in the name of the same creativity. Spiritually, Venus gives the search for truth through form and creatively expresses it in form. Mentally, Venus gives mastery of the thought-creating process, that is, logical deduction, and creates creative intelligences. Mentally, Venus creates types of artists, creators, and gives art the polarisation of love. Venus creates a difference of potentials in the personality itself, which is expressed by the searching. Longing for the ideal comes from tension, created by Venus. Etheric-physical Venus creates harmony and beauty of form with a slight hint of asymmetry, as the beginning of the search for higher harmony.

The moon has three aspects of influence. The waxing moon gives individuals the desire for refinement, for the separation of the psyche from the material framework, that is, it contributes to the psychic phenomena of exteriorisation in all planes of life.

The full moon manages the law of polarisation of processes, patronises the incarnations of souls, that is, the process of conception and birth, as well as the process of implementing creativity into earthly material, but the idea of creativity does not depend on it at all. Therefore, it inclines to phantasmagoric and devoid of spiritual values realisations of psychic material in artistic and other forms.

The waning Moon manages the process of decomposition of matter, that is, it acts destructively at the same time and associatively. In addition, it causes an illegal process of materialisation of negative entities seeking to touch the Earth, and forcibly, that is, without the presence of subjective preparation, causes a partial exteriorisation of the psyche of people subject to lunar influence. Spiritualism and mediumism should be included in the area of immediate influence. Spiritually, the Moon causes anxiety, the search for an indefinite higher principle and attracts the personalities subordinate to it to the solar personalities, the centres of spiritual life. Mentally, the Moon manages the process of induction, that is, the search for higher syntheses on the basis of dissatisfaction with concrete thinking. Mentally, the Moon will give passivity, instability and good nature. Etheric-physical-gives phlegm, due to the lack of expansive solar energy, and easily creates vampiric types that use the life force of others.

Mars spiritually gives the ability to concentrate the spiritual tension of the environment and identify with other set ideals. This gives an extremely powerful force for the implementation of these ideals. Mentally, Mars bestows concentration of thinking, at the same time narrowing it so that it makes it impossible to merge with the general flow. Mars does not have oversight of the general plan, but it perfectly focuses on the particulars.

Jupiter gives an awareness of the reliance on regularities, and therefore, softens and facilitates responsibility. He also introduces the principle of hierarchy into consciousness, that is, the joyful recognition of the Higher and caring for the lower. Jupiter supports the consciousness of a common chain of cooperation. Spiritually, Jupiter gives the ability to transmit spiritual influx from top to bottom with full trust and recognition of the highest spiritual authorities. Therefore, he is the patron of all existing churches and religions on Earth, built on the principle of hierarchical and cosmic cooperation. Mentally, Jupiter gives an awareness of the regularity: his thinking is formal, figurative and not inclined to abstraction. Individuals under the influence of Jupiter recognise someone else's regularity, but do not introduce it into the circle of their thinking. Psychically, Jupiter will give complacency, a tendency to patronage, unshakable devotion to once recognised authorities. It also gives the ability to friendship, that is, to systematic mental cooperation. Etheric-psychically, Jupiter, being the distributor of mental and vital force, is the main factor of health, that is, the order in the regular distribution of the body's forces.

Saturn gives the ability to narrow consciousness in the process of concentrating spiritual tasks. He also closes the consciousness in the orbit of arrogance, builds partitions protecting it from the influence of others and firmly fixes the will in the spiritual core, as in the centre of his personality.

Spiritually, Saturn makes it possible to realise spiritual values within ourselves, can create the possibility of a personal example; mercilessly dismissing everything that hinders, he gives our consciousness objective knowledge and an impartial assessment of the method of the path.

Mentally, Saturn gives analytical thinking, creating a filigree accuracy of our consciousness. He also rewards us with the ability of criticism, that is, a clear examination of objectivity; illegal criticism generates doubts, distortions, and then the influence of Saturn can be devastating. Saturn also inclines to economy, to a balance between the arrival and expenditure of vital forces. Saturn is prudent, and sometimes this prudence is expressed in avarice in all its manifestations, and avarice-in absorbability. The legitimate absorption of Saturn is always justified by its self-creation. He always encourages the individual to give self-transformation to the world treasury of what is taken from it. The principle of duty is the principle of Saturn. With its influence, Saturn gives us a sense of loneliness, but it will give us the strength to endure this loneliness in order to forge our psychic core. Etheric-physical Saturn will create endurance, inertia, melancholy, lack of cheerfulness, that is, it creates a type of psychic old men. As for the three planets following Saturn, they do not belong to the creative seven.

This is the general characteristic of planetary influences.

The details of capturing their laws and signs relate to the seventh principle of reading the natural symbolism of the Book of Nature. Thus, the creative seven of secondary causality manifests itself everywhere in the universe: it creates life in the Solar System, as well as on Earth and in all its kingdoms. These seven creative forces, therefore, are imprinted everywhere in the symbols of true knowledge.

The seven keys of the worldview symbolise the seven points of view on each thing. We can consider each phenomenon as a form consisting of planetary principles: physical-etheric, an expression of psychic life, an expression of the usefulness of existence for other forms. And each phenomenon can be viewed from three points of view of spiritual vision: as an expression of an idea, as a manifestation of the meaning of life and as a manifestation of love. The seventh key reveals the very essence of things.

The seven candles of the sacred lamps denote these seven creative forces; and the Hierarchy of angels symbolises them; and these seven principles are reflected in the symbolism and legends of the East, deeply imprinted in the popular consciousness. And every spiritual impulse given to humanity has seven spectres of its manifestation.

Seven mysterious Kumaras, Spirits from Venus, who came to help humanity, create seven Initiatory Schools and Paths, seven religions. And not only on earth, but also in the sky, this seven is in the seven stars of the Big Dipper, in the seven stars of each truly grouped constellation. For truly the number seven, representing the three fundamental principles of the world, reflected in the Quaternary Law of World Dynamics, is the number that governs the life of the Cosmos.

The three Higher principles rule over the four lower ones and possess their elements. This is the basis of what people call the right of ownership, because without the possession of materials, it is impossible to show creative initiative and carry out spiritual construction in the form.

Each consciousness, according to the size of its internal potential, determines the possessions of its spiritual, mental, mental and physical potential. In this way, everyone is measured according to his measure, and in this way the scientist ultimately determines the size of his possession and his right to this possession. This is how God owns the world, and this is how each consciousness owns that part of the cosmic material that it needs for its conscious creativity. No one has and cannot have any other property right, and illegal seizures of subtle or condensed energies from the common treasury without the possibility of their creative processing entail severe retribution, terrible cosmic kata stanzas, the consequences of which are quite difficult to predict.

Justice

The Eighth Arcanum

Justice

1. Balance in motion
2. Regularity
3. Karma (causality)
Numeric designation: 8
Astrological correspondence: Cancer

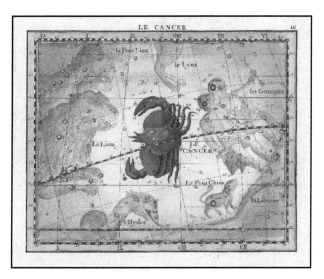

John Flamsteed, Le Cancer (Cancer), 1776

The symbolic picture depicts a woman sitting between two columns on a cubic stone. She is dressed in long clothes, her eyes are blindfolded; in her left hand she holds a scale, in her right - a raised sword. The Romans used this picture to depict Themis, the goddess of Justice.

The domination of the spirit over the object, asserted by the seventh principle, would lead as a result to the destruction of the world, that is, to its immersion in the Divine Subject, because the world cannot exist without the balance of the two forces acting in it. The apparent predominance of the centripetal force is compensated by the fact that the potential of the central Divine Consciousness includes opportunities from the inexhaustible source of the Absolute. The more the centripetal force is loaded, the more consciousness leaves the world, the more the Divine

Consciousness is strained by the radiation of new creative possibilities, and, as the evolutionary process intensifies, the creative force also increases. Therefore, nothing is ever repeated in the world, but creative possibilities are always manifested in it. The world is not at all a once-and-for-all set static material, the dissolution of which is engaged in consciousness in the process of evolution. The domination of the spirit over the form does not mean the destruction of the form, but it only makes it possible for its boundless transformation. Therefore, the universe is eternally renewed and never ceases. The days and nights of Brahma should be understood not as periods, but as a constant process of two cooperating forces. Without the balance of these forces, no phenomenon, no form can exist. A violation of the equilibrium in the direction of evolution burns the form, a violation of the equilibrium in the direction of involution leads to ossification and decay.

A living form, a living phenomenon, is the result of the balance of forces. In the earthly world, in which involution is illegal for humanity, this balance acquires an ethical character - the balance of good and evil. In the total sum of the ethical manifestation of the earthly world, these forces are the same. The general evolution does not at all consist in defeating evil with good, but in refining the forms of ethical manifestation, forcing the opposite force to refine the methods of struggle, and refinement is possible only with the spiritualisation of consciousness. Thus, when evil becomes more refined, it loses its sting, rivalry grows out of struggle, and a commonwealth of power grows out of rivalry, spiritualising and realising power. This equilibrium is not an exact account of both forces at each acting moment, it must be understood in dynamics. The higher the ideals that the best part of humanity lives by, the more terrible is their distortion by the rude part.

The lower the ethical level of peoples, the stronger the thirst for search and religious aspiration among the best part of people. That is why often the highest aspiration generates the most nightmarish blasphemous grimaces, that is why terrible crimes often lead to the awakening of consciousness, and that is why the teachings of the average height are usually better realised in the masses, although they do not give insights of the highest tension. Symbolically, this can be represented as follows: The higher the right scale rises, the lower the left one falls. The higher the left cup rises, filled with the longing of the hearts for the Spirit, the lower the right one falls, illuminating the consciousness of the lower planes. In the name of the strength and power of construction, it is necessary to take into account and balance these two forces in every activity, which means that the highest spiritualisation of one's own consciousness, the "subjective side", and taking into account the lower side are necessary.

The balance of phenomena and the form depend on the proportionality of the whole and the parts. It is the incommensurability of the parts with the whole that causes all the tragic misunderstandings in the life of mankind. All self-abasement and self-aggrandisement have a disastrous effect on our life and activities. We must remember that our personalities have a price, as diverse vehicles of Creativity for the Common Good. But any overestimation of the importance of the personality and its experiences, as well as an underestimation of its creative forces, destroy our consciousness and general construction.

In the ethical world, balance is reflected by justice. Justice consists of two scales: the scales of Severity and the scales of Mercy. Rigor takes into account the legality of Causality and raises the sword of retribution, as a consequence of the generated causes. Charity takes into account the future, the possibility of expedient development of consciousness and forgiving the past in the name of the future. Only those who take into account the Law of Mercy have the right to raise a punishing sword: not in the name of revenge for a violation of the balance, but in the name of cleansing consciousness. And only he can show real balance, who knows how to judge with rigor. Such mercy will not be an indulgence of weakness, but will help to open up new opportunities.

The Great Law of Nature also works in its relations with humanity. The law of Causality governs all natural phenomena, that is, the environment in which a person acts, and the part of human consciousness that belongs to this environment. And only his creative initiative, that is, the subjective world of a person, is governed by the Law of Expediency.

These are two naturally acting forces of the world. The Great Quaternary Law of Dynamics governs the universe, so every initiative must take into account the environment and manifest itself accordingly. If the environment is not suitable or if an individual initiative cannot join it, then no evolutionary creativity will occur. The natural results of Universal Creativity depend on the spiritual potential of creative individualised initiative and on the intensity of life in the environment. In addition, an individual initiative is connected with the results of its past actions, in other words, the environment, the conditions of activity, as well as thoughts, feelings and volitional impulses are objectively the result of pre-existing causes, and it is actually impossible to escape from the Law of Causality anywhere. The great law of Universal Dynamics, as it were, builds a square around the subjective initiative, enclosing every manifestation of creativity in its cage. It would seem that there is no way out of this cage, built by the Dynamic Law manifested in the objective world, because every cause must have an effect that binds the subject. If we want to get rid of this fate of the objective cell, the consequence of previously created causes, then there is only one way left, namely, to force ourselves to go inside ourselves, to direct the Law of Universal Dynamics in the opposite direction, and not passively wait for the consequence, giving ourselves up to the flow of life. By freeing our consciousness from the impressions produced by these consequences, that is, by developing a dispassion towards the objective world, we can neutralise them for ourselves.

The path of man in the Subtle World goes against nature, against its dynamics, which embodies causes into effects, spirit into form. This path against nature must be carried out, first of all, inside your own consciousness, namely, by directing it into the Spiritual World, increasing its strength, and not being carried away by the whirlwind of life.

This striving for the spirit twists the cycles of the Dynamic Law in the opposite direction - the direction of spiritualisation, that is, evolution, and the goals of spiritual achievements are set by the subject, and are not sought in the objective world. Therefore, the Law of Expediency, according to which the flow of evolution is moving, although it excludes complete freedom of creative manifestations, but in itself, at its root, is a product of inner spiritual freedom.

Thus, the ideal of consciousness and subjective freedom are opposed to the materialism of nature in the cell of the objective world. But this freedom is realised only if the forces of our consciousness are directed to the construction of a subjective ideal, and not objective values. In this case, the ideal struggles with the forms of the world, the goal with the cause, evolution with involution, human consciousness with nature. And only in this way, building subjective ideals, a person can not only get out from the constraining framework of the environment, but also to influence the nature of their activities, as well as the transformation of natural conditions and the thinning of the forms of the environment. Of course, this struggle takes place in the Subtle World, the rape of nature in the physical world is unacceptable. By this process of freeing consciousness from the framework of natural regularity and building a new regularity, a subjective square is symbolically created inside the objective square, directed by angles to the sides of the first and striving to break through them. For an explanation, let's turn to the following example.

Nature encloses our personality in the framework of material instincts, awarding them to our etheric body. These instincts are the instinct of self-preservation of one's own person, the instinct of the struggle for existence, which includes nutrition, procreation and gregariousness. A person sublimates these instincts, that is, he does not manifest them as required by the natural law contained in him, but forces them to serve the achievement of his ideal. The instinct of self-preservation, which causes mainly cowardice, he transforms into the heroism of self-defence in the name of the ideal. The instinct is the struggle for existence-in self-affirmation of oneself as a spiritual worker who gives spiritual values to the environment instead of the received matter. From the instinct of preservation he creates a spiritualised love, which encourages him to creative creations of cultural values, that is, the sexual instinct. He transforms the herd instinct into a social cooperation of mutual exchange. Of course, this inner square must rest against the walls of the outer one, that is, spiritual constructions must take into account objective facts, otherwise they will be utopian and will not produce the desired effect.

And the action is the following: while the person lives and works in the world, he never can get away from the actions in this world Quaternary law of motion, that is to break through the wall of the square, he could not; but as you expand your consciousness, inspired and grow their personality he pushes the inner square of the external wall, that is part of a more broad, General, and therefore more spiritual, the cycles of the World Law. Thus, by pushing the boundaries of nature, he fills them with new content. This is the way of man against nature, which results in the cooperation of two forces and two laws. Symbolically, this is expressed by two intertwined squares. The outer quadrilateral encloses our subjective aspirations and the great Law in its cage. Causality is the law of World Dynamics, directed towards differentiation and involution. It can be called a "Quadrilateral of Karma".

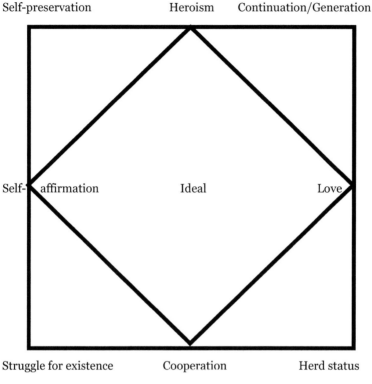

Figure 45

Karma is the reverse effect of the generated chain of causes and effects on the subject who gave birth to it. Although we develop and grow by the evolutionary path of Expediency, our objective causes, our objective manifestations, that is, actions, are links in the causal process, because we ourselves are the result of our creative manifestations. Everything generated, isolated, is bound to the parent by a great bond of responsibility and, in turn, affects him, causing further evolutionary work.

Therefore, all our actions aimed at the Common Good strengthen us, as Vivekananda says, "by the forces of a thousand angels," and all our actions aimed at harming the world are like a tiger ready to tear us apart. So we all constantly receive return blows from our actions. Some accelerate our spiritual growth, others slow it down, but both are strictly connected with everything that we have done and spawned.

In the general Universal construction, initiative creative consciousnesses are connected with the environment of action and the results of work, and this connection allows the creative consciousness to leave the environment of activity prematurely, until the possibilities are exhausted, and protects the forms from premature dissolution. Karma is the history of the development of our consciousness, the history of our journey in the universe and our repeated stay on Earth.

Earthly humanity, having one common task of cultural construction, binds all its members with a common Karma, and only the fulfilment of its task can completely free our consciousness from Universal Karma. This means that the Karma of humanity falls on all its members, and everyone, no matter how pure and high he himself is, is responsible for all the mistakes of humanity. Therefore, the last task of the Higher Forces is to indicate to humanity the ways out of the situation created by it and to teach it the formation of its Karma.

In addition to universal Karma, a person, being born in the environment of a certain people and race, performs the tasks of this people and this race and is connected with them by a common psychological traits, bearing the consequences of these. Thus, it is impossible to consider a Person's Karma separately from the Karma of all Mankind and from the Karma of the People to which he belongs. This Is a Common Karma.

Against this background of humanity and nationalities, his Personal Karma is determined and develops, that is, the Chain of Causes and Effects that he has developed during all his earthly lives. The human soul cannot immediately reveal all its possibilities to achieve perfection during one incarnation, but the whole series of incarnations, gradually unfolding its creative potential and the path of its evolution, builds a ladder of the soul's ascent to perfection. This is Personal Karma, since it is made up of the actions of a person determined by his character. Each incarnation is full of actions and deeds that determine the formula for the next incarnation. This general formula is developed in the next incarnation by its karma: specifically, by the nature of the new personality in which the soul is clothed, and by the special conditions of the environment of its birth, suitable for its further development and the repayment of previous debts. This Incarnational Karma, living, acting, manifesting in its new stage, again forms a chain of causes and effects, which is eliminated by the Fate of the Incarnation of this person. Thus, a person carries a triple karma: General, universal Karma (racial, national, social); Personal Karma and

Incarnational Karma. Of course, as a being belonging to the Cosmos, a person embodies the Karma of the whole World. Only a strong person can comprehend all the responsibility that lies on him. We must understand that Karma is the resultant of all our existences at every moment of our life, that we manifest it all in every action, and therefore karma or, as it is vulgarly called, "fate" is inside us, and not outside. Having taken this point of view, we translate karma into an inner square, create from it the actual steps of our ascent and turn the Forces and Cycles of Causality into Forces and Cycles of Expediency, and thus we obtain internal and external power over events and the surrounding environment.

Thus, the sides of the outer square break through, and Causality and Expediency are intertwined into an octagonal star of cooperation. So the Subject overcomes and transforms the Object, and the person - nature.

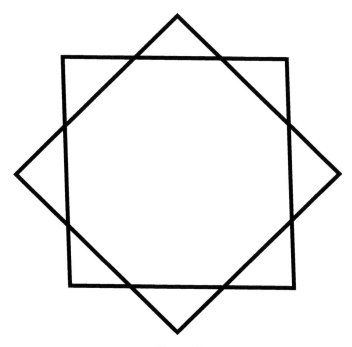

Figure 46

All beings of the world, if they act and create, are connected by karma with generation. Similarly, God, the Creator of the Worlds, is bound by the World Karma and carries it, which means that He carries the karma of all beings and each of people. Whoever understands this, it is easy for him in the world, because he can put all his burdens on God, in return embodying His Spiritual Ray and doing His Work. In this way, a person is freed from the Karma of the Incarnational and universal humanity and bears the Karma of God, "the yoke of which is easy".

Another expression of the same is "performing an action without a seed", that is, without personal interest in the action itself and its results, but perceiving them as fulfilling God's orders and tasks, moreover, the whole life can be perceived as such an assignment. Such actions do not multiply either incarnational or personal karma, because God is responsible for them.
Of course, the condition for such a victory over karma and throwing off its yoke is complete selflessness, non-attachment to one's own personality and the results of actions. The one who understands and is able to implement this is freed from the outer square and is called "liberated".

The Hermit

The Ninth Arcanum

Astral light

1. Dedication
2. Managers
3. Caution
Numerical designation: 9
Astrological correspondence: Leo

John Flamsteed, Le Lion (Leo), 1776

The symbolic picture depicts an old hermit, wrapped in a cloak with his head. This cloak forms three folds along his body. Under the cloak, he holds a lighted lantern in his right hand, and in his left a staff crossed at the end with three horizontal crossbars. Three folds and three crossbars. The first means knowledge of the three planes of manifestation of creative power, the second-power over the totality of the three worlds in which it manifests. The light is the acquired light of the Spirit, carefully protected from the ignorance of the profane and the attack of enemies.

The Ninth Principle as a whole synthesises all the previous Principles in itself, adding to them an element of their subjective implementation in itself. This realisation of the Divine spiritual principle of Love and Life and the creative force resulting from them, its laws and applications - is Wisdom. Wisdom is the legitimate heritage and the only property of humanity, forgotten due to the fragmentation and narrowing of consciousness, identified with earthly objects. The Path of Initiation - this is the way of regaining Knowledge, Wisdom and Strength, which belong to man forever. Its search is associated with the separation of consciousness from the Earth, the awakening of the immortal Soul, the finding of a Spiritual Source or God in it. And only those who have found God in themselves are given power over the creative force and a true knowledge of the laws of its manifestation. Therefore, the preparation for the Initiatory Dedication, the path is difficult, because, tearing our consciousness away from the objects of our desires, we go through the stages of death, the death of our earthly personality every time. Therefore, Initiation was symbolised in ancient times, the sphinx, which must be overcome, challenged to a contest, because otherwise he will defeat the audacious.

This struggle, of course, is purely subjective, because you need to overcome your false nature, created by many incarnations, in which attachment to earthly objects and selfish desires formed the karma of pseudo-personality. And only by tearing out our consciousness from this personality with all the prejudices, superstitions, habits, attachments, passions and desires that have developed in it, we will be able to feel our true divine nature; to know the Universe as our home, creative power as the radiation of our spiritual core and God as our source. And then knowledge and strength will be able to gradually develop in us. This knowledge will unfold into a new deep creative vision of the previous principles, into the forces and possibilities of their application in the name of the Common Good.

The Ninth Principle is illustrated by the Emerald Tablet of Thoth Hermes Trismegistus, which reveals the achievements of the initiate in its Testaments. Let us comment on some lines of these Testaments.

Truly, without falsehood, reliably and to the highest degree truthfully...

"Truly, without lies" - this statement refers to the spiritual plane of consciousness, where the truth is perceived directly and therefore there can be no lies. "Reliable" - this refers to the mental/psychic consciousness, where everything can be verified by personal experience. "Extremely truthful" refers to material facts that are natural symbols of spiritual phenomena.

That which is above is like to that which is below, and that which is below is like to that which is above, to accomplish the miracles of one thing.

This great Law of Analogy, the method of world creativity, is found in the sixth Arcanum and is sufficiently illuminated in it. It summarises the mechanical process of the Universe. Therefore, each of us is a thread of Divine Creativity that passes through all the Worlds from Spirit to form.

And just as all things came from the One through the One, so all things were born from the one essence through adaptation

The first half of this position speaks of the first principle - the One All - Knowing Power of Love, the radiation of the One Spirit through Its own expression and manifestation - Life. Thus, the Divine Spirit, the one and indivisible Love, and Life, the dynamics of Its manifestation and Its differentiation, are actually one and the same and are unthinkable without each other. The second half of the statement speaks about the third principle - the birth of a single Essence of the World Mind and the generation of creative world processes by it through adaptation to the cycles of the Great Quaternary Law of Vital Dynamics. This is the end of the cosmic part of the Emerald Tablet and then there is a description of the adaptation of the World Truth to our system:

The Sun is his father, the Moon is his mother The Sun is the father of creative power.

Esoteric science does not diverge from the scientific theory of the incandescent matter or about the centre of the magnetic field - it is generally accepted to consider the Sun as such. But esoteric science still considers the Sun to be an open door to the World of Spirit, as if a window of cosmic substance, through which a stream of Divine Love and Divine vital force flows into the cosmic environment from the Spiritual World (this window appears spherical to our three-dimensional point of view). There is no matter in the Sun: The Sun is the entrance to the Divine World of Unity, in which every form burns, the Sun is an immaterial prism that concentrates Spiritual Energy in itself and pours it into space.
In this prism, the spiritual energy of individualism is divided into secondary prisms or individual solar rays gifted with thought-

creating abilities. Thus, the entire flow of spiritual, psychic and vital energy, individualised into radiating consciousnesses, pours out from the Sun into the Cosmic Environment of our Solar System and determines life in it. All the beings inhabiting this system, gifted with creative consciousness and individualised life, are essentially solar spirits sent down to build in different circles of the periphery, and their consciousness and tasks defined by them are formed accordingly with the place of their activity.

Thus, the Sun is the father of all things that think and create in our system. The Sun, drawing us back, determines our spiritual religious searches; through the doors of the form of the Sun, we enter the door of All-Being, All-Bliss and All-Knowledge. The sun is the eternal presence of God in our system; and all of us, as children of the Sun, are eternal in the very depths of consciousness, like it, and through it we will someday merge into the Absolute.

Of course, in every system of the boundless Cosmos there are the same centres, the same open gates to the Spiritual World, the same windows through which the Divine creative power of Love flows; but we do not need to make a circle through the infinity in order to reach God. According to the Spiritual Ray of the Sun, a return to God is provided for each of us from any place on the periphery.

The mother of creative power is the Moon. The moon is considered here as a symbol of the Cosmic Environment, because in fact the Moon outlines the periphery of the influence of Winter weather, and the Cosmic environment, captured by the influence of the Sun, like our Moon is subordinate to it. The nature of the creative force and its actions are determined by the nature of the environment in which it operates. The creative power of Solar Love, refracted in the Cosmic environment of the planets, it is in it that it acquires its specificity, which distinguishes it from manifestations in other systems.

The wind carried her in its womb

The creative force, passing from one sphere of the periphery to another, passing through the spiritual, creative, intellectual, psychic and material world, forms, as it were, tornadoes or Cosmic winds, and the fact or form is their final realisation.

The Earth is its nurse

Realising itself into a material form or fact, the creative power of the Sun absorbs the vibrations of the environment, is nourished and enriched with intense possibilities. This is the meaning of the form and the meaning of the material embodiment, because only in a form that has been completely objectified is it possible to fully come into contact with the surrounding Cosmic environment, exchange with its energies, pour out one's subjective creativity and draw new experience. Truly, the lands of our system feed the creative power of the Solar System in Love.

A thing is the father of all perfection in the whole universe.

The same creative force, but of the opposite direction, leading to the spiritual source, spiritualises, refines and perfects the forms in the surrounding environment. Therefore, it gives birth to every perfection, that is, it leads every form to the source.

Her powers remain intact when she transforms into the Ground.

Its forces remain whole when it turns into the Earth, which means that every materially formalising fact is like a bomb, in which the entire vortex of creative force with all its special vibrations arising from the passage of various planes of consciousness is condensed. In each material form, the entire history of the passage of the Spiritual Ray and all the possibilities of its return are condensed, and thus all of us inside the embodied form, as if inside a bomb, carry a spiritual charge, a fire of thought-creating power and a vortex of psychic energy, and only by introducing it into the earth can we get a lightning quick return. That is why it is said that in order to achieve perfection, the Gods must become human, that is, incarnate.

You will separate the Earth from the Fire, the subtle from the gross, carefully and with great skill.

In the seventh Arcanum, it was said about the domination of the Spirit over the form, that is, Fire over the Earth, the psyche over the mother, that is, the subtle over the gross. For this domination, it is necessary to distinguish in each phenomenon, and above all in oneself, what belongs to the Spirit, that is, to Fire, and what belongs to the form, that is, to the Earth; what belongs to psychic impulses, that is, to the subtle, and what belongs to material instincts, that is, to the gross.

Since the worlds mutually penetrate each other, then in this understanding it is necessary to show extreme caution so that the seemingly crude, that is, primitive expression is not taken as belonging to matter, and also be able to distinguish the subtly materialised from the truly spiritual. Incorrect and careless recognition in this case can distort one's own character and harm the karma of other beings.

It is on the wrong recognition of the gross and subtle that all the tragic mistakes and false paths of humanity are based. Thus, all unselfish creative impulses in the name of achieving Truth and service are for the greater good, they will belong to the subtle spiritual, however primitive these impulses may be, even the most refined self-interest and selfishness should be attributed to gross material instincts. In separating the Earth from the Father, it is necessary to show great skill, that is, to be able to separate the levels of one's consciousness from someone else's, without defeating any of the threads. For example, when disciplining the body, it would be unwise to damage health by too abrupt and premature separation of its interests from the general psyche.

This force ascends from the earth to the sky and descends again to the earth, perceiving the forces of both the higher and lower regions of the world.

The only Divine creative Force of Love rushes from the form back to the source of Unity, dragging all consciousness with it, spiritualising and refining them. And, having come into contact with the Spiritual World and taken root in it, it again rushes to the self-realisation of the form, that is, to a new creativity on Earth. In the Spiritual World, the creative force feeds on the light of Wisdom and perceives new creative opportunities. In the lower strata of the world, the creative force is enriched by the vibrations of the environment and increases intensity. Thus, the light of Wisdom feeds the creative flow at the top, and the power of concentration feeds it at the bottom.

Thus you will gain the glory of the whole world

The consciousness in which the creative force operates through self-manifestation and self-giving in selfless service, the Spiritual potential becomes possible Light, thought-creation, mental tension and the realisation of experience by enriching it with the glory of the whole world.

Therefore, all darkness will depart from you.

The consciousness that realises the Solar Creativity cannot be subject to the eclipse caused by non-knowledge, desires, greed, misunderstanding, because all the knowledge and all the powers of the world are open for selfless service. Darkness is a limitation. But the stirrup - he who strives objectively for the truth strives for the limitless and overcomes the darkness of limitations.

This force is the force of every force, for it overcomes every most refined thing and penetrates every solid thing.

A single Creative force is Life itself and, as such, lies at the basis of all forces and processes. The one who goes with the flow of Life, carries Love in the soul, conquers the entre Spiritual World and transforms the material world.

This is how the world was created, from here there will arise specific adaptations, the method of which is described.

We already know that every form is a cycle of applying the creative force to a specific Cosmic environment. Having the creative power, that is, spiritual energy, you can find an infinite range of possibilities for its application and achieve amazing results.

Therefore, I was called Hermes the thrice greatest, since I have knowledge of the three parts of the universal philosophy.

The one whose consciousness lives in the Spiritual World directly sees and knows the processes, forces and facts operating in the mental, psychic and physical planes. His worldview will be precisely the Universal philosophy.

What have I told you about the work of Solar doing has been completed.

Therefore, all darkness will depart from you, the consciousness that realises Solar Creativity cannot be subject to obscuration caused by the so-called Great Solar Work, which is the immediate task of humanity. The Initiate becomes a real Adept who is aware of himself.

The Solar Consciousness, the conductor of the Divine Spiritual force on Earth. Everything that he does bears the seal of Solar Creativity on Earth, and therefore every work of his carries a Blessing, because it is spiritualised and infinite. To become Sons of the Sun in cultural work and to transform the psychic atmosphere of the Earth means to create a Great Work. In the state in which humanity is now, most of which is striving to obtain material goods and low pleasures, the implementation of All Kinds of Solar Work is very difficult. The aura of the planet is poisoned by low-quality earthly emanations and earthly deeds. Therefore, the Higher Forces have established a special spiritual order on Earth, according to which the Great Solar Work is carried out thanks to the participation of the Great Teachers of Humanity and the White Brothers who reside in a special spatial zone of the planet - the energy centre of the Earth. And it is from this centre that the Great Teachers send spiritual energy to the seeking consciousnesses, where the Cosmic energies that feed the Earth are transformed by the Adepts of the Himalayas, and from there They send their messengers and collaborators to help the peoples.

In the process of Guiding people, nations and students, it is necessary to exercise caution. Caution is the basis of wise Guidance on the path of Initiation. It is expressed in the words: "Give to everyone according to his measure," because an overloaded consciousness is not only harmful, but can have a destructive effect on the subtle vehicles (bodies) of students. That is why Initiation is esoteric and occult. Premature knowledge and premature possession brings harm, not benefit. Only the full growth of consciousness will make it possible to master the fullness of power and the fullness of knowledge, in the name of selfless construction. Only gradually passing through many stages of accumulation of positive and negative experience, consciousness is spiritualised and grows. Therefore, it is to preserve the possibility of self-consecration that the White Brothers occasionally set milestones on ways, as humanity develops, revealing the treasury of knowledge. "Throwing pearls in front of swine" is irresponsible, careless - it is a consequence of ignorance of one's responsibility. Thus, dedication, self-consecration, guidance and recognition of leaders, caution and responsibility will lead the one who goes to the Heights of Wisdom.

The Ninth Principle symbolises the riddle of the sphinx. The Sphinx carries all the nine principles outlined above and is called the "synthetic great secret", the solution of which frees consciousness from the formal world, and therefore from a detailed study of all other Principles. We offer this solution to everyone's intuition, because everyone must find it subjectively for himself.

To make the task easier, let's say that the upper triangle symbolises the three Great Spiritual Principles, reflected by the principles of the All-Knowing giver-Mind, the All-Bliss giver-Heart and the giver of All-Existence-expanded by the spiritual will of Consciousness. The same triangle symbolises the mystery of the union of Love and Life into a creative force, and it also speaks of the Divine origin of man. Of the elements, it refers to Air.

The six-pointed star of the middle part symbolises the mental-psychic world, and the triangle turned upside down - the inverted reflection of the spiritual triangle is symbolised Water and depicts the flow of psychic forces. The triangle with the top up, the triangle of thought-creation, mental construction is symbolised by Fire.

The lower part of the symbol captures in the circle of Cosmic Life the square of the Great Quaternary Law of Universal Dynamics, the Law of Causality, that is, the Square of Nature. The cross behind the centre, a hidden quadrangle, symbolises the path of humanity against nature, the expediency of which everyone must find and establish in himself, as the hidden centre of the cross.

Wheel of Fortune

Implementation

The Tenth Arcanum
The Covenant
Worldview
The wheel of life
Numerical designation: 10
Astrological correspondence: Virgo

Virgo, Johann Bayer, 1603

It is a state in which all consciousnesses can freely seek the Truth and manifest the creative initiative of the spiritual core of consciousness, applying the Great Creative Power of God to the realisation of their potential. All beings of the Universe are called to build the Common Good, to be an assistant of the Creator in the creation of Worlds, that is, in the objective expression of his plans. This is the Testament of God to all consciousnesses. This is a testament to man.

The picture of the Arcanum shows a wheel that is strengthened. It is placed on a pole resting on a wave, entwined with two snakes forming three circles. Inside the wheel is a hexagram. At the top of the pole, relative to the wheel, a platform is fixed immobile, on which a winged sphinx lies with a sword raised in its right paw. On the right side of the wheel, Anubis, that is, a man with a dog's head, holding a rod entwined with snakes in his right hand, climbs to the platform. From the left, typhon falls down the wheel, that is, a dragon with a human head, holding a trident in his right hand, pointing down.

Some gloominess of the image of the tenth Arcanum can be explained by the fact that in the human consciousness, disconnected from the Spiritual World, the wheel of earthly life seems to be a closed circle with no outcome, and therefore the previous evolution - Anubis - entails a new involution - typhon, because the circle of life, disconnected from spiritual sources, rotates hopelessly. An explanation of the other symbols of this picture, in which the breakdown of human consciousness is imprinted, will be given below.

The Tenth Principle tells us about the objective realisation of the spiritual achievements of the initiated Subject, which are disclosed in detail in the ninth principle. Subjectively acquired Knowledge of God, Dedication, Life Wisdom, mastery of Thought-creation and Creative Power, objectively translates into the construction of the Common Good. The Common Good is the natural state of everything, it is a state in which all consciousnesses can freely seek the Truth and manifest the creative initiative of the spiritual core of consciousness, applying the Great Creative Power of God to the realisation of their potential. All beings of the Universe are called to build the Common Good, to be an assistant of the Creator in the creation of Worlds, that is, in the objective expression of his plans. This is God's covenant to all consciousnesses. This is His covenant to man. This natural state of the all-encompassing Common Good on Earth is called "cultural construction". The concept of culture translated into Latin means service to the light. In its essence, it is the embodiment and manifestation of spiritual values in the conditions of the existence of the planet Earth. These conditions are expressed mentally - in the development of a combinatorial mind (small manas), psychically – by individualisation and materially - in the mastering of three-dimensional space.

In the picture of the tenth Arcanum, cultural construction is a pole entwined with two snakes. The covenant of the realisation and objective manifestation of spiritual ideals developed on Earth by Higher Consciousnesses is the basis of all religious teachings ever given to humanity. If culture is a process of realisation of spiritual values in the forms of earthly existence, then the basis of any cultural construction should be Spirit, not matter, ideals instead of profit, unselfishness rather than self-service. Looking dispassionately at the history of human development, we will certainly notice that all great cultures were built on the foundation of religion and Covenants. The concept of religion, as we know, means a connection, that is, a channel laid to the Spiritual World, through which knowledge of Cosmic Principles and Laws flows to humanity, knowledge of those ideals that are based on these Principles and implemented by these laws. And the most powerful force - the Spiritual World-religion - is then expressed by ideology into a general worldview that bears the colouring of the time, changes in the existence and character of peoples. Further, this worldview is embodied in the forms of philosophies, sciences, arts, social order and material construction. All attempts to build a culture on the basic economic and political ones are doomed to failure, because they do not provide a direction for spiritual life for cultural realisations. Every culture is the realisation and construction of the Common Good, and the Common Good must be understood broadly, not only in the sense of material well-being, but also in the sense of deep mental satisfaction, the ability to reveal the riches of spiritual life and get everything necessary from the common treasury for each servant and for cooperation in general in its entirety.

The Universal Good is the realisation of God's Plans in the earthly world, and each servant is a thread of the Divine Spirit, a thread of the Absolute, realising one of His opportunities during all transformations and incarnations. Thus, the Universal Good represents for its realisation a strict hierarchical system of conducting the spirit into forms. And in this system, each part, each working consciousness, has its own place, its own meaning, the meaning of its existence, and, consequently, its own happiness. No element can be removed or damaged from this chain of cooperation and creative construction without general harm to the construction as a whole.

The construction of the Universal Good is based on the dynamic balance of two world forces - evolution and involution - and there is not a repeating flat circle or a wheel rotating in place, but an unfolded Infinity is a spiral, the turns of which are never repeated, but are always analogous to each other. The infinite diversity of the universe and, at the same time, its harmonious rigor, in the depths of which the same law operates, depends on this. The subjective growth of creative servants who embody the diversity of the Creator, the unlimited and even the return of consciousness, which has completed its spiral by approaching the original source, only excites and strains It to reveal new creative spiritual possibilities. The construction of the Common Good has no end and never ends in time and space. If the construction of the Universe is infinite, since it itself has no end, then each part of it is infinite in time, although it is limited by space, because space is the possibility of the coexistence of two or countless consciousnesses, different in their range and colour, and time is the unfolding and movement of an unchanging Eternity.

Each part of the universe in its dynamics manifests one of the possibilities of the Absolute, and in its depth is eternal, that is, it rests in the Absolute.

The construction of the Common Good presupposes (since it is construction, not chaos) a Common Plan and a Common Divine Plan of the Universe. Each consciousness participating in the construction knows about this general plan in its subjective reflection, that is, insofar as it accommodates this plan according to its role and place in the general construction. Therefore, each consciousness contributes its own note of understanding of the General Plan, but it can never cover it as a whole. Only the Divine Consciousness can fully embrace it, and God's closest collaborators transmit it in the language of symbols to other consciousnesses, offering them to everyone's intuitive understanding.

Thus, the construction of the universe is based on a Divine system that embodies the living worldview of God. All actions, conscious or unconscious, are always conditioned by the worldview of their producer. Thus, the worldview of each person is reflected in the whole structure of his life-activity. Worldviews cannot be understood as an independent abstraction far from life, on the contrary, it is the worldview that has always been an effective force in the history of human development and has been imprinted in all external events of peoples and individuals. We already know that the only creative force is Thought-creation, but every Thought-creation presupposes a background, the basis of a specific worldview from which it develops.

The Great Consciousnesses close to God have transmitted to us the Divine System of World Construction by the symbolism underlying the Single Great Esoteric School and its sectors. Here we will use the symbolism of Egypt, transmitted to us by Moses under the name of the Sephirotic system, that is, the sacred numbers, which is the basis of the esoteric school of Pythagoras. This system says: we can perceive, understand and reason only about what has at least the most subtle form. We cannot talk about the world of pure Spirit, and everyone can perceive it only subjectively, with the greatest effort of the heart and the establishment of a spiritual connection. The Absolute is incomprehensible not only for the sick earthly mind, but also for the World Mind, because It is above it and, reaching It, the Mind fades away. The Absolute is also incomprehensible to the Heart, that is, to spiritual feeling, for the Heart merges with Him and melts in Him, having reached Him. But the first processes taking place in Him, His fundamental forces of Love, Life and General Plans are available only for the subjective perception of the spiritual development of the Heart.

The mind can realise and create only starting from the realm of the most subtle spiritual realisations, and since the realisation of spiritual possibilities is the realisation of the Truth of the Universal Good, this system can to be recorded and transmitted by such a subtle symbolism as only the mind is capable of. Therefore, we have an incomprehensible Absolute, the Ocean of the Spirit, which carries all the creative abilities in itself. In this all-consuming and All-pervading Ocean, there is always a process of life or movement that reveals its possibilities. This dynamic process causes the self-emission of the Absolute, called Universal Love, and is embodied in Universal Life. The general Plan of this manifestation, that is, the Plan of the Creative God, cannot be comprehended by man, because he himself, since he is a man, is only a part of this plan. Therefore, all disputes and all theories about the root cause of the world are fruitless. The part cannot comprehend the measure of the whole, but can only reach it and then merge with it. But the general plan of its implementation with the Law of World Dynamics is open for comprehension.

The indeterminate first three foundations, as the very essence of things, exist in the universe in a reflected form. And these three Principles establish the spiritual connection of each form, its true living immortal part, and at the same time the Spiritual World of the Universe. In this Spiritual World, the system puts, as its primary basis, a Great Unity, against which the Universe will unfold, that is, the Unity that we talked about in the first principle. This means that in the general flow of life, everything is as deeply rooted in the Absolute as the entire Universe with its Creative God is rooted in It.

But like the process of polarisation into Love and Life that takes place in the Absolute, this Unity of the Plan, manifesting itself, is polarised into a subjective and objective part. The individualised subject is the carrier of Divine Love, and the chain of objects of the Universe are the carriers of Life, because Love is the deepest subjective secret of each individual consciousness, and Life is a stream of transformation to which the shells of consciousness are subject. This upper triangle of the Spiritual World is the Higher World, or the World of Radiance, where the songs of life sound, fully revealing their meaning, where the manifestations of One Love are infinitely diverse and where consciousness is immersed in the Ocean of Divine Unity. This triangle contains the secret of the interaction of the two great poles of creativity, the secret of the universal androgyny, the secret of the union of Love (+) and Life (-), Subject and Object into Unity, that is, of god. And since the Spiritual World is reflected in every form, in the same enclosed secrets forever and ever - men's and women's deepest meaning androgynous love creating and leading to God, this World of Radiance, the Spiritual world, for realisation, must, as it were, return, that is, turn down the vertex of the triangle as a result of interaction or the generation of the dual power acting into it.

We have already talked about the birth of the World Mind and thought-creating processes. The general scheme of this birth is as follows (Fig. 47). The subjective principle asserts the Principle of evolution, that is, the expedient flow of individual striving for God. The objective principle, Life, asserts the process of involution, that is, the sequential passage of the cycles of life in the process of differentiation according to the law of causality. The subjective consciousnesses that establish evolution together generate a general picture of the Universe in its energetic creative form, as a set of creative processes. This general picture is an energetic unfolding of the general plan, it is the world of Thought-creation or the Creative or fiery World.

Further, the overall picture reveals the aggregates of subjects acting in it. This Is The Hierarchy of the Cosmic Brotherhood of Consciousnesses. Objectively, the parts are revealed through the natural forces that weave the shells of these. The chain of natural forces preserves the forms that embody the picture of the Universe. These three principles make up the Subtle or Formational World, where form is understood as a set of energy vibrations embodying the Forces of the Fiery World. These created forms are then embodied in the tenth beginning, as it were, in seven facts, which are then developed by the historical process into what we mean under the material form of things. Each material seed, unfolding, again imprints in itself and the material world the ten basic principles of the Great System of Building the Universe. Thus, the seed is in the reflected form the first, the most subtle the beginning of the physical world, in which the entire process of the Universe is being developed again (in a particular form - at least a tree).

Absolute Manifesting		Emanation
Object (Life)	Subject (Love)	Spiritual World

Creative Involutionary Impulses of life	Evolutionary the picture of consciousness	Generation
	The overall picture of the universe	The Creative World

World Forces of nature	Cosmic Hierarchy historical deployment Consciousness	Formation
Forms-ideas of systems and the lives on them		The World is Thin

---

Deploying forms In space and time	Realisation the material world

Figure 47

Unity of design

Radiation

The Sprits of Nature are the
Divine essence

Natural Individual cycles
Of the Earth, the soul

Spiritual World
Fiery

Subjective Consciousness

The causal chain is

Expedient

Creation

Creative
Mental Energy

volitional
initiative

Creative World
Individualistic

Militaristic

Prototypes

Natural
Power
Energy
(mental energy)

Hierarchical
ladder of
consciousness

Formation

Energy forms
Thought forms, representations

The World is thin
Energy
Formational

Seeds of Facts

Realisation
The World of Incarnations

Realisational

Figure 48

Table 47 demonstrates that the Beginning - or the Sephirs of the right and left columns vertically - reflect each other and flow from each other. The same can be said about the Sephirs of the middle column. The general scheme is represented by Figure 48.

The right column (vertically) contains the development of the subjective principle, which reduces to the identification of consciousness with objective shells and the acquisition of the power of their transformation. This is a symbolically depicted world of the "I", integrating the particular into the general. The left column symbolises the creative development of the world of "not me", in order of differentiation by The World Law of the Dynamics of life cycles. The left column restricts the right one in the same way as in the eighth principle, the outer square restricts the inner square.

In the middle column, the world 'I' and the 'not I', touch, and the last secret of their fusion is in the Sephirah of the upper triangle. The divine creative power is symbolised by the channel passing through the entire middle of the Sephira, that is, the middle column. Therefore, the secret of mastering the creative power lies in a deep understanding of the subjective principle and the ability to arbitrarily connect it with the objective world. And involuntary submission to the objective world will make a toy of the universal creative force out of consciousness.

In relation to humanity and to the ways of its creative development, the Sephirotic system symbolises three main streams:

1. The path of knowledge-Jnana Yoga - the path of the right column, the world of the "I", the path is subjectively active, and objectively inactive.

2. The Path of Love and Sacrifice-Bhakti Yoga-the path of the left column, the world of "not me", in which the Divine " I " is distinguished by absorbing its shells by the objective world. This path is internally passive, and externally active.

3. The middle way is a combination of the first two. Its lower part is symbolised by Karma Yoga, the middle part is Raja Yoga, and the upper part is Agni Yoga. This is a kind of androgynous path, where self-creation and creativity go hand in hand and where the Subject is always in harmonious combination with the Object. In the terminology of Rosicrucianism, these paths are energetic forms based on:

1. The Way of the Rose.
2. The Way of the Cross.
3. The path of the Pelican.

The sephirotic system, as a plan of world construction, can be applied to the construction of each of its parts and in each of its planes. So, in relation to our solar system and its structural part, its beginnings are represented by the Sun and the planets:

Hades

Neptune		Uranus

Mars	The Sun	Venus

Saturn		Jupiter

Mercury

Moon

Figure 49

In relation to the creative development process life on our Earth can be represented as follows:

Solar Energy

Passive object	Active
Positive side	Subjective Side
Involution (The Creative God)	Evolution of the Soul
	(Individuality)

Causal Law	Appropriate Initiative
Numbering	Initiative
(forces)	Spritiualisation

The general plan of the planet's life

| Efficiency | Cultural Construction |
| Nature | |

The general picture of the life of the Earth

The history of the development of the planet in time

Figure 50

Do not forget that by the horizontal connection lines between the Sephiroth, I denote between 'I' and 'not I', the shells of consciousness are woven and transformed back into the initiative consciousnesses of the cycles of life. In all four planes of the Earth's life, construction and therefore recognition, is also built according to the plan of this great system. So the Basics. The Spiritual World is symbolised by ten attributes. The unknowable. In religions:

Omnipresent
(the one who is the Absolute Being)

Omniscient

All-creating

God is in Himself
Metaphysical God
The All-Blessed One

All-Good

God of Forces
(Of the Universe)

God of Hosts
(the Almighty)

The Almighty
(God who works miracles)

The Lord
(Lord of Karma)

Figure 51

In the Intellectual World

The Idea

Objective   Subjective
Shell   Initiative
Involutive   Evolutionary
Mental Environment   Ideological Impulse

The World of ideas

Law   Law
Causality   Expediency

Law of Harmony
The World of Representations

Figure 52

In the physical world, the sephirotic system is displayed in the structure of bodies, in the main nerve centres of organisms

Figure 53

The centre of the Bell

(connection with the spirit, the world and the Cosmos)

Laryngeal centre	Occipital Centre
(recognition)	(connection with spiritual World)
Left shoulder	right shoulder

Heart
(anahata)

Solar plexus	the centre of life force
The will of emotions	in the navel
(manipura)	

Sexual centre

The centre of the spine in the sacrum

Figure 53

The process of writing The Sephirotic system was used by the sages and initiates in all their actions. So, it was displayed by the ten Commandments of Moses and the prayer of Jesus Christ. The sephirotic system is a system for deploying the creative process, and therefore every wisely performed action with a comparable result is performed according to it (Fig. 54).

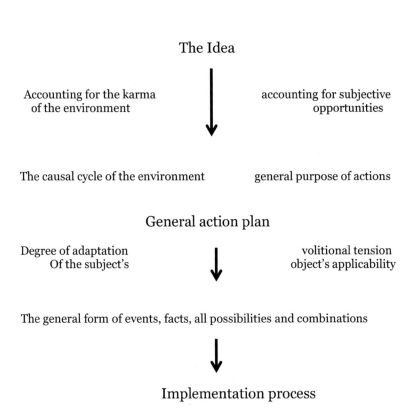

The Idea

Accounting for the karma
of the environment

accounting for subjective
opportunities

The causal cycle of the environment   general purpose of actions

General action plan

Degree of adaptation
Of the subject's

volitional tension
object's applicability

The general form of events, facts, all possibilities and combinations

Implementation process

Figure 54

In relation to the writing of a book, a picture, to the creation of systems of social movements, mystical teachings, to the creation of harmonious relations between people.

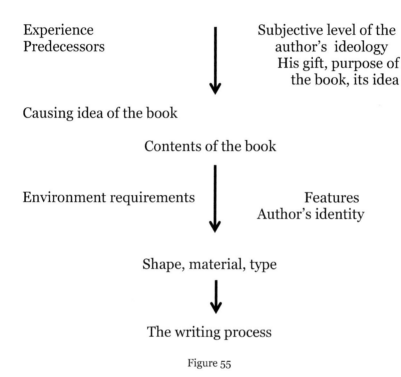

Idea of the book

Experience
Predecessors

Subjective level of the
author's ideology
His gift, purpose of
the book, its idea

Causing idea of the book

Contents of the book

Environment requirements

Features
Author's identity

Shape, material, type

The writing process

Figure 55

It will be clear to a thoughtful consciousness that the presentation of the Ten Principles, or Sephir, is nothing more than the ten Principles of the foundations of the Universe that we have considered, and the order in which they are arranged is a system of their influences and dynamic radiations. This system ends the principal part of the presentation of the Foundations of the Universe and the consequences generated by them. The following ten Principles, starting from the tenth to the nineteenth inclusive, are power psychic energies. The four last Principles, from the nineteenth to the twenty-second, synthesise their manifestations on the four planes of consciousness. These

Twenty-two Principles make up the wheel of life, in which the beginning, meeting with the end, denotes the new spiral.

Man has forgotten that the world was created by the word, and that all parts of it are embodiments of individual words. The elements of this sacred universal language are the Twenty-two Principles that correspond in all people.

There are twenty-two main sounds in Russian languages. Modern human languages have become vulgarised, that is, they have materialised, simply imprinting concepts about the objective world. Human consciousness has forgotten that the words that make up its languages are formulas, the spiritual utterance of which causes psychic energy to act, helping to translate it into facts. Thus, from a combination of the corresponding special words-formulas are created from the symbols-letters, which activate the creative force and produce creative vortices of psychic energy. This forgotten sacred language remained, however, in the memories of mankind in the form of the special sacred words or special magic formulas-spells Thus, the highest word is Aum among the Hindus, Emesh among the Jews, Amen among the Egyptians, which turned into the Amen of prayers among the Slavs, is the essence of the formula that sets in motion the most subtle and the most powerful spiritual vibrations. In the same way, special magic words appeared, which activate psychic energy and consist of sounds in which the World foundations are imprinted.

These incomprehensible words, which we ironically call "abracadabra", are actually formulas that activate combinations of World Principles by the will of the operator. In their magical practice the Jews used twenty-two letters of their sacred alphabet for the most powerful psychic and material perturbations, combining the spelling of the letter symbols of psychic energy with the corresponding forces and events. So, in revenge for the persecution, they caused the earthquake of Lisbon, linking the life of this city with the twenty-two sacred signs of their alphabet and making chaotic movements in it.

The ten basic Principles, refracted in four worlds, create a system of forty of their applications, called small secrets. These forty combinations of the imprint were hidden in the signs of a card deck with its four suits:-

10 signs of clubs or wands correspond to the structure of life in the spiritual world;

10 signs of hearts or cups correspond to the structure of the psychic world;

10 signs of spades or swords correspond to the structure of the intellectual world;

10 signs of pentacles correspond to the structure of the world of forms.

Initially, the four figure cards denoted four degrees of initiation into the knowledge and possession of these basics in the four worlds. The degree of a cavalier, or a king, or a warrior was lost in the clouds.

The Ten Foundations of the world system are ten Principles that burn with eternal lights, like the stationary stages of its creation-dissolution. The same ten in the dynamic aspect plus twelve represent the wheel of life of the twenty-two Principles. Their combination is shown in Fig. 56

A thoughtful awareness of this scheme reveals all the secrets of creative paths and will give a full understanding of the principles and forces operating in the world, their combinations, correspondences and dynamic radiations. Therefore, it is said that knowledge of the system, the ability to apply it to different areas and the ability to concentrate saves a person from a detailed study of any area of knowledge and will give him a special Omniscience, which in any moment of the process of cognition can be consciously and correctly applied to any science, any studied and unexplored area. As applied to the composition of the human individuality and its shell-personality, together with the interchange between the planes of consciousness and the relationship of the principles that establish these planes, the system is depicted in Fig. 57

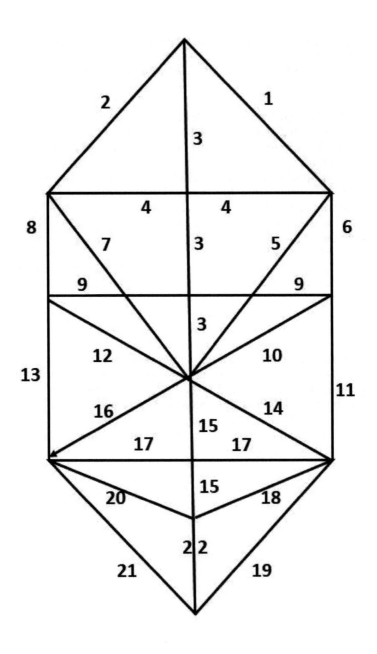

Figure 56

In this scheme, it is extremely important to take revenge on three intersections along the middle line:
- The first intersection of the third and fourth channels in the upper triangle - the point of balance of "I" and "not I", the point of the highest tension of the actions of subjective consciousnesses and the forces of Nature, the lightning of the meeting of the Male and Female principles, plus and minus, is the source of creative power up to God and down to the world, and in it is the Great secret of the universal androgyny, reflected in all truly androgynous actions. To master this mystery is to master the mystery of the Universal Androgynous-the Creator, and that's why Love, man plus woman, is experienced by a person on Earth only at the same time - creatively and materially.

The second point - the intersection of the third channel with the ninth, that is, with the channel of initiation, is the point of intersection of Consciousness and Spirit. For an earthly person, this is the point of intersection of his immortal trinity Idea, the essence - Spirit, Soul and Creative Mind - with the shells of the earthly personality, of which the first and highest is his earthly intellect. The same intersection point corresponds to the heart centre. That's why the connection of the earthly man with his Universal part occurs through the awakening and the highest tension of the Heart.

The third point - the intersection of the fifteenth channel with the seventeenth-is the intersection point with the subtle body, the connection of the higher shell with the psychic personality. Just as a constant power supply should go through the intersection of the third channel with the fourth Personality spirit, so the intersection point of the fifteenth channel with the seventeenth conducts constant psychic nutrition into the material body of a person and thereby ensures its plasticity, which protects it from wear, old age, and death.

The Tenth Principle ends the system of manifestation in the world of Principles and Laws in their spiritual and creative aspect. The following Principles, which give rise to these Principles and Laws already in the aspect of acting forces, in the aspect of their application to Psychic Energy, are set out in the system of Twenty-Two Principles applied to the humanity of the Earth with the introduction of corrections caused by the breakdown of human consciousness from a spiritual height into the limitations of matter, its separation from the World of Spirit, the breaks between the planes of manifestation of his essence and those corrections of his crooked paths that the Higher consciousnesses who came to his aid brought into him by their work. In other words, the statement of the following Principles is consistent with what is called the fall of man in the Bible. To determine the meaning, cause and consequences of the fall means to state the tasks, the place in the chain of Cosmic Cooperation and the ways of evolution of earthly humanity.

In the Great World Cooperation, each centre of consciousness is given its own place, role and significance in the general construction of the Creator's Plans. But at the same time, each consciousness is given the freedom to express its initiative in the specific creative possibilities contained in it, which develops the details of the general Plan. Thus, in the highest chain of Global Cooperation, everyone occupies exactly the place and performs the tasks to which he is inclined and which they are close to him, and large consciousnesses transmit the details of the part of the spiritual Plan entrusted to them for development to subordinate consciousnesses, and so on. There is also cooperation with our planetary system, where the Spirits of the Sun transmit part of the general Plan to the planetary Spirits for special development. Thus, each of the subordinate Spirits, receiving a spiritual impulse from the highest level in relation to him, is always subject to the hierarchical ladder to the beginning - to God, for the hierarchical ladder of consciousness is completed by the Divine consciousness.

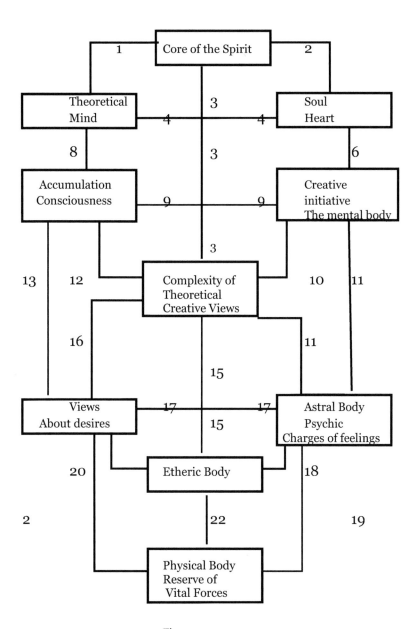

Figure 57

Each consciousness is a servant of God, a servant of the Creator and a collaborator. The spirit of the planet Earth contains special opportunities, thanks to the place that, from a spiritual point of view, it occupied in the Solar system. He took the stage on the hierarchical ladder of consciousness at which the involutive and evolutionary flow, Subject and Object, "I" and "not I" were balanced. In other words, he seemed to live at the tree of the knowledge of good and evil. It was these conditions that were suitable for the outbreak an individual consciousness that seeks God not on the hierarchical ladder of the universe, but in the depths of itself.

It was this task that the Spirit of the Earth took over, since then called by his brothers "the Light Bearer" (in Latin - Lucifer, and in Hebrew-Shatalael). The Spirit of the Earth resisted being just a carrier of one of the Creator's tasks, to be a part of the Creator. Feeling the Divine principle in himself, that is, the power balance of the ray of Divine self-consciousness that fell on him, synthesising the Subject and the Object, the world of "I" and "not I", and therefore the process of evolution, he conceived to carry out an unheard-of task - to reflect the whole being of God, namely the Divine essence. This he made his task: the part conceived to embody the whole.

To fulfil this task, it was necessary for him to stand out from the chain of Cosmic Cooperation that hierarchically transmits the Spiritual World of the Creator, but at the same time he could not break the connection with the Spiritual World, that is, with God; this established connection, going directly from God to the Spirit of the Earth, thanks to the balance of forces in the Spirit of the Earth, gave the possibility of implementing such a plan.

As a consequence, this plan also implied the mastery of the world creative force, that is, the treasury of the Creator's forces. After all, this creative force is born just at the contact of the Subject and the Object (the second intersection), the worlds of "I" and "not I" (the first intersection), and also, the knowledge of involutional and evolutionary currents (the third intersection). This creative force is thought-creation, which is possible when the World Mind is embodied in itself. The first step to mastering the World Mind is an understanding based on the recognition of God, His essence and His manifestations, that is, the Absolute and the External Subject, as a representative of the Divine Essence in his own consciousness and the greatest Subject who creates his shells and forms in this consciousness. So, Lucifer took upon himself the task of becoming God, that is, to find God directly in himself, to recognise the world of "I" and "not I", to master the key to the Divine Creative power. Since every initiative in general creativity is allowed by the Creator, this plan of Lucifer was also admitted. Since then, it has become necessary for the creative Spirits of the Universe to know God, that is, to feel God within themselves, to incarnate on Earth. Therefore, earthly incarnations, no matter how difficult they may be, are the most blessed and valuable. Only by incarnating in earthly human forms could they reach those states of God-knowledge in which they felt the fusion of their being with God, in which they embodied God in themselves, "became God". This is the subjective aspect of the task of these Spirits on Earth, along with their objective aspect - helping humanity. Earth people, like the Spirits of Nature incarnated on Earth, are Solar Spirits who have long been seconded to obey the Spirit of the Earth.

Every human being has as his highest goal the realisation of finding God in himself, in addition to the entire Universal Hierarchy, and then the royal entry again into Cosmic Cooperation by the Son of God, to whom all the forces of the world are subordinate, and not by the servant of God. Under the guidance of humanity, the entire nature of the Earth is individualised, and if a person embodies the Divine self-consciousness, then the earthly nature is also individualised. and if a person embodies the Divine self-consciousness, then the earthly nature is also called upon to individually embody all the stages of his life manifestations.

To fulfil this task, Lucifer had to isolate himself and his armies from the Hierarchy, to be independent of the transmission of the spiritual impulse, without breaking his connection with God. This means that He had to immerse his mind inside himself and master the source of creative power and thought-creation primarily within himself, create his world in the likeness of God, precisely recognising and owning both power flows. In his heart, he had to be connected with God, constantly feeding on the Divine power that he intended to embody in himself and the supply of which would thus become inexhaustible.

The Divine
Self-awareness

Not Me   I
(Object)   (Subject)

The source of creative forces
(Suspension point)
The place of the break of the former
A continuous series of hierarchies

Nature Spirits   Lucifer
(Objects)   (Subjects)

Lucifer's Consciousness

The place of connection
And realisation of the world

Ground
(fulcrum)

Figure 58

Let us turn to the above diagram (Fig. 58). The centre of Lucifer's consciousness was located in the sixth principle, that is, just in the centre of the Sephirotic system of the Earth. The Spiritual world was his own spiritual world, the middle Sephirah was his synthetic personality, woven from the materials of the Earth, and the lower Sephirah was the planet Earth itself. Lucifer took as the fulcrum of his task precisely those features that the physical energy of the Earth gave him, that is, its special balance of power. Therefore, he had to move the centre of his consciousness into the middle of this material, weaving his personality out of it, and not only influencing it from the outside, as the Spirits of other saints do, living constantly in the Spiritual World, that is, identifying his knowledge with Higher Principles.
Having made the "sun of the earth sphere" out of his consciousness, Lucifer surrounded the psychic atmosphere of the

Earth with the radiation of his initiative, symbolically-the Serpent, mentioned in Bibles. But his heart, located at the intersection of the third and ninth channels (or Arcana), always remained in a living connection both with his own spirit and through it with God. Lucifer's assistants helped him in carrying out his task, because their goal is to reach God, find Him in themselves as their hidden essence, as well as master His creative power for cultural construction on Earth, reflecting the Great process of the Universe.

Things were moving smoothly while creativity was going on in the Fiery World, that is, in the field of thought-creation, the mastery of which is based on an accurate and clear recognition of the world of "I" and "not I" and the merging of the latter at the creative moment. After all, the line of creative power runs along the middle column and, in other principles and stages of creativity, both elements merge. This moment of merging of "I" and "not I", Subject and Object, we can catch in true human creativity, that is, in moments of identification with the created idea or image, and these moments are called inspiration. This is the secret of creativity, that is, in the ability to be both creative and creative at the same time.

But when the matter has passed from the World of Thought-Creation into the World of Formation, into the world of energetic creation, into the world of preparing formulas and forms, preparing creative ideas, such a distribution of the world into "I" and "not I" has become impossible, because then the thread of the created image and plan is lost, that is, the average, in my principle.

And there is a gap between both worlds. In addition, the sixth creative Sephira is connected with the Spiritual World and separation from it means the termination of the nourishing spiritual flow, and this means the exhaustion of opportunities and the termination of both planned evolution and the receipt of energy material. And when the consciousness of humanity has come in the area of construction of the cultural forms of all that exists, that is, his mind went in the ninth principle, he pointed to the inadmissibility of the rupture of the peace of "I" and "not I", the need to stay in balance, not to eat of the tree of good and evil, not to touch the evolutive and involutive stream (fifteenth Principle), but in order to learn to operate them in all your synthetic consciousness (ninth).

The previous recognition between Subject and Object, which is necessary in the Fiery World for the performance of a specific task, tempted us to do the same in the Subtle World. But in the

Formational World, human souls are already clothed in the shells of earthly personalities, and therefore the separation of "I" and "not I" in this world means the recognition of one's earthly personality as "I", that is, the substitution of the spiritual "I" with the subtlest form of the earthly personal "I " and the identification of one's earthly consciousness with earthly shells. Therefore, the realisation of one's personal "I" led to the deprivation of domination over the Subtle World and entanglement of oneself in its currents and energies.

Having preserved the general task of the Earth Spirit, the Solar Spirits decided to change the situation of the planets in order, firstly, to protect it from the upcoming decomposition, and secondly, to purify human consciousness, to enable the souls that have broken up into separate personalities to find themselves. The spirits of Nature have received an order to condense the material shells of the planet and the spiritual shells of people, and the human consciousness, henceforth incarnating in a dense material form, falls into a cage that protects it from mental infection by the world created by people - owls, or larvae. This is the meaning of shells. But because of the density and non-plasticity of the material, these shells lag behind the evolution of consciousness and therefore wear out, not accommodating its tension. Thus, physical death appeared and with it the break of consciousness between the Subtle and physical Worlds.

From now on, both the Spirits of Nature and the souls completely began to incarnate in the coarsened matter of the Earth. All the middle principles fell out, forming a larvic world of empty illusions. The world of "I" and "not I", having suddenly lost the connective connection, became in opposition to each other in conditions of earthly materiality. The vague preservation of memory in the human consciousness about its immaterial origin forced man to enter into a struggle with the forces of nature that constrain him, which have preserved the shells of his consciousness. This struggle for one's liberation has become a way of knowing oneself as a Divine essence, and the conquest of nature has become an incentive for Cultural Construction.

The illegal split of the world into "I" and "not I" in the common earthly psyche, caused by humanity, also resulted in an internal split of humanity into two poles, that is, the separation of spiritual and psychic androgynes embodied in different bodies. There was a division by gender, and the androgynous halves lost each other in the general chaos. This consequence of the fall occurred in the middle of the third Lemurian race. Instead of spiritual creativity, the law of human existence has become the creation of their own kind, because the spiritual poles of androgynes have been replaced by material poles. In addition, the psychic atmosphere of the Earth also thickened with the condensation of the material, and the larvae and demons inhabiting it, karmically connected with their human producers, began to break through material cells and attach themselves to the newly formed psychic entities in earthly incarnations. Negative vibrations of the coarsened thought-creation and the burning of selfish motives, distorted waves of psychic energy poisoned by egoism, passions and vices, threatened to spread their influence into the surrounding space and infect the consciousness of other luminaries. Therefore, just as Lucifer previously shielded himself from the influence of surrounding consciousnesses, leaving at the same time the possibility of influencing other Worlds through the third channel, so now it was necessary to isolate the Earth from cooperation, but at the same time allow the influence of the healing currents of the environment on it. The earth was surrounded by a crystal dome, that is, a layer of atmospheric crystals that did not allow its radiation into space, but allowed more subtle vibrations of solar and planetary energies to pass through. Of course, the negative waves, hitting the dome, began to reflect off it and fall back to Earth and humanity, like the return blows of Karma.

The distortion of human consciousness, the loss of Cosmic Cooperation, the forgetting of their Spiritual tasks and their creative purpose, the distortion of self-selflessness of the individual affected the entire rest of the Nature of the Earth, reducing and coarsening the level of the creatures inhabiting the EU, especially the level of the nearby animal kingdom. Instead of a spiritual and ideological creator, man has become a rationalist. The animal kingdom should have been the combinator of earthly materials, as well as the representative and carrier of the tasks of the small earthly mind, whose duties included the preparation and individualisation of the mental flow of the Earth for the realisation of those ideals that humanity was building.

Now the human race itself has descended to the animal level, and the task of animals has become the individualisation of the Spiritual World of the Earth with the distortions introduced by the perversion of humanity. The vegetable kingdom should have been the carrier of psychic energy, but now the role is reduced to the organisation of the etheric flow of the Earth, the sublimation and synthesis of burnt-out physical materials. The Mineral kingdom has become coarsened and condensed to the limit of the lottery of plasticity and consciousness. It has become just a material stronghold, decomposing the matter of the Earth into elements and their innumerable natural combinations, and the role of the alchemist in the laboratory of his own bodies is played by nature. Thus, humanity is responsible for its own affairs and before the entire nature of the Earth, the management of which is entrusted to it. If the manager is bad, then subordinate servants are corrupted and materials are spoiled.

The task of the Earth Spirit Lucifer is to become a beautiful image. But inside Lucifer himself, a disease was born, a dark psychic condensation caused by the mistake of people, their incorrect understanding of his great self-creative task - the embodiment of God in himself and the great creative purpose - the inclusion of the entire Universe, that is, the formation of a microcosm and the reflection on Earth of all universal possibilities.

The mistake of humanity is in the fall of the Spirit into matter and in the application of the principle of freedom not to Spiritual creativity in life, but to the needs of one's personality. This dark formation inside Lucifer has partially lowered its consciousness, and the legend about him says that he became blind, that is, the thread of perception of the Spiritual World that connected him directly with the Divine Principle was interrupted in his consciousness.

The Solar Spirits came to help in fulfilling the various tasks of the earthly Spirit, and some of them descended to Earth, taking the synthetic essence of the Archangel Michael, transforming the Spiritual World with their creativity. Taking over the fulfilment of Lucifer's tasks until the evolution in solving Lucifer's tasks destroys the dark growth in his mental organism and until his consciousness restores his connection with God. In the legend of man, this was expressed in the formula:

"And Michael took the throne of his brother until the time of his epiphany."

So, the fault of the temporary failure of the implementation of all Lucifer's plans lies with the responsibility of people. People, out of their weakness, dump this responsibility on the Great Spirit of the Earth, making him Satan, the Devil, allegedly pushing them to all bad deeds, the "scapegoat" of their own sins.

We must not forget that the sixth Principle, that is, the middle part of the Sephir, with which the centre of consciousness, the consciousness of the earthly Spirit, has merged, fully embodies the principle of Freedom of Choice that has remained with all mankind.

Acceptance of it means taking responsibility for one's own affairs and, no matter who humanity would blame for its mistakes, in the end each of its members will have to answer for himself. Humanity has also forgotten that the whole world of larvae, or demons, is the product of its own mental decomposition, individualised by the psychic flow of the Earth, and that people are responsible for the existence of the whole world, and not the world for them.

The Solar Spirits, having decided to help the Spirit of the Earth, began to help humanity first of all, so that it would create a new connection with the spiritual impulse brought by them and the Spiritual World built up by them with human ideals and tasks. And with the highest ideal, they illuminated the task of Lucifer in this Spiritual World - to find God in themselves and embody Him in themselves and in their lives, to include the Soul of the Universe with all its laws and principles and realise this in their activities. This highest ideal shines as the last achievement of all religions, and all other ideals are only milestones to its understanding and accommodation. The Solar Spirits thus brought people an ideal in the diversity of religions.

This ideal is symbolised by the five-pointed Star of Redemption. The action and its reflection in religions was analysed in the Fifth Principle. The Solar Brothers, together with the part of humanity cooperating with them, filled in the principles of the ten-fold scheme with new material, instead of the perverted one.

Perverted psychic energies, which are nothing more than corrupted resonators of planetary vibrations, still break into the psyche with the so-called vibrations of negative properties of planets, which are subject to correction and purification by the stresses of the human psyche, because humanity is obliged to correct the consequences of its guilt.

Thus, the Spiritual World itself has come closer to people so that they can get closer to it. This is the Great Spiritual Sacrifice of the parts of the synthetic Spirit of Michael. The Subtle and Fiery Worlds and their principles are partly developed by humanity with the help of Solar Spirits. The redeemers of humanity have become the bridges of the ascent of the human personality into the World of the Spirit, and the Principle of the Heart is the instrument of this connection.

Initiation is an understanding of one's tasks, as well as knowledge of all methods of dealing with power directions for their implementation. Therefore, cooperation with Nature and the mastery of the creative realisational force must be restored by the creativity of humanity itself and, first of all, by each person in himself. This means what is said in the Emerald Tablet: "Be able to separate the subtle from the dense and with great care", that is, without damaging the material, to separate the world of "I" from the world of "not I", to process in yourself the materials given by the world of "not I", that is, Nature, and an instrument for fulfilling a subjective spiritual task. That is why the Initiation is called "victory over death" - both spiritual and physical.

The second stage of Initiation is the connection of the Earthly World - psychically-materially - with the Heavenly World - spiritually-mentally (according to the scheme on S. overcoming partitions between these worlds by restoration of the centre of the system, the sixth Sephira, Harmony and Beauty). The connection between the Worlds and Beauty flares up from the penetration of the radiations of the Heavenly World into the Earthly World.

Force

The Eleventh Arcanum

"Purity"
The Divine Power
Human strength
The Power of Nature
Numeric designation: 20
Astrological correspondence: Mars

Hans Thoma, Mars

As a result of the breakdown of consciousness, humanity found itself in a helpless state, because it lost power over the continuous source of creative life. After all, it is possible to possess the creative power that will be experienced in the creative ideomotor and psychomotor process only if consciousness is anchored in the Spiritual World and rooted in a spiritual task.

An ideomotor process forms a spiritual task and ideals, that is, it takes place in a world of fiery intensity of mental energy, and these formulas are not empty abstractions, but living individualised and radiating light centres inhabited by consciousnesses that are now higher than the embodied man, but must be subordinated to him in principle, because there is no being in the world higher than the Cosmic man.

Further, these organised centres are grouped in the circle itself, the mental energy, which in its waves reflects and refracts in the form of representations and images of and ideas, and this creates a differentiated, repeatedly reflecting the ideological truth, psychic, Subtle or astral world; this, the last, as if it photographed the lightning of Eden, flashing in time of manifestation and unfolds into the historical, developed with facts (that is, ideas are reflected in the subtle astral, which is like a succession of images of events). In this process, continuity is important, because it ensures its correctness, that is, in the final account, a clear impression of the facts.

It is clear from the above that this continuity is possible only when the creative consciousness stands above the areas of creativity, directly perceiving the flow of life, laws and forces with immutable evidence. Human consciousness, detached from the spirit, has lost the overview of those areas in which it is called to create, has lost the perception of their living values, as well as the possibility of continuous possession of creative by force. The human consciousness, enclosed in a cage of coarsened matter, has materialised itself, identifying itself with the material world. But this material world, after the breakdown of human consciousness, was created by the spirits of earthly nature without the participation of man, and therefore man has become powerless even over his own body. In his mind, the single creative force was torn into three parts. The spiritual and intellectual aspect, where he had previously been the master, became not for him-accessible and in its essence incomprehensible. The forces and facts of it were forgotten, only a vague memory of something that is higher and that guides remained, and man called this aspect a Divine force. The spirits of the earthly nature, previously subordinate to man, intended to be his servants, executors of his creative will, broke out of obedience and even enslaved him, overwhelming his consciousness with materiality.

To both worlds, the Higher World - a manifestation of Divine power, and the lower world - a manifestation of natural power, man could oppose only a vaguely conscious human power based on unconsciously rooted in it will and individual manifestation of creativity and struggle.

In short, man has found himself in the position of a savage who has lost consciousness of his cultural task, is struggling with a hostile nature and, from old memory, sometimes appeals to the Higher World, too alien and incomprehensible. The tragedy was further intensified by the isolation from the general planetary cooperation that the Earth was subjected to so that the perverted psychic, astral world, inhabited by the personifications of negative human impulses, would not infect the surrounding world space with heavy incorrect vibrations. The result of this isolation was, firstly, the inability to communicate with the surrounding cosmic environment, and secondly, the constant reflection from the created dome of psychic vibrations that are generated by incorrect thought-creation of a person and aggravate his karma.

In this trouble, the high and developed consciousnesses of other planets, mainly the consciousness of Venus, as the closest in the planetary system to the Earth and the highest in its development, came to the aid of earthly humanity. The esoteric doctrine says that since the fall of the Earth, it has been adapted by Venus. These consciousnesses, or Brothers of Humanity, took upon themselves the fulfilment of the task that humanity had forgotten about, the task of Lucifer the Light-Bearer ("Lucifer" is the name of the planet Venus). This task is the individual incarnation of God in himself (the sonship of God) and the implementation of the Universal Divine Plan on Earth.

The brothers of Humanity came to Earth and, psychically constantly staying in its atmosphere, from time to time they incarnated in earthly bodies, bringing people their own high ideal and milestones to achieve it. They entrusted people with the task of improving their nature, thereby fulfilling the Highest Hierarchical Will.

In addition, they founded Dedicatory Churches on Earth Centres, attracting the best of people for training and serving this task. These Centres, where the Brothers of Humanity lived in their special bodies, more subtle than the bodies of Earthlings, were always located in the mountains, that served as antennas for conducting to the Earth Cosmic Energies.

Historical records preserved in the existing similar centres speak of the Sacred belt of the Earth that continuously bordered our globe during the time of the third race. This mountain belt can be traced to this day. It begins with the Himalayan chain, continues with the Hindu Kush, the Iranian plateau, The Caucasus, the Crimean mountains, the Carpathians, the Alps. Then it is interrupted by the Atlantic Ocean, passes through a mountain range along its bottom, continues in America by the Cordillera and the Andes. Then the bottom again - The Pacific Ocean with individual peaks rising above the surface in the form of islands and again the transition to the Asian chains. Once this belt was continuous, but then catastrophes during the change of times tore it apart, and this gap of physical mountains corresponded to the loss of consciousness of unity in humanity and the differentiation of its cultures.

This Sacred Belt was the place of residence of the Brothers of Humanity and the Initiatory Schools created by them, which transmit to people, according to the subjective growth of their consciousness, the knowledge of spiritual truths, world principles, universal laws, cosmic forces and correspondences, that is, everything that people call Dedication. The disciples of the Brothers of Humanity, growing up, entered their cadres, freeing their Teachers from their assumed duties, and became spiritual leaders of humanity. Many stayed on the mountains for exclusively spiritual and pedagogical work, while others assumed the duties of public leaders, religious leaders, that is, priests, kings, and other responsible posts. They were links connecting the general mass of earthlings with the chain of cosmic cooperation, and mainly they were bridges between degraded man and God - representatives of Religion in the true sense of the word, because they restored the connection between the worlds.

They filled the Higher World, the spiritual atmosphere of the Earth, with conditions corresponding to these idols, which are called Rasm, inhabited the highest spirits of nature - Angels, high consciousnesses and spiritual egregores who fulfil the plan of the Brothers of Humanity. And people were entrusted with the responsibility of implementing these ideals of life, that is, cultural construction. Therefore, any cultural construction, that is, the manifestation of human power, is possible only on the basis of religion. Only under this condition can the forces of nature be again subordinated to man, and the Spirits of nature can become the executors of his laws. But by religion we must understand the true connection made with the Higher World, for only such a connection has been established-rotates the human consciousness to the highest place in the Highest. The world creates an Initiate from a person, before whom all junior servants willingly bow.

This connection with the Higher World occurs through the transmission of a spiritual impulse, a spiritual emanation from the Brothers of Humanity to their chosen disciples. The initiatory school sets milestones for the ordering of initiation and the improvement of the earthly personality, that is, for the student's subjective work on himself in the sense of the discipline of the mind, feelings and will. The very act of Initiation is a direct transfer of spiritual emanation, which connects the perfected human personality of the student with his own immortal principles and transfers his consciousness from the sphere of influence of the Earth to the Spiritual World, the world of God-knowledge and life-creation.

The religion of antiquity was created in the narrow walls of temples, where the true Religion was available only to a select few who were able to perceive the spiritual impulse. These chosen ones developed spiritual and philosophical systems in the beginning. For the masses these spiritual and philosophical systems were expressed in the images of myths available to them and in rituals, the execution of which was purely disciplinary in nature. With the further differentiation of humanity, such initiatory centres turned out to be too few.

The breakdown of consciousness deepened, the forms of earthly existence and the materialistic instincts associated with it increasingly flooded the consciousness of the Chosen Ones, who could not cope with the task of educating discipline and cultural organisation of these masses. It happened that their consciousness was obscured by a chaotic perception of the world, self-interest and material instincts. After all, due to the change of races and the geological catastrophes accompanying these changes, the Sacred Belt of the Earth was torn and the unity between the spiritual centres was lost. By the arrival of the fifth race, only two centres were already playing the role of centres of the Spiritual life of humanity, only in two places could the true Initiatory School concentrate. The first centre is still located in the Himalayas, in a place corresponding to the Heart Centre of our planet (by analogy with human centres).

The Himalayan mountains have become the only antenna for conducting cosmic energies to the Earth, and around this antenna brought together the initiates who settled in the Protected Valley. This centre is now called the White Brotherhood, in which most of the Human Brothers have already been replaced by inhabitants of the Earth who have grown to the level of consciousness of their teachers.

The second centre was not in the mountains, but in the valley of Egypt, and was founded in the same sacred place, the solar plexus of the Earth. The Egyptian centre had a realisation task, the task of conducting the spiritual impulse captured by the Himalayas into human consciousness and into the body of the Earth. If all religious philosophies were born from the Himalayan Brotherhood, then from the Egyptian One hermeticism was born, which is based on the principle of the transformation of earthly forces, energies and other materials, as well as the sublimation of the earthly personality of a person in the name of the Kingdom of God on Earth. Thus, the Himalayan impulse had two accents of subjectivity - self-knowledge and spiritual self-creation - while the emphasis of the Egyptian centre was placed on objective transformative and creative work. Both centres, of course, are based on the entire esoteric tradition passed down to our race as the legacy of Atlantis and received by the Atlanteans from the Chosen previous races.

This division of all the forces acting in a person into two poles is generally characteristic of humanity after the breakdown of consciousness: after all, one of the main consequences of this was the differentiation of the subjective and descriptive worlds. And, especially, it is characteristic of our fifth race, which embodies the intelligence associated with the manifestation of the sexes.

These two centres could not cope with the task of spiritualising humanity, and therefore emergency measures were taken. It was necessary to give the entire human mass spiritual impulses and ideals. Firstly to raise consciousness and secondly as the cornerstones of construction on Earth. Those who have achieved perfection, the Spirits - already perfect in their nature, who agreed to help humanity and formed an Invisible Brotherhood in the atmosphere of the Earth in the form of a redemptive type - strengthened their help by incarnating and living among earthlings. They agreed to embody a Redemptive Cliche, that is, to lower the spiritual impulse closer to the consciousness of people, while at the same time taking on a part of the Karma of humanity. In other words, they agreed, in the name of saving humanity, to become bridges between the degraded human consciousness and the spiritual world, embodying the human earthly nature and the radiations of the Spiritual World. These spirits have become what we call the Teachers of Humanity. Living in a human body among people, overcoming the weaknesses of human nature themselves, they brought to people:

1. A powerful impulse that stirred up the consciousness of the people
2. An example of what people should be like.
3. Teachings that, in the form of philosophy, reveal the basic human ideals of lost and forgotten tasks.
4. The prototype of the state control over psychic energy created by people.

And on these four red-cornered stones they built their Religion for the masses. The scheme of building a Religion is given in the fifth principle.
Here we will only note that this scheme, which reflected the pentagram of the human essence before the breakdown of consciousness, is called a Redemptive Cliche precisely because the founders of religion had to be not only the powers of God, that is, spiritual, cosmic workers, but also the Sons of Men, taking upon themselves and transforming in themselves all human weaknesses, all the Karma of earthlings.
Each of the Teachers, bringing with him the knowledge of all world principles, the power over forces, emphasised in his teachings those principles and forces that were needed to fulfil the next part of the differentiated common human task and therefore corresponded to the cultural epoch and the racial psychology that was in the line of implementation.
The Great Teachers of Humanity have made the task of reintegrating people even easier by building up the spiritual atmosphere of the Earth even with verbally formed ideals and spiritual forces adapted to the human level, concentrated in their earthly bodies.
In summary, we can say that the great Initiatory centres with their esoteric schools are symbolised by the religion of the Father, that is, the direct connection of man with the Divine essence, in addition to intermediaries and ideals built by them.
The religions brought by the Teachers of Humanity can be called the Religions of the Son, because they are the result of a spiritual thought-creating process that has built ideals for people and does not require them to independently produce this spiritual work.
Both the Religion of the Father and the Religion of the Son require a hierarchical structure of humanity.

The coming religious revelations are the Religion of the Mother of the World, the Universal Life, the Holy Spirit. It will erase all the differences between the levels of human consciousness and will allow everyone to experience God directly, in addition to schools and disciplines. Of course, the possibility of its occurrence is due to the previous spiritual experience of humanity, which transformed its Karma.

Such is the Divine power in its manifestations on the fallen Earth. Human power manifests itself in the realisation of spiritual ideals in the formulas of life on Earth, that is, in cultural construction. The main condition of cultural construction is the mastery of psychic energy and domination over psychomotor processes. Developing a worldview based on these materials, collecting and mastering creative cultural ideas is a mental power over psychic energy. The implementation of the plans is possible only if the coordination and tension of the psychic flows that create psychic or astral vortices.

Of course, knowledge of the laws of psychic energy and power over the manifestation of the latter are possible only if consciousness is anchored in the ideals of the spiritual world. For the same rooting, it is necessary to meet the requirements of the eleventh Principle: Purity. What has clouded the human consciousness? Self-interest and material impulse. Purity is freedom and unselfishness, freedom from material impulse. True unselfishness is possible only if you give yourself to the service of the ideal, and the wider and higher the ideal, the more the principle of unselfishness manifests itself, the more powerful the psychic force that flows from it. Freedom from the material the impulse is achieved by detaching consciousness from the Earth, that is, awareness of oneself by the spirit, and not by the body. And here we see a manifestation of the same duality, that is, the fulfilment of the main condition for transferring consciousness to the Spiritual World and mastering psychic energy is divided into two parts and is carried out in two human sexes.

The separation by gender was a consequence of the loss of connection between the subjective and objective worlds, which was expressed in the human consciousness by the opposition of the Heart and Mind. The Woman became the representative of the Heart, the representative of the Mind - Man. The search for their common source has become a special form of Love between them, and all the cooperation of the sexes is built on this relationship, at the root of which is the same God - seeking, and as a result of which is life-creation.

The invisible part of the Teachers' mission, namely the breath of a spiritual impulse, has been transferred to the female part of humanity, the female heart, the Love that dwells in it and the ability to directly perceive spiritual truths. That is why during the historical development, a woman has always been the inspirer of men's creativity, and why during periods when a woman lost the power of Love and religious attitude and forgot her mission, men's cultural creativity dried up, became flat and historically insignificant.

A woman is a teacher, not only of her sons, but also of her husband and friends around her husband, and education is an alchemical work of spiritualisation, which without religious foundations cannot be carried out. But for the purity of Love and for spiritual perception, chastity is required from a woman, that is, freedom from material impulses. Thus, unselfishness is inherent in the female heart only if it is free from the material impulse and is turned to the Spiritual World.

The purity of the male representatives of the world Mind, to whom the Teachers have inherited the entire visible part of their mission, that is, the teaching, the personal approach and the power of domination over the psychic energy in the name of cultural construction, is in selfless activity. Selfless service to ideal under the influence of a spiritual impulse given by a woman frees a man from identification with his evil personality and gives him dominance over the material impulse. That is why the ancient wisdom says: a chaste woman can even send a saint out of a criminal.

Thus, the most powerful psychic vortex occurs when the conscious work on the psychic energy (that is, magic) of two people, the cooperation of psychically complementary men and women, creates a powerful astral vortex.

Any cultural construction is based on the principle of cooperation. One person is not able to do as much as a group of people can do. You need to be a psychic giant, or a genius, to create great cultural values in solitude. Not everyone is capable of this. The same applies to the region works on psychic energy. Of course, everyone eventually grows up to the level of a giant in this field, able to create and direct mental vortices that move planets and peoples, but even these giants often resort to the help of less developed servants in this field, establishing magical chains of influence. A collective action is always stronger than a single one, provided that the consciousnesses are equal and the same mood. The contours of a thought outlined by one consciousness are four times weaker than the same thought outlined by two consciousnesses. Astral cliché thoughts created by three consciousnesses many times surpass the work of two consciousnesses in their clarity and strength. The same can be said about the created vortices of psychic energies. The strongest chain consists of twelve people, differently coloured in the sense of the zodiac constellations and harmoniously corresponding to each other.

The psychological work of such a chain can change the historical development of an entire nation. Further expansion of the chain is undesirable, but it is desirable for each member to create a new secondary subordinate chain. So you can weave the desired mental pattern of an entire nation. So, a chain of twelve always has its own leader, the thirteenth, who determines its work. Less strong (because the number of subordinate consciousnesses must be even, otherwise there will be no balance), but just as good are chains of three, five, seven, nine people plus an initiative element that makes the whole chain dynamic.

The same subtitle -"Human Power" also applies to the picture of the Arcanum: a girl, above whose head the sign of infinity is depicted, closes the mouth of a lion with her hands. This figure symbolises the spiritual task of a woman who is calm and confident (for above her the sign of the Divine world hangs) closes the toothy mouth of worldly self-interest and directs the gaze of the lion - the fiery creativity of a man-up into the world of ideals.

The lowest servants of man are the forces of nature. In his evolution, man must first free himself from the cage of earthly nature into which he has fallen. The slogan of esotericism: "the path of man lies against nature". This opposite of "man-nature" should not be understood aggressively, in the sense of introducing an element of hostility and destruction. To get rid of nature and subjugate it does not mean to outwardly break and deny the connection with it, running away from its beneficial physical and mental influence on cities. It is wrong to understand the subordination of nature to man as his violence against the forces of nature and the beings produced by it. Liberation from nature should be understood as the purification of one's consciousness from one's own body, as the subordination of the needs and desires of the body to spiritual tasks and mental activity.

The struggle with nature is a struggle with oneself, since the elements of living nature dominate in our consciousness. This struggle includes the discipline of the will, which conquers the natural needs of sleep, food, rest, sexual instinct, etc. to dominate them and rationalise their manifestation. And only when we have mastered the materials given to us by the Earth, we have the right to begin to rule over the forces of objective nature. Any illegal violence will eventually turn against the person who uses it. The slave will rise up against the master and kill him. A careful look of objective consciousness can observe the latter precisely in the modern era, where the illegal acquisition of natural forces and the aggressive use of their actions does not elevate, but causes the human consciousness to degrade deeply.

Only those who know the psychic forces underlying its physical manifestations, who love their colleagues who ensure the earthly existence and the possibility of the cultural work of mankind, can legally own nature. The main forces of nature are reduced to the four spirits and elements manifested in it: from the combination of Air, Earth, Fire and Water, all earthly forces and forms were created. Their diversity depends on their various proportional combinations. The elements should not be understood as mechanical force manifestations. The elements are based on spiritual emanations, and the spirits of the elements are by nature high. In Western schools, their names were Latinised:

Spirits of Air are called Sylphs, Earth Spirits are Gnomes, Fire Spirits are Salamanders and Water Spirits are Undines. A clairvoyant eye can catch their outlines. It is easiest to catch the outlines of Undines in the waves and Salamanders in the flames. The elements are extremely beautiful in their purity because they reflect the four main spiritual vibrations of the Sun. Further, the combination of elements into chemical elements also occurs on the initiative of spirits, in which the Earth element predominates. The great alchemical work of converting chemical elements into healing bases and psychic radiations into nutritious materials is carried out by the spirits of the vegetable kingdom, in which Fire manifests in various combinations. The spirits who create the bodies of animals and people belong to all four elements. The energy radiated by all these spirits is physical forces and energies that act constantly and form the face of the earthly nature. Therefore, the study of nature requires respect for nature and should be put on the rails of study the psychic basis of natural phenomena. Mastering nature means attracting the spirits to conscious cooperation with man. And, of course, such cooperation can only be based on mutual understanding and mutual trust. By his thought-creation, a person constantly influences the work of natural spirits, and therefore the quality of the work of natural spirits partly depends on the quality of a person's thought-creative work.

Thus, deserts arose due to the impoverishment of the human heart and the materialisation of the burnt mind. Thus, thunderstorms, hurricanes, storms were often caused by the psychic whirlwinds of collective human passions. So, even the subordinate natural forces often take revenge for the selfish abuse of all sorts of explosions and catastrophes.

Of course, the person standing in the middle of the cross of elements is potentially the master of its branches. Therefore, a person in potency is the master in the world of earthly nature, but he should love, study, manage his farm, and not frivolously ruin it. Then the paths will be open to the ways of fulfilling his/her role as the owner of the Earth and people will become People from the Earth.

Image from "Undine," by Friedrich Heinrich Karl Baron de la Motte Fouqué, 1919

The Hanged Man

The Twelfth Arcanum

"Sacrifice"

Mercy
The Soul of the Messiah
Zodiac
Numeric designation: 30
Astrological correspondence: Libra

Astrologie & Sternzeichen & Kalender

The picture of the Arcanum depicts a man hanging upside down by his right leg. The left leg is tucked so that it forms a cross with the right leg. The arms are outstretched and converge above the head in the form of a triangle with the top down. Gold falls from the man's hair and from his pockets to the ground. The unfortunate man is suspended between two pillars, each of which has six branches. Geometrically, the entire figure of the suspended one is represented by a triangle turned upside down. The cross of the legs depicts the quarternary system of the Evangelist John.

The general title of the twelfth Arcanum says that after the breakdown of human consciousness, the concept of sacrifice was introduced into every power manifestation of a person by an active psychological element, that is, the rejection of one that is lesser/lower in the name of achieving one that is a greater and higher.

Human evolution is not going smoothly - as a gradual transformation of a person's personality and activity - but makes leaps, often painfully affecting the psyche. This loss of psychological flexibility, of plasticity, arose as a result of the identification of consciousness with earthly forms, which, in turn, led to the appearance of attachment generated by self-interest. Every sacrifice, is nothing but liberation from attachment, either to an objective form or to a subjective state of consciousness. Non-attachment to norms and to one's own personality is achieved by Selflessness.

Thus, the process of separating co-knowledge from more or less egoistic attachments – that is, the sacrifice - is a consequence of unselfishness and its realisation.

The concept of sacrifice must be treated carefully, as this concept is just as worn out and vulgarised by people as are the concepts of love, heroism, and the like. In human everyday life, it is customary to call a sacrifice both the giving of unnecessary things and the purchase of forgiveness of sins for money, and the rejection of secondary attachments in the name of a passion that has taken possession. That is, a selfish element is introduced into the concepts of sacrifice and everyone needs, therefore, to check this concept in relation to life.

The concept of sacrifice is twofold, because sacrifice happens in the name of the realisation of two fundamental human ideals: the search for truth and the service of the Common Good. In the first case, we must define sacrifice as the rejection of the usual lower state in the name of achieving an unknown higher state, because the rejection of this orientation is always a leap into the unknown. In this case, the word "sacrifice" is well replaced by a combination of the words "freedom" and "fearlessness".

In the second case, the direction of the victim is reversed downwards. In the name of serving the ideal of the Common Good, one has to stop at a certain stage of one's own search for the sake of giving the values received to others. Therefore, sacrifice in this direction is the realisation of extreme selflessness, expressed by self-sacrifice, self-forgetfulness, self-denial, even in the spiritual plane. In both directions, the sacrifice is effective on the four planes of consciousness:

1. The material sacrifice in the first direction is expressed in the words of Christ: "Give away all your wealth and follow me."

In the second case, it is also expressed in words of Christ: "To the one who asks for clothes from you, give a shirt," that is, even the most necessary things for you. In both cases, the willingness to sacrifice detaches consciousness from the material world.

2. The psychic sacrifice in the first direction frees from the emotions, passions, and habits that possess a person in the name of achieving a more perfect mental level, in the name of organising and cleansing the astral vehicles. This sacrifice can be called self-control. In the second direction, the victim's psychic energy is the ability to adapt to his neighbour by curbing unpleasant traits for him and acquiring new ones.

3. Mental sacrifice in the first direction means the rejection of existing prejudices, conventions and superstitions, that is, the excess ballast of past experience, and the acquisition of new measures of expanded consciousness for further cognitive work. Rarely does anyone know how to make such a sacrifice.
In the second direction, it is a sacrifice due to conclusions from personal experience in the name of recognising the experience of another. The words of Christ refer to such a sacrifice: "Do not judge, so that you will not be judged." A person should give up the conceit of being a militant measure for all ways and phenomena.

4. Spiritual sacrifice in the first direction means a willingness to become a poor spirit, that is, to accept the insignificance and illusory nature of all your spiritual achievements and built-up ideals in front of the boundlessness of the Spiritual World and divine possibilities. This sacrifice leads to direct knowledge of God. In the second direction, spiritual sacrifice is again expressed in the words of Christ: "There is no greater love than if someone lays down his life for his friend." This is the bestowal of all your spiritual achievements in the benefit of others, so that not himself, but others, use the results. Such a sacrifice frees the soul from the impact of the results of its activities on it, from personal karma, and merges it with God.

From all the above, it is clear for thoughtful minds that there is no sacrifice, as we understand it - with elements of suffering or deprivation - in fact, because every sacrifice is paid for a hundredfold by the acquired great values: Separation from the material world relieves the suffering associated with it and makes it easy to live like a bird of heaven with the certainty of innocence. Mental sacrifice enriches with new talents, frees from heavy habits and attachments and gives the possibility of countless sympathies, providing warmth of life. The mental sacrifice expands and enriches all forms of consciousness, introducing more and more new interests into its circle. The spiritual sacrifice gives us the knowledge of the only treasure of the world - God. There is, therefore, no sorrow of the victim, but her joy is confirmed everywhere. "I want mercy, not sacrifice," Christ said, for mercy is joy to the one who gives it and to the one who receives it.

Despite the apparent gloom of the twelfth Arcanum depicted in the picture, the greatest sacrifice to people in the image of the Messiah, Bodhisattvas, Human Brothers, if you look at it from the perspective of the Spiritual World, is not painful, but joyful. Let's remember the words from the Upanishad: "And the Gods must come and become men in order to be perfect." Of course, from the point of view of human consciousness, this sacrifice is associated with the greatest rejection, and therefore with the greatest deprivation, because its Perfect Souls refuse Nirvana, or from merging with God, from a state of the greatest bliss in order to bring Spiritual Light to an environment that does not understand them and in every possible way crucifying them. But from the highest point of view, it is only by such a sacrifice that they can give up the last shadow of the self, that is, an unnecessary element in the desire to achieve All-Existence, All-Bliss and All-Knowledge of God. For in the most difficult conditions, they must establish the All-Blissful Divine presence in their consciousness. So, even in this case, the sacrifice is the last karmic chord.

In the East, Great Souls who have renounced Nirvana in the name of helping humanity, that is, who have renounced the results of their knowledge of God in the name of the greatest service to the Common Good, are called Bodhisattvas or Buddhas of mercy. The love of the heart for stragglers is a downward love – mercy - caused by compassion. Compassion is a statement of connection with the world and with everything that is in it. Moreover, this connection, no matter how painful it may be, cannot be broken until all the accumulated spiritual gold is poured out into the circle of these backward people, because only a poor person in spirit, that is, who has given up all his spiritual values, enters the Divine World, where there is no material world. Compassion causes empathy or willingness to help. This willingness to help is based on forgetting or forgiving all the past causes that caused unfortunate conjunctures, and on opening the gates to the future, the milestones of which are being set. Therefore, charity is always directed to the future of a person or humanity, as opposed to severity, which is directed to the past of causes. Charity brings to life the tension of purposefully creating a better future. But since the consequences that have arisen from the causes of the past have not been destroyed, the one who shows mercy takes it upon himself to eliminate them. After all, in the human in life, it is compassion and mercy that makes an innocent person suffer internally and bear burdens for another person, thereby facilitating his karma and opening up the possibility of the future to him.

The Buddhas of mercy and compassion are giants of feelings, thoughts and will compared to us. The souls who reached the highest spiritual states lived out the karma of entire peoples with compassion and mercy, and this opened up the possibility of getting out of the confusion of mental chaos into the Spiritual World. The Messiahs took upon themselves the sins of the world. The covenant of all the Teachers of humanity was the manifestation of mercy, and if the law of causality says: "an eye for an eye, a tooth for a tooth", then the expedient law of spiritual aspiration, commanded by the Teachers, speaks about forgiveness, that is, about the repayment of negative karma of its oblivion. All vindictiveness (an eye for an eye), no matter how fair it may seem, will cause a return blow of vindictiveness, and the chain of negative causality will lower the level of consciousness associated with it more and more. And only forgiveness, that is, the rejection of retribution and forgetting the past, can extinguish this fire.

Thus, mercy is the only force that can once and for all, by forgetting the past and revealing the prospects of the future, destroy the evil of the world and affirm its good. Charity is a statement of the future.

So, the main psychological impulse of the Brothers of Humanity is charity, and it is also the main Covenant that they collectively passed on to people. Let's delve into the psychology of these Great Souls. If we go through all the Teachers of humanity known to us, we will be struck by their fundamental similarity: the same level of consciousness, the same spiritual experience, penetration into the same depths of the Spiritual World, the same motives for actions and the same attitude to the world. Truly - The Soul of the Messiahs.

In their very depths, they have reached the fundamental Divine Unity and have reached the Unity of the Spirit. By their essence, they confirm that there are no different souls, but there is only one Divine Universal Soul that manifests in the forms of different personalities. By implementing this unity, they are truly all "Sons of God", that is, they have realised God in form. But this One Soul, this Divine Unity, always identical with itself, can neither change nor reincarnate. At the same time, the personality of each of the Teachers of humanity bears the features and experience of a long evolution and is extremely different from others. Here we come to the great mystery of the duality of the nature of the Great Teachers, to the mystery of the so-called Avatar.

The personality of each of the Teachers was created by the past experience of mankind, and the peculiarities of the epoch of the people to which it belongs have put their seals on it. The mental body formulates spiritual truths in accordance with these accumulations; the astral body reveals the world attitude characteristic of the best people of the epoch; the etheric body bears traces of heredity. Of course, the personality of the Great Teachers developed according to the evolutionary human orientation, and therefore, there is also a Consciousness that guided this evolution through the centuries, in addition to the Divine Consciousness that illuminated it.

Each of the Great Teachers embodies the mystery of the union of two Souls, two Principles. The man of evolution, working on himself, will finally reach religion, that is, connection with his Higher Principles. And it is when he reaches this connection, and when, thanks to the specific task of the Earth, he has to directly embody God in himself, that compassion for the stragglers takes possession of him and allows him to embody God in himself, to go into the Divine World, he, who is still connected with humanity with all his human nature, draws the Divine Soul into his perfected soul and personality, as into a funnel. These moments of the union of the human soul with the Divine Soul are vividly captured in the biography of the Teachers: the Buddha united with the Divine Soul and became the Messiah, meditating under the Bodhi tree; Moses heard a voice from a bush burning with an Incandescent Fire; Mahomet prostrated himself dead in the desert hills of Arabia, and this connection with the Divine caused a temporary madness, since his mental vehicle was not yet ready for accommodation.

The duality of nature then remained throughout the entire life of the Teachers. The divine nature has not destroyed the nature of man, for this is precisely the task - to be God while remaining Human. But because of the imperfection of the materials that now make up the vehicles of the human personality, this accommodation of the two natures could not be completely harmonious, and every disharmony entails suffering. "The Spirit is awake, but the flesh is weak" not only in the disciples, but also in the Teachers themselves, and in the words of Christ we see a deep understanding of this, testifying to our own experience. Let us recall the longing of Christ, the longing of great loneliness among people: the human heart longed for warmth and understanding, but met with misunderstanding, hostility and rudeness.

Let's remember Ramakrishna's tears because of Vivekananda's misunderstanding; let's also remember Ramakrishna's purely human addiction to sweets. Let us recall the anger of Moses, the impulses of burning impatience and the repentance that follows them. Let us remember the sadness and tears of the Buddha, abandoned by his disciples. After all, it was not the Divine Soul that felt all this in them, but the soul of the Sons of Men. These weaknesses, manifestations of "infirmity" complicated their lives, but, of course, did not interfere with their Mission, but rather the opposite: Personal suffering brought them closer to the suffering of others.

The role of the Great Teachers was to bring the Impulse of the Spirit in order to connect the disparate planes of consciousness and fill the Psychic Energy of the Earth with creative power. The environment reacted to this by creating active mental circuits around the Teachers. The teaching of All the Teachers was reduced to the adaptation of the ten Great Principles, that is, the Eternal Covenant, to the environment of a certain epoch and race for the fulfilment of the spiritual tasks facing this epoch and race. The environment reacted with the formation of a religious and mystical school, in which the teaching was coloured by the peculiarities of the historical stage. The activity of the Teachers was manifested in Spiritual Guidance, and by their spiritual thought-creation they introduced an element of initiation into the environment. The result was the creation of dedicated consciousnesses, which, in turn, spread Spiritual Ideals.

For the Earth, the task of the Teachers was for the Earth to unfold the cycle of a Dynamic Law, having established creating a new balance in cultural construction. The consequence of this, every time, was the introduction of a new pattern into the karma of humanity. The goal of the Teachers is to create conscious pentagrams out of people who would dominate the psychic world of the Earth through being rooted in the Spirit. The achievement was the spiritualisation of life forms, only under the condition of which more perfect personalities could develop and new energy planes of the Earth could be individualised.

The third subtitle - "Zodiac" - seems strange in connection with the other subheadings - "Mercy" and "The Soul of the Messiah". But there is a deep logical connection between them. The fact is that after the breakdown of human consciousness, it was necessary to establish other conditions of earthly existence. The condensation of the matter of the planet and the Earth caused the need to change Cosmic influences, and the very existence of the Earth in its materialised form was possible only with a change in energy vibrations in the surrounding Space environment. Thus, a small visible cause often causes large effects in its range.

The earth was like a big child who had to be put to bed. A doctor and a nurse were needed. A sick child focuses the attention of the family on himself. The mother interrupts her usual activities and cares, often the father is forced to leave his self-employment, and all attention is focused on a small creature whose illness affects the entire atmosphere in the house. So the" disease " of the Earth caused the need to introduce new and rearrange old factors in the surrounding Space environment.

The nearest constellations surrounding our planet The solar system and defining its formal life, is the circle of the zodiac constellations. Before the" disease "of the Earth and its confinement in a" blanket " of coarse matter, there were ten constellations, and each of them reflected one of the ten Principles. Since the separation of the Earth from the general chain of planetary cooperation, it was necessary to introduce two new constellations that entered the Zodiac circle from other Cosmic circles, namely, constellations appeared in the zodiac circle Virgo and Pisces are "doctors" and "nurses". These appearances in the Zodiac circle have somewhat changed the vibrations of Solar energy in relation to the planet Earth.

The Zodiac, as a factor determining normal life on Earth, distributes the Cosmic Energy it receives into four groups of vibrations, which are reflected on Earth by four states of matter (physical, etheric, psychic, mental), known as the four elements. That is, the Zodiac determines the Solar cross of the elements. At the same time, conducting spiritual energy through its prism, the Zodiac reflects the Principle of the triplicity of the Spiritual World and determines the essence of each element.

Thus, symbolically, the Zodiac can be expressed as four times three. Under this basic aspect, it is necessary to study the Zodiac, at the same time denoting its correspondence with the Principles, and in relation to the Earth, and these correspondences have changed, because the carriers of some of the Principles, in relation to the Earth, have become the refracting planets. And the whole system of ten Principles has developed into Twenty-two Principles, because the twelve following Principles relate to those adjustments that were made to the spiritual and psychic atmosphere of the Earth.

According to the principles already discussed, some zodiac constellations are known to us.

The constellation of Aries is considered the beginning of the zodiac circle, because this constellation gives the initial power impulses to the planet Earth.

The first four constellations (Aries, Taurus, Gemini, Cancer) establish with their radiations mainly the life of earthly nature and human life insofar as it relates to nature, that is, since man is part of earthly nature. After all, we know that his etheric and physical bodies are not created by himself, but by the forces of earthly nature - the guiding Spirits of Nature.

The following four constellations (Leo, Virgo, Libra, Scorpio) determine by their vibrations the psychic materials from which the human personality builds its personality.

The last four constellations (Sagittarius, Capricorn, Aquarius, Pisces) conduct spiritual impulses to the perception of human consciousness and determine the main tasks of the CSO cultural construction.

The first four planets

Aries-Fire, the fifth principle, vital impulses.

Aries spiritualises the earthly nature with the instincts of sex, that is, ignites the fire of love in it in the conditions of its materiality and thereby makes it possible to overcome the partitions created as a result of self-interest. The instinct of sex is the most primitive and original overcoming of egoism, and it is as such that it is the conductor of Spiritual Fire, the Instinct of sex forces us to abandon the isolated state, forces us to transfer our consciousness to another, to which it is attracted. The result of this is procreation - the transfer of consciousness from identification to identify oneself with one's material body with the genus, that is, with the etheric principle.

The sexual instinct thus transfers consciousness from the gross physical body to the more subtle etheric plane. The sexual instinct is the most spiritualised of all material instincts, and its spiritualisation is confirmed by all nature in the vegetable and animal kingdom. The flowers of plants and the wings of the mating sex in insects are natural symbols of their spirituality.

In a person, the sexual instinct is exalted and sublimated into his mental aspect, raising creative forces in consciousness and giving inspiration. The influence of Libra opposite to Aries refines this fiery natural impulse in a person, and under the influence of intense psychic love, a person becomes more active.
Thus, Aries brings an element of tension into human life, and intensity into creativity, which accelerates the pace of its evolution. In this acceleration of the pace of evolution, in the separation of consciousness from gross materialistic egoism, lies the secret and meaning of the division into sexes and the awakening of the instincts of sex in consciousness. Thus, the sexual instinct is the possibility of accommodating spirit in matter.

Taurus is the Earth, the sixth principle, Earth's resource materials.

Taurus determines the resources of the earth's nature. After all, after falling out of Cosmic Cooperation, the Earth is a closed system, the supply of vital force of which is limited. Taurus defines the cycle of material life on Earth, that is, manages, so to speak, the storerooms of the Earth, the distribution of their reserves and the process of universal nutrition. This process of nutrition has two aspects: mental nutrition and material nutrition.
The flow of material nutrition goes from the bottom up on Earth, that is, its more materialised floors or kingdoms serve as food for the upper - more individualised and organised-floors. Thus, the basis of universal nutrition is the mineral kingdom of material and chemical elements. This mineral kingdom nourishes the vegetable kingdom. The Athanor (alchemical furnace) of the earth's nature, in which these elements enter into various combinations, determines the forms and functions of individual species of the plant kingdom. The vegetable kingdom prepares food for the animal and human kingdoms. On the other hand, the reverse process takes place: by its dying, more seriously by the products of its decay - by garbage corpses - the animal and human kingdoms nourish the vegetable kingdom, and the vegetable kingdom - with the products of decomposition-again replenishes the reserves of the mineral kingdom. The process of psychic nutrition, that is, the filling of forms of earthly nature

with psychic energy, is underway from top to bottom, that is, from the human being, who determines the psychic impulses and the quality of psychic energy, to animals, who individualise the psychic properties of humanity in their species. From the animal kingdom, the psychic flow goes to the vegetable kingdom and freezes in the mineral kingdom. But this fading determines the processes of individualisation of the material kingdom, called crystallisation, that is, it makes living beings out of minerals, which in their further evolution pass into the vegetable kingdom, from there into the animal and human, again replenishing the stock of human psychic energy.

Humanity, as it were, constantly throws back, downwards, the used and unnecessary reserves of psychic energy that go to the psychic nutrition of nature. On the other hand, it constantly draws etheric-psychic reserves from nature. By this cycle, Taurus binds a person to the earthly nature.

As long as humanity leaves its physical and mental corpses in the earthly nature and depends on the general nutritional process of nature, it cannot get rid of the Earth. The practice of asceticism and cremation of the body is aimed at weakening this connection and freeing a person from the restraining fetters of nature.

Gemini is the Air, the seventh principle, hierarchical cooperation of kingdoms.

The Twins contribute to the materials of the Earth a hierarchical distribution, the domination of the Higher Kingdoms over the lower, the perfect over the imperfect. Man, as the determinant of the psychic tonality of the Earth, is the visible ruler of nature, because his psychic work invisibly determines the life of the earthly nature, which in its forms embodies the psychic vibrations sent by man.

The closest collaborators of man, in nature, are animals, but humanity did not realise this in time and went on the wrong path, replacing its natural servants, whose powers and abilities it did not use, with artificial formations, that is, machines. It created a world of pseudo-animals, gifted with a psychic essence that is coarser and less perfect than the psyche of animals.

This underestimates the role of the animal kingdom, which is doomed to extinction over time, and with the extinction of the animal kingdom, the mental and physical nutrition of the vegetable kingdom is doomed to impoverishment. The first sign of this threat is the need for artificial fertilisers, the use of which has a harmful effect on the physical health of people who eat cereals and other plants grown on such soil, because the amount of vitality (vitamins) in such plants is reduced.

The hierarchical structure of the kingdom of earthly nature should not be understood as a ladder of gradual development from one kingdom of nature to another. Each stage of the earth's nature was self-sufficient and is not a transitional stage from the highest to the lowest. There are several lines of evolution on Earth, and each of these lines fulfils its own task. The vegetable kingdom is not at all a further stage of the evolution of the mineral kingdom and in its evolution does not at all pass into the animal kingdom, also the animal kingdom, will not need at all to pass through the human kingdom for its evolution. Of course, spiritual evolution is meant here. This means that the psychic essence or soul of a plant does not need animal incarnations, in the soul of animals-in human (that is, in their forms). The lines of their evolution continue in other worlds, on other planets after they fulfil their task on Earth, but the common life cycle of the Earth, the common work on our planet makes them dependent on each other, and a common responsibility binds them into one Brotherhood.

Psychic, etheric and physical interchange charges representatives of different kingdoms with common properties and makes possible individual incarnations within the boundaries of another kingdom for the accumulation of cognitive experience. But these are temporary phenomena, and the general evolution of individuals depends on the nature and line of evolution of the kingdom to which they belong. The difference between these separate lines of evolution is as follows:

The sign of human evolution is expressed by individualisation in a material form, that is, the soul and personality of a person seem to flow into his body, and together form an evolving spiritual-psychic individual.

In the other three kingdoms of nature, the soul, that is, the spiritual-psychic essence, is not embodied in one body, but is the ruler of a number of psychic bodies that form a species. Such souls are called group souls, although in fact the soul is individual, and the group body is a body fragmented in space and time, which the soul controls from the outside. In the animal kingdom, the soul is embodied individually up to the etheric body, and then the etheric body is expressed in a group of physical bodies of this type. In the plant kingdom, the soul is embodied in the astral body, and the multiplicity of physical-etheric bodies corresponds to it. In the mineral kingdom, the soul is embodied in mental shells, and differentiation begins in the astral region.

Man, as the zenith of the cycle of nature, introduces the principle of individualisation, which is most reflected in the nearby animal kingdom. Especially dogs often embody an individual soul. The nadir of the earth's circle - the mineral kingdom-introduces an element of collectivity that reaches a person, infecting him with a sense of gregariousness.

Cancer is Water, the eighth principle, the regulation of material impulses.

Cancer introduces a new causality into the material life of the Earth, namely, horizontal causality, on which materialistic sciences are now based. Vertical causality is difficult to grasp and establish on Earth, because the discontinuity between the planes of its consciousness, or between the worlds, closes each world into its own conditions of existence. Although the causes existing in the Higher Worlds cause consequences in the lower worlds, but the sequence of actions of these causes, and therefore the corresponding series of consequences, caused in these worlds limited from each other a direct horizontal sequential mutual contact and mutual influence of the effects alternating in time. This pseudo-causality caused a special spike of phenomena within each circle and prevented the possibility of chaos even if the emanations of the Higher Worlds did not reach the lower planes. This pseudo-causality is most clearly reflected in the law of heredity. The real causality of human incarnations, which determines the character and properties of the earthly personality of a person, is the sum of the accumulated experience of past incarnations, which makes us look for suitable conditions for a new incarnation. Thus, the incarnating soul is looking for parents who are able to give the elements necessary for its development. These elements relate to the etheric plane, that is, to the character and quality of the vital force, to the properties of the material impulse with which parents supply the child. The astral and mental body, that is, his personality, a person creates himself during his incarnation, depending on the available incarnation experience, as well as those etheric-physical materials that are given by parents.

The law of heredity, as a determinant of further evolution, of course, plays an important role in earthly life. The significance of the law of heredity is especially great because human consciousness in the overwhelming majority of cases is just identified with material impulses and rarely consciously builds its evolution on the basis of spiritual experience. Since the etheric body of a person is not built by himself, but is given by nature, the parents in this case are also not conscious builders of the child's etheric body, but transmitters of the vital force of nature, broken in their specific prisms. Therefore, the qualities and properties of the etheric body are often transmitted almost in purity from generation to generation, determining the generic similarity: both ethereal properties and physical traits. Parents transmit to a child according to the law of heredity:

1. The reserve of vital forces, that is, the quality of the etheric vibration that determines physical health.
2. Temperament, that is, the degree of intensity of life perception and life determination.
3. The properties of the etheric body, called passions or inclinations to certain attachments, that is, the qualities of the material impulse.
4. Diseases of the etheric body, called vices and causing physical diseases in their last stage.

This significance of heredity makes a person who does not know how to shift the emphasis on spiritual life dependent on a natural material impulse and organises his personality in accordance with this impulse. Such dependence on the material impulse, that is, on the forces of the Earth, causes the magical slavery of man to nature, which is expressed in the dependence of his thinking abilities and mental moods on natural phenomena. And a person becomes a part of nature, and the more he harmoniously merges with it, the more hopeless his slavery is, on the one hand, and on the other hand, the more enlightened his psyche becomes. After all, the forces of nature "did not fall" like man and his psychic power. The spirits of nature remained unaffected they perform their work as harmoniously as before, although the results have become rougher and due to the lack of cooperation, the refining influence of the non-fallen person. Therefore, merging with nature means, as it were, a way out of the chaos and obscurity of consciousness created by man, but at the same time it knocks out of the normal, evolutionary life intended for man. A person who merges with nature is deprived of individual initiative creativity, ingenuity, struggle and victory of responsibility, that is, everything holy, which is a specific human treasure.

An example of such a departure from the line of cultural evolution to the impersonal world of nature can serve as feral peoples-degenerated carriers of once high cultures. An example of the enlightenment of consciousness with the specific wisdom of adopting natural laws can be representatives of a special psychological type, which is common among the peasantry, who live in deep harmony with the life of nature and do not rush to show individual creativity associated with unprecedented novelty. These enlightened, calm types with deep wisdom and knowledge of natural paths and with a natural religious feeling can be found among the peasantry.

The second four planets

The Lion is fire, the tenth principle.

The impulse given by the Lion corresponds to what in religious worldviews is called the Baptism of Fire or the Kindling of Fire. Not everyone can be satisfied with the enlightened wisdom of natural types. A person feels that he is something more than a part of nature. Even after the breakdown of consciousness, he still had memories of his task to dominate the nature of our planet, control it and remake it. But the purpose, ways and milestones of such management were lost in his consciousness. In addition, the force of nature has so outgrown the human force that it constantly fills the human consciousness with material impulses and thus, through the manifestation of bodily instincts, puts obstacles to the manifestation of typically human creativity even in the human organisation itself.

The Leo impulse reinforces in a person his ability to master the creative force, that is, it takes the human consciousness out of the Ocean of Nature. Only the consciousness carried from the ocean of nature is capable of understanding its typically human cognitive-creative individuality, as well as, through self-discipline, to forge trunks and branches of a personality independent of nature.

The first steps in this direction are expressed by the rebellion of man against nature. This departure from nature explains all the beginnings of human sociality, all attempts to manifest their own creativity, which often violates nature. Awareness of the line of one's development going against nature will give a person the impulse of a Lion, and this impulse in the historical development of mankind gives cultural development, and individual individuals are brought to the top of initiation, that is, deep knowledge of their historical task, and to full possession of creative power. In the initial stage, Leo's impulses affect the human psyche with longing for himself, the desire to get out of the usual conditions and a vague search for his destination.

Virgo is the Earth, the tenth principle.

The constellation Virgo entered the Zodiac circle after the breakdown of human consciousness. Just under the impulse of Virgo, the matter of the Earth condensed and the partitions of corporeality were created in the elastic waves of etheric vibrations. These partitions were saving the created mental chaos. Human personalities who had lost the suspension point, that is, the consciousness of their spiritual-creative individuality, were threatened with dispersion in the general psychic sea of the earthly astral world. In order to preserve the purity of human individualities, therefore, it was necessary to create a support base below, to place them in cells in which they could create an instrument of their manifestation, the mental and astral body of the personality, concentrating vibrations corresponding to this task in these cells.

Thus, the body for a person is: The necessary point of support for attracting the psychic vibrations of the personality that creates him, the point of support from which the axis of his consciousness begins, the desire to find the point of the lost suspension, that is, his rational and creative individuality, his spiritual "I"; a safe haven, in which the tired human consciousness can always hide from the pressure of negative psychic waves, larvae and psychic waves at once; the organiser of his psyche, because healthy material instincts often cure the psyche of flaws; an obstacle to penetration into the realm of the Subtle and Fiery Worlds, the overcoming of which develops human strength, expands consciousness and strengthens the core of the human personality, that is, the spiritual "I", because only with a sense, at least dimly, of this core, it is possible to overcome bodily obstacles.

Under the impulse of the Virgin, the wheel of earthly life acquires rotation, because human activity begins where the activity of nature ends, goes against its movement and changes and potentiates the dynamics of nature with its dynamics, all the time processing the energies of nature at its fulcrum, that is, the body. This process is invisible, because it occurs in the field of manifestation of psychic energy. But its results are reflected in changes in natural conditions due to changes in the cultural structure of people. Thus, the materialising impulse of Virgo returned to humanity the opportunity, even if not quite consciously, to realise the Object of its purpose, which is expressed in the transformation of earthly material.

Libra is Air, the twelfth principle.

Libra, as the name says, establishes a balance of forces on Earth. Through the constellation of Libra, spiritual impulses brought to people by the Brothers of Humanity pass to the Earth. The materialisation caused by the influence of Virgo created a fulcrum. Libra, conducting spiritual impulses into the psychic atmosphere of the Earth – thinks about the spiritual point of suspension and creates a new point in the human consciousness to replace the lost old one.

Thus, human life and cultural construction on Earth take place between spiritual search and the desire for material self-realisation. This is formulated by the two main ideals of humanity, which are spoken about by all religious teachings that connect the fulcrum with the suspension point. These ideals are: The search for truth; the ideal of knowledge and Knowledge of God and service to the Common Good - cultural construction. The material point of support is the foundation for the growth and development of the human Mind, its cognitive ability and its creativity. The suspension point is the foundation for the development of the human heart, the development of religious knowledge and its spiritualising work of the alchemist. The impulse of Libra establishes the balance of these two principles of the Mind and Heart - in human life and human construction, and the oblivion of one of them leads to cultural collapse and life chaos. The representatives of these two principles are determined by the two sexes, into which the whole person has disintegrated. A woman became the bearer of the Beginning of the Heart, a man became the bearer of the Mind. Since both have both cognitive and creative abilities and are looking for self - manifestation, both are symbolic triangles, and the Heart is looking for self-manifestation up, that is, the possibility of spiritual life, and the Mind is looking for self-manifestation down, that is, imprinting itself in the activity of earthly construction. The cooperation of both is necessary, so they can be represented as two triangles woven into a hexagram.

In the general cultural construction, the role of a woman is reduced to a subjective direct experience of the Spiritual World and its ideals; to the knowledge of the feeling that establishes warmth in relationships; to the sublimation of earthly life in relation to education in a broad sense, that is, to the alchemical work of spiritualisation of general cooperation and its results. The role of a man is reduced to an objective knowledge of the world with the desire to realise the truth or God through His manifestations; to the processing of the conditions of earthly existence in accordance with the knowledge achieved; to assert oneself as a rational being over everything irrational. Cooperation between the two sexes is established by their spiritual attraction to each other, provided mutual trust, respect and mutual understanding. The influence of Libra spiritualises the sexual desire, ignited by the impulse of Aries, and makes it a powerful tool for self-improvement, Knowledge of God and cultural construction.

Scorpio is Water, the fourteenth principle.

The influence of Scorpio establishes the principle of individual reincarnations. Material shells, due to their condensation, that is, slowness, cannot tolerate the intensity of mental changes that accompany the development of individual human consciousness. They wear out and therefore die, that is, they decompose into their component parts. The created psychic complex loses its point of support, but it will not disintegrate in the general world of Psychic energy due to the created axis of consciousness, called the human "I", in its manifestations on different planes of Cosmic Existence.
But together with the disintegration of the body, that is, with the loss of a fulcrum, a person loses the possibility of further evolution of his consciousness and the development of horizontal planes through which this axis passes. After all, the body with his nervous system, he is a magnet of attraction of psychic energy. If a suspension point is found and consciousness is firmly identified with it, then the evolution of the development of cognitive and creative abilities is possible without a fulcrum. But while this suspension point is not stable, that is, until the spiritual " I " is fully embodied in consciousness, it is necessary to create a new fulcrum for further evolution, a new magnet for further attraction and transformation of Psychic energy. Such a new incarnation seems to continue the previous one and, through the chain of these incarnations, the axis of consciousness is strengthened and an increasingly strong, perfect and broad personality is forged, which can become a conductor of spiritual creativity.

Scorpio, protecting the human personality after the death of the physical body from being dispersed in the general flow of psychic energies, at the same time establishes plastic transitions of this personality from one incarnation to another, making each new personality a successor and heiress of the previous one and a carrier of the rudiments of a new personality. The same applies to collective mental formations, called the People's or Racial Soul, and the physical body of the people also dies, as well as the individual, and a new body is often born in other, more suitable for subsequent development, conditions. Thus, it is possible to take revenge on the reincarnation of the People's Soul, and the lines of reincarnation are noticeable by the continuation of the task and the general national character, as well as by the People's Karma. For example, we can give the line Egypt-Byzantium-Russia. Another line is Carthage-Later Rome-England.
Ideally, there should be only seven racial and individual incarnations, but mistakes and the chaotic nature of the human psyche have increased the number of group and individual incarnations many times.

The third four planets

Sagittarius, fire, the fifteenth principle.

The influence of Sagittarius helps to develop a specific role for earthly humanity. The spiritual will is defined as the creative self-emission of the spiritual core of consciousness. This is the will to self-government, to spiritual self-realisation. With the loss of the spiritual suspension point in the human consciousness, this will, that is, the initiative to self-manifestation, has also been lost. Creating a point of support the body was conditioned by a new manifestation of the will, called desire, which is always based on polarisation in the consciousness of the Subject and Object and on focusing attention on the latter, the Spiritual will is radiating, and the material consciousness is absorbing.
Since at the fulcrum a person has objectified himself in relation to his spiritual essence, the desire aimed at searching for the axis of consciousness and achieving a subjective knowledge of his spiritual "I" is the only possibility of his self-development.
A material person always wants what he does not have, that is, his will is directed to the absorption of the object and its transformation into a subject. This is the basis for the expansion of consciousness, therefore, from now on, the will is called the expedient aspiration of consciousness, since the stupid causal

impulses of the desired object are colloquially called "desires". These desires often contradict each other, because different human vehicles may need the opposite for their development. Therefore, these desires must be coordinated around the main expedient axis of human aspiration, which is called "education of the will".

This ability of concentration of consciousness on the goal and concentration of desire gives a person the influence of Sagittarius, setting him the task of developing a new one from material desires, purposefully aimed at growth consciousness, will, as the spring of its cultural evolution. Such a will groups the vibrations of psychic energies around itself, creates a force vortex from them, which takes consciousness to the spiritual and intellectual plane, that is, to the plane on which a person is destined to live and create. Only by raising his consciousness to this new level, a person can become the master of psychic energies and control the life of the planet.

Capricorn is the Earth, the sixteenth principle.

Smooth transitions from one stage of evolution to another are disrupted due to the breakdown of human consciousness, which has lost control over the general plan, ways and methods of its cultural development. This consciousness of continuity is lost due to the disruption of the connection between the Worlds, because the cause that unites the various effects always lies in a more subtle plane, which is now elusive for the materialised consciousness.

The constellation of Capricorn establishes the timing and sequence of the fulfilment of cultural human tasks and introduces - instead of the lost principle of continuous evolution - the principle of revolution. Revolution, in essence, is the destruction of the ossified accumulations of already obsolete cultural tasks that the human consciousness has outgrown. Such purges of the old are necessary so that the sprouts of a new level of consciousness and the corresponding cultural tasks can manifest themselves. The influence of Capricorn thickens the shadow of the old one for a clearer display of the path travelled and the obstacles that need to be overcome. Thus, the constellation of Capricorn establishes a new Karma of humanity with a change in the terms of individual cycles of cultural construction.

Aquarius is the Air. The eleventh principle.

The influence of Aquarius will help humanity to bring together the torn planes of consciousness again and erase the illusory boundaries between the Worlds. Aquarius detaches human consciousness from the illusory perception of earthly objects as absolute values. Its influence opens consciousness to the perception of Cosmic Infinity and sets before man the task of Cosmic Cooperation, which he has lost.

Of course, this task manifests itself in a person's consciousness as a material aspect, and only spiritual impulses given by Teachers spiritualise this perception. Therefore, the epochs that take place under the increased influence of Aquarius are marked by individual attempts of people to penetrate into other Worlds and an increased interest in occult knowledge.

Pisces is Water, the eleventh principle.

The influence of Pisces forces the human consciousness to turn deeper into itself, because objective knowledge and searching in the objective world do not create the desired connection between the worlds: for the perception of these worlds, it is necessary subjectively develop new organs of perception.

The influence of Pisces helps to move consciousness into the formed new Subtle human body and feel the world through new organs. Therefore, the influence of Pisces contributes to the subjective growth of consciousness and the development of Higher human bodies.

Such work can be done by each individual only independently, because the development of consciousness and Subtle vehicles is a highly individual thing. Therefore, Pisces contributes to the process of individualisation of humanity and set it the task of independence.

This independence by no means contradicts the consciousness of being connected with the Cosmic Hierarchy, because the Earth is given to humanity as an independent possession and "the temple must be built with human feet and hands" with a full sense of responsibility for its construction.

All the influences of the zodiac constellations on the Earth and humanity just listed should not be understood as a complete dependence of human consciousness on the vibrations of the surrounding cosmic environment. Rather, they should be understood as decrees given and forceful assistance to a drowning person for swimming back to the surface of the Ocean of Psychic Energies of the Earth. Humanity is free to use these influences or to reject them. It is also free in the coordination of the received force flows for individual conscious goals.

All these influences do not force humanity, but only put new opportunities into its hands, and also remind it of its royal position in the planetary system. They are like subjects taking on the duties and functions of a sick king who, after his recovery, will again rule them.

The influences of individual zodiacal constellations vary over time, creating a special individual psychic colouring of the epochs of the cultural development of mankind. The sun, in its journey through the zodiac circle, moves in the direction from Aries to Pisces, and it swims in front of each constellation for about two thousand earth years.

For the last two thousand years, it has been passing near the constellation of Pisces and now it will enter Aquarius, whose influence on Earth is growing stronger.

In its annual rotation around the Sun, the Earth in a small circle also seems to float among the zodiac circle, and the influence of the zodiac constellations is reflected on the life of its nature by the aspects of the months of the year, and each such aspect begins on the twentieth (according to the new style), and the movement goes from Aries to Taurus. The point of the spring equinox, on average - March 20 - corresponds to the entry into the sphere of influence of Aries, the summer solstice into the sphere of influence of Cancer, the autumn equinox into the sphere of influence of Libra and the winter solstice into the sphere of influence of Capricorn.

The characteristic features of the life of nature, that is, the phases of its annual evolution, correspond to the nature of the influence of the zodiac constellations, and it is easy to determine them by observing the peculiarities of individual months of the year. We will only note that for human life, the summer months, from the spring to the autumn equinox, contribute to the tension of creative work, while the winter half-year contributes to cognitive work, In addition, birth in one or another month determines the general temperament in all planes of consciousness of the person who appeared, creating his zodiac type:

Aries - fiery natures, tense, truthful, fearless, resolute;
Taurus - inert, materialistic, causal natures;
Gemini is a frivolous nature, easily adaptable;
Cancer is passive, receptive nature, susceptible to influence;
Leo is an expansive, open nature;

Virgo is a hardworking nature and self-absorbed;
Libra is a balanced, calm, spiritually-creative nature;
Scorpio-natures are prone to melancholy, absorbing,
psychologically cowardly, prone to lies;
Sagittarius is a domineering, quarrelsome nature;
Capricorn has a closed nature, wearing a disguise, distrustful and
uneven;
Aquarius is a visionary with a bold nature;
Pisces is a self-absorbed, meek nature, often suffering.

Zodiac constellations in astrology are divided into alternating
day and night signs. This is an indication of their influence -
either on objective shells or on subjective consciousnesses.
In astrology, the zodiac constellations of their influence are taken
into account by horoscopic houses, and the circle of these houses
begins with Aries and moves to Taurus, ending with Pisces.
Accounting for these influences is as follows:

Aries is the first house - Life. It takes into account the total
reserve of vital forces and human health.
Taurus is the second home – wealth – where the material
conditions of incarnations are taken into account.
Gemini - the third house – Brothers, both of blood and spiritual
servants.
Cancer - the fourth house -Parents, physical superiors and
spiritual leaders.
Leo - the fifth house - Children and public figures
Virgo is the sixth house of Subordination in the field of activity.
Libra is the seventh house - Marriage.
Scorpio - the eighth house - Death. The time, conditions and
environment of death, as well as the half-hour inheritance.
Sagittarius - the ninth house - Piety. Travel as a condition for
expanding consciousness (sometimes traveling to other Worlds,
exteriorisation).
Capricorn is the tenth house - the Kingdom, that is, the main
task of a person, the main sphere of his activity, taking into
account the results in this activity.
Aquarius is the eleventh house - the Patrons and helpers of man.
Pisces - the twelfth house - Dangers. A house that takes into
account obstacles and threats.

Horoscope houses do not coincide with astrological houses,
which are individual for each person, starting in one or another
zodiac sign. Horoscope houses are the houses of the ideal

horoscope, which serves as a background for taking into account individual deviations.

In conclusion, we note the three crosses of the elements formed by the twelve constellations of the Zodiac:

- The first cross is formed by crossing the elements of Fire (Aries), Water (Cancer), Air (Libra), Earth (Capricorn). This is the spiritual cross of the elements or the Cross of the Teacher.
- The second cross is formed by crossing the elements of Fire (Leo), Water (Scorpio), Air (Aquarius), Earth (Taurus). This is the mental cross, or the Cross of the Disciples.
The third cross is formed by crossing the elements Fire (Sagittarius), Water (Pisces), Air (Gemini), Earth (Virgo). This is the Psychic Cross of Nature.
The development of these hints is provided to the initiators - the faith and knowledge of everyone.

Death

The thirteenth Arcanum

"Change of life stages"

Immortality in essence
Death and reincarnation
Energy transmutation
Numeric designation: 40
Astrological correspondence: the constellation of the Big
Dipper or Great Bear

A Chart of the Constellations Great Bear and Little Bear

The symbolic picture is somewhat crude and has become trivial: Death in the form of a skeleton (the skeleton, as a relatively non-decomposing part of the human body, symbolises the first subtitle of the principle) mows down a head that has grown out of the earth, but on the path passed by Death, legs and arms grow out of the earth, that is, the organs of new formations.

In the Universal life there is no death, as we understand it, there is no sunset. Life is governed by the principle of transformation of one stage of consciousness into another, and, accordingly, with the transition of consciousness to the next stage, the form of its manifestation and the conditions of its existence change.

The principle of life is manifested everywhere, and the dynamics of life are symbolised by rows of waves. The coordinates of these waves are their fractures, that is, the upper - the culmination point and the lower - the fading point. Transitions of consciousness through these points is what we call death, because when these points are crossed, a new stage of life and manifestation begins each time. The discontinuity of the Worlds, that is, the loss of continuity of the transitions of consciousness from one stage of manifestation to another and the identification of consciousness with the stage of each manifestation, introduced the concept of birth and death into the worldview of mankind instead of the concept of continuous transformation. These false representations were the reason for the loss of humanity's power over the materials of its personality (body and psyche) and the loss of self-knowledge.

Birth and death are phenomena of the same order. The transition through the culmination point is a spiritual death, that is, leaving the higher planes of consciousness for the immersion of the human "I" into matter.

Death is the leaving of the material plane for the transition to a Higher and more Subtle state, that is, birth to other Worlds. The tragedy of the process lies only in a wrong understanding of the moment of death and depends on the oblivion of previous states. The core of consciousness - the spiritual "I" of a person, expressed in it by self-consciousness on any plane of manifestation - always remains identical to itself.

The restoration of the continuity of the memory of the previous stages is always the result of finding one's spiritual "I" and the non-identification of consciousness with the individual stages of its manifestation.

To be the master of changes and not to identify with them means to find your unchanging immortal essence, in religious language - your Immortal Soul. This Immortal Soul consists of a spiritual core of consciousness, clothed in the thinnest energy shell, which carries the dynamics of its development - the Principle of Life - and gives the opportunity of contact with the objective world, as well as giving the ability of creative cognition and self-manifestation, called abstract Reason, in Sanskrit - "Buddhi-Nikaya". The result of the activity of these shells is the creation of transitional forms and bodies depending on the conditions of objective existence.

Everything, except this upper Trinity (the Immortal Soul), is constantly changing and, objectively considering the course of even a single incarnation, we can easily take into account the intellectual, psychic and etheric-physical changes taking place with us, according to the development of our consciousness, the accumulation of experience and favourable external conditions.

In fact, we are constantly dying and being born into a new cycle of existence and even nightly we pass our consciousness into other Worlds during sleep. It is the phenomenon of sleep that can explain to us the phenomenon of so-called death. In both cases, the same break of consciousness with the loss of memory: on the higher plane - the lower and on the lower plane - the higher. At the same time, we are perfectly aware with our inner consciousness that the same "I" experiences both the dream of earthly life and the dream of the Subtle World. Our immortal "I" - an unchanging part of our being - is like an axis on which the spiral of objective existence is wound, creating from each time it has a shell corresponding to the turn of the spiral.

These turns of a continuous spiral are the chain of our incarnations not only on the earthly, but also on the general cosmic scale, because the Immortal Soul is only temporarily connected with the conditions of earthly existence and the chain of a number of earthly personalities conditioned by it. After the exhaustion of earthly experience and the fulfilment of earthly tasks, our Soul goes to Other Worlds, continuing the chain of its incarnations on other planets, as it was before, in the times preceding the earthly incarnations. Our earthly incarnations are extremely confused due to violations of a certain norm, due to errors, false identifications of consciousness and a network of misconceptions and concepts in which we are entangled.

Since this network of ideas is extremely individual for everyone, since everyone carries a world created by himself, then everyone's karma is individual, and therefore both the terms and lines of incarnation are individual. Of course, there is a general law regulating human incarnations, but the application of this law is extremely diverse and depends on individual karmas. During the incarnation, a person will accumulate experience, and by his actions he will generate a whole chain of causalities. This experience does not exhaust the cognitive possibilities and requires continuation. The consequences generated by these actions do not have time to get out of life during one incarnation and, thus, provide for the following incarnations, because the worn-out conductors, the secret of transformation - which a person has lost - are not able to accommodate stresses exceeding a certain limit. When this limit is reached, the human consciousness leaves the conductors, first of all the physical conductor, that is, the body.

After leaving the body, a person remains in his mental, astral-energetic and etheric-force shell. But with the loss of the body, he loses the necessary conditions for contact with the earthly objectivity, that is, with the surrounding planetary world, so the state of the departed from the body is relatively subjective. After all, consciousness is the ability to consider the accumulated experience, to recognise the true from the false in it, to separate good from evil and determine the lines of its next manifestation. In the first moments after leaving the physical body, the lower, coarser shells of the astrosome are still in contact with the physical body.

The etheric body is finally separated from the physical body 48 hours after the heart stops beating. During these 48 hours, it is recommended to leave the body in complete peace and silence, without shaking the mental atmosphere with lamentations and sobs. High concentrations, called prayers, are good, which introduce high-order vibrations into the vehicles of the outgoing person and facilitate the process of leaving the body.

On the ninth day after death, the final division into the constituent parts of the etheric shell takes place, and its higher part - the life force (prana) - goes to feed the astral body, and the lower part, borrowed from the treasury of nature and not converted into human vibrations, remains with the body and accelerates the process of decomposition. This is the part of prana that nourished the material instincts of the body, therefore, overcoming the material instincts leads to the non-decomposition of the body (the Relics of the Saints).

After the ninth day, the consciousness of the astrosome is focused on the astral plane, where it re-emotionally experiences the pictures of its incarnation, restoring them to the smallest details forgotten during earthly life. At the same time, there is a reckoning and the allocation of the main moments of life, as decisive for the karma of the following incarnations. Attention is focused most of all on negative cliches and on the adjustments that can correct them.

This state is called in Sanskrit - "staying in Kama-Loka", in Christian terminology- "passing through Purgatory". Having highlighted the main moments of the incarnation, having exhausted the astral experience, the consciousness of the departed leaves the astral shell, which dissolves in the general psychic vibrations, remaining in consciousness only as the resultant of the experience passed.

Consciousness passes into a mental shell, where there is a revision of the worldview and the elimination of the ideal. This state is called in Sanskrit - "staying in Devachan", and in the religions of other peoples - "staying in Paradise". Here consciousness experiences its best aspirations, the ideas of the ideal created in life, and gradually reaches the highest states once outlined in earthly life, experiences them in their entirety until the power of concentration invested in them during earthly life is exhausted. Then the longing for a new one begins, the search for which forces you to leave this culminating point, to descend from the highest, happiest mental plane again into the emotional-psychic world to acquire an energy impulse to search. And from there-to the material world, where a new tool is being created-the body - for contact with earthly objectivity in the name of continuing experience, correcting detected errors, expanding consciousness and the evolution of mental creativity.

Approximately the same process occurs in other kingdoms of nature with their inhabitants.

The consciousness of animals, more accustomed to the physical world, perceives the moments of transition more acutely.

But after the transition of its astrosome, the animal does not experience an individual subjective state, but, as it were, transfers the stock of its experience into the group consciousness of the species to which it belongs. This group consciousness refers to him in approximately the same way as in the generally accepted concept of God refers to a person: It judges the astrosome of the animal, and in the form of a reward - draws it into itself, and in the form of punishment for poor performance of the task - awards it to a new incarnation.

The soul of the plant easily leaves the physical plane. In the astral world, the astrosomes of plants are centres of harmonisation and association of psychic energy - this is their task there. The group soul of plants is located on the mental plane, and the "paradise flowers" symbolise this group soul.

The soul of minerals, passing directly to the mental plane, is transformed there into the main types of mental-spiritual flow.

Returning to the human being, we note that the duration of stay on different planes of consciousness, in Kama-Loka and Devachan, depends for everyone on the level of consciousness that he has manifested during his earthly life, and on the degree of aggravation of his karma. The timing of the incarnation also depends on this.

Thus, a person with a rich spiritual life and unselfish in his manifestations quickly passes the stage of separation of the etheric body and staying in Kama-Loka and stays for a long time in the Devachan of his spiritual-mental formations. A person, burdened with egoism or crimes, confuses and complicates his stay in Kama-Loka, and the stage of Devachan passes unconsciously, as if in a psychological dream, and reincarnates much faster than the first.

A person who is absorbed by materialistic instincts does not go further than the etheric plane and, trying to satisfy these instincts, seeks contact with the physical world through mediums and at spiritualistic seances, and uses the first suitable opportunity for a new incarnation.

The inveterate criminal or suicide is still attached by consciousness to the moment and the situation of the crime or suicide, until despair forces them to escape by passing into matter, that is, into a new incarnation that will appear to them as Paradise.

Spiritually highly developed people, who are aware of the subjectivity of post-mortem states, quickly pass through all the stages without identifying with them, and, bypassing all sorts of paradises and devachans, either go to another planet, or they would they are incarnated again on Earth to continue their service to humanity.

Early deaths also usually entail a new incarnation, which is often a direct continuation of the interrupted one. In this case, the passage through the Kama Loka and Devachan is postponed until the next time, and the preservation of the personality ensures the clarity of the memories of the previous incarnation (since the same astral and etheric body is used for the new incarnation as in the interrupted incarnation). The same category includes deaths in childhood, and it happens that a child is born twice to the same mother. In this case, the death of the first body indicates some kind of error in the process of the incarnations of the guides.

The incarnating soul seems to radiate from itself the main skeleton of the future mental body, consisting of a general formula of the experience gained in the previous incarnation, which will then develop into a new worldview. This mental formula radiates from itself the emotional resultant that the mental body absorbed after leaving the soul of KamaLoka and which will unfold during the next incarnation into the world relation and the emotional possibilities associated with it. This embryo of the future personality is looking for suitable conditions for its development and for its embodiment on the physical plane and which will give him an etheric body suitable for solving his tasks. At the moment of physical connection, the parents strongly radiate etheric energy, which the incarnating soul uses as a connecting bridge with matter. Through this bridge, it connects with the material world, connects with the embryo and animates it. In the process of uterine life, the etheric body of the child is created, the axis of which is the etheric charge of the father's family, and the shell is the etheric vibrations of the mother.

From the moment of birth and independent physical existence, the emotional axis begins to be absorbed into the etheric body, and full absorption occurs by the age of seven, when the infant passes into adolescence. Then there is the development of this axis into the astral body of a new person, the main tonalities of which are established by the age of thirteen. From the age of thirteen, the absorption of the mental body begins, which is also associated with the achievement of puberty, because gender is determined in the mental plane. This is the transition from adolescence to youth. At approximately the age of twenty-one, the unfolding of the mental formula into the main determinants of the incarnational worldview ends. This finally establishes the Karma of the Incarnation. The moment of coming of age is the moment of the full incarnation of a person on the ground. Next comes his self-manifestation of the accumulation of a new conscious experience.

The breakdown of a person's consciousness separated him from the Higher Worlds. A person seems to have died in the spirit, and religion is a way of connecting him with his own spiritual essence and with the Spiritual World. It is not for nothing that it is said that religion leads to the Resurrection of consciousness. The result of man's isolation from the Higher Worlds, that is, the result of his spiritual death, was the condensation of matter and the associated phenomenon of physical death. These suitable conditions are created by finding consonant souls who will be his parents on the surface. If religion returns consciousness to his spiritual homeland, then the so-called Initiation gives him knowledge.

The Principles, Laws and Forces operating in the intermediate worlds and transfer his consciousness beyond the threshold of physical death. Initiation can begin only when the religious consciousness of a person is firmly strengthened, because without this condition, the axis of consciousness passing through the above-ground worlds up to the Spirit cannot be established. Penetration into these Worlds without a stable axis of consciousness threatens the daredevil with mental illness, falling under the power of negative formations of the Subtle World and Black magic.

Initiation is the lost human knowledge of the metaphysical worlds, the knowledge of their actual experience, the mastery of ideomotor and psychomotor processes, that is, the creative force in its earthly manifestations, and the discovery of Cosmic Citizenship and Cooperation. The highest point of Initiation is the victory over Death in the three earthly Worlds, that is, the restoration of the continuity of consciousness, the ability to master the apparatus of the transformation of spiritual materials - the secret transmutation of energy within oneself and in the descriptive world.

The result of the first stage of Initiation is a theoretical victory over death - a theoretical recognition of the continuity of consciousness and the laws of transformation - associated with the ability to observe the transitions of individual spiral cycles into each other. Theoretical knowledge of the continuous Law of Dynamics and the ability to apply it in the dynamic consideration of facts leads the human mind out of the repeating flat circle of physical earthly life, introduces it to the phenomena of other Worlds, makes it notice these phenomena in earthly life, creates confidence in the reality of Other Worlds and potentiates its thought-creation.

The second stage of Initiation brings a person into practical contact with Other Worlds and practically introduces him to the apparatus of transformation, which leads his consciousness to Other Worlds and from there back to the earthly world. This practical familiarisation is achieved by exteriorising consciousness from one's physical body to other Subtle Bodies operating on other planes. The first stage in this case is the separation of the mental, astral and, partially, etheric bodies from the physical body. Moreover, the physical body with the lower part of the etheric arrives at this stage in a state of trance, similar to death. With longer exteriorisations, this condition is called lethargy. In fact, the human consciousness passes the threshold of death, but not after the wear of its shells or for a karmic reason, but voluntarily and consciously, with full possession of the abilities of its magical and mental bodies. In this state, after a short stay in his own KamaLoka, a person gets acquainted with the Astral World of the Earth and returns to the body again with the acquired knowledge.

With the repetition of such exteriorisations, the knowledge of the Subtle World, the understanding of its laws and methods of action deepens and expands, and the ability to arbitrarily project one's astral shell to earthly distances is acquired by storing the memory of the impressions received and the actions performed. Further stages of exteriorisation separate and separate the mental body from the astral one. Then the state of lethargy is not necessary. The body is in a half-trance, the astral body gives its power to the mental body and is also in a state of half-trance. The mental body, imbued with the power of the astral and transformed by the power of the etheric, penetrates into the Creative Mental World of the planet and, temporarily concentrating in its Devachan, learns the general mental sphere of the Earth with the Suns of ideals burning in it and Spirits building it up with subtle beautiful images.

At this stage of exteriorisation, the mental body, at its highest tension, can leave the earthly spheres, come into contact with the mental entities of other planets and partially penetrate the consciousness. One enters the sphere of life and activity of these planets, directly acquiring knowledge about them. Directed by concentration to the Spiritual World, the mental body comes into contact with the highest vibrations reaching the Earth and through these vibrations directly learns the life of the Spiritual World, coming into contact with the Solar consciousnesses.

These stages of exteriorisation are called ecstasies, the highest degree of which – Samadhi - refers already to the transition of consciousness from the mental body to the immortal soul through the bridge connecting the Higher and lower Minds. In the stage of Samadhi, the highest Knowledge of God will be revealed, the knowledge of one's true Essence and the direct accommodation of Cosmic Laws in consciousness.

When such exteriorisations are achieved, associated with the passage of the first stage of isolation, a person acquires the ability to dissociate consciousness and act simultaneously in several bodies, in which his etheric shell will also be dissociated. During the experience and training, the physical body may not arrive in a trance, but show normal activity.

Awareness of the circulation of the psychic flow along the fibres of the nervous system and conscious possession of the centres of the body contribute to the constant influx of new reserves of Psychic energy into the physical body, change its composition (in the sense of thinning the vibrations of its tissues) and bring it closer to the etheric body.

The last task of the Initiates is the ability to immortalise their physical body in the case of staying on Earth and "not leaving a corpse behind", that is, when leaving the Earth, the dematerialisation of the physical body by transmutation of its energy. The third stage of Initiation is, therefore, a physical victory over death, achieved by the ability to transmute energy from the higher planes to the lower ones and from the lower ones to the higher ones. At the same time, the earthly personality changes its composition. The lower mental body is firmly connected with the higher mental principle of Reason: the practical earthly reason with its opportunism and egoism disappears. Active creative idealism replaces it, leaving only the ability to orient oneself in earthly conditions (the mind becomes visionary).

The old astral body is completely replaced by a new one - a woven stellar body consisting not of earthly physical vibrations, but of vibrations of the surrounding cosmic environment, reflecting the principle in purity Buddhi, that is, the Soul. The astral body becomes, as it were, the dynamic of the Soul. Such subtle vibrations of the astral body constantly renew the composition of the etheric body, feeding it with cosmic energies. The constant nourishment of the etheric body and the plasticity of the new astral and mental bodies protect the physical body from the process of dying.

Temperance

The Fourteenth Arcanum

"Personality"

Deduction
Comparability
Reversibility of the process
Numeric designation: 50
Astrological correspondence: Scorpio

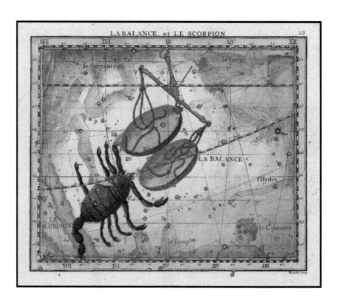

John Flamsteed, La Balance et le Scorpion (Libra & Scorpio), 1776

The symbolic picture depicts a solar genius holding a golden vessel in his right hand, and a silver one in his left. From a tilted golden vessel, he pours a stream into a silver vessel.

The Fourteenth Principle explains the mechanism of conscious construction of personality as an instrument of human manifestation in earthly life. The first subtitle - "Deduction" - hints at the source of the creativity of the individual. Personality is not a random result of accumulated objective experience. What is usually called a personality is not really such yet, but is only the psychic material for creating a personality.

There are few personalities among people, because personality is conditioned by the stability of consciousness. What is colloquially called a personality is actually an unstable mental formation that threatens to crumble and collapse under the influence of the first, stronger pressure of Psychic energy. These ordinary personalities change according to the subjective conditions of their existence. They are a product of the environment and depend on the environment, they do not have a subjective orientation and a creative element. They are absorbed by the general nature of the environment and after death they break up into composite psychic flows that are not soldered around the common axis of consciousness. Therefore, most people after death and stay in Kama-Loka - "fall asleep", that is - losing consciousness and with it the memory of the past incarnation. They pass into a new incarnation with a weakly expressed experience that makes them dependent on the influence of upbringing and the conditions of the surrounding environment.

The Egyptian wisdom says: "We will create our soul on Earth," that is, a person who is able to preserve the main features of his character and continue his existence in the chain of incarnations. A personality cannot be created without a stable axis of consciousness, and the stability of the axis of consciousness is determined by purposefulness. The first stage of personality formation depends on the certainty of the goal set in life, even if this goal is not high. At first, you need to learn to know what you want and achieve what you want. A person who has set himself a goal, remakes his own material according to this goal in the name of achieving it. The goal itself indicates to him the need for self-discipline, which expresses the degree of mastery of his mental material.

In other words, a person is always a product of deduction, the main postulate of which is the goal set. The breadth of personal consciousness and the volume of personality depends on the height of the level of this postulate. The strength of the personality axis depends on the intensity of field tension to achieve the goal. So, both ambition, and the thirst for wealth, and other earthly goals can serve as postulates for the formation of persistent personalities pursuing their goal on the way from one incarnation to another one. The higher the goal, the larger the personality. The personality deduced from ideal, that is, from the potency of its spiritual individuality, which builds these ideals, is the most solid in its construction, broad in its consciousness, full-fledged in its spiritual aspiration and large in volume. Of course, the wider and higher the ideal, the more perfect the listed personality qualities are.

Personality is an imprint in the psychic material of the spiritual value that fills the human consciousness. From this spiritual value, an axis is formed that meets the axis of the will contained in the etheric body, and spiritualises this will, making it a constant aspiration to the ideal. The mental material and the worldview that follows from the basic ideal and depends both on the past mental experience and on the target postulate that gives it the main tonality are grouped around a single axis. Further, around the axis of the personality, coloured in the tonality of a certain worldview, the entire complex of mental material captured by consciousness is grouped, which, through self-discipline, is transformed into energies and forces that move consciousness along the path of achieving and realising the ideal. This transformed psychic world is the main power part of the personality, its attitude to the world and its influence on the environment. This created centre of psychic life transforms the etheric vibrations, that is, the world of material instincts, passions and habits, by discipline, forcing him to carry out the ideal in everyday life.

And finally, the transformed etheric body acts on the physical body, improving the ego and keeping the psyche inspired by the ideal in subjection. Thus, by gradual deduction from the spiritual postulate, the personality is built as an instrument of the earthly manifestation of man - just as God builds the Universe in all its aspects from His potential possibilities.

The same can be said about any organic or inorganic formations. So, a circle of acquaintances is not an organisation, but a random gathering in which, at least, causality can be traced. But people who have gathered in the name of an idea and its implementation develop a common plan, rebuild their psyche accordingly, and their association becomes an organisation with a mental face and a mental collective body. According to the same law of deduction, all sorts of organisations are created. Thus, clusters of matter, called nebulae, are not yet worlds but they become worlds, organising themselves according to the plan of the mind that guides the process of deduction.

The personality is located on the axis of consciousness, which can be conditionally divided into higher and lower parts. Each of these parts is associated with certain qualities, properties and characteristics of a person, some of which can be called positive, others - negative manifestations of character and soul.

The totality of qualities manifested in the state of daytime wakefulness forms a stable everyday consciousness of a person, clothed in a constant degree of tension of his psyche. And these coordinates with their points and scales are necessary for knowing that the psychic material that a person has inside his own vehicles, because without such self-knowledge, it is impossible to develop his personality.

Positive qualities are grouped around the upper part of the vertical scale and in total give the degree of general spirituality of consciousness. Negative qualities are grouped around the lower part of the axis of consciousness and show the degree of filling of consciousness with material impulses and egoism. Abilities and talents are grouped around the left side of the horizontal axis and show the wealth of psychic materials. The limits of stress and the results of the manifestation of abilities and talents are grouped around the right part of the horizontal axis and show the possibilities of further development.

Work on yourself begins not from the nadir point, but from the zenith point. Clear, relief perception, the development of ideals and ideas arising from it transforms the intellect, purifying it from ideas that are inconsistent with the ideal and harmonising its mental energy. The work of the intellect, its thought-creation, is composed into a worldview around the axis of the ideal, and all the streams of thought are brought into a harmonious hierarchical order under the influence of the illumination of their ideal. Of course, the volume and coverage of a larger or smaller range depends on the degree of height and width of the ideal.

The spirituality and harmony of the intellectual world pushes its ideological thought-creation on the emotional world of a person. We call this pressure inspiration, because in this case the emotional world begins to embody the elements of the soul, that is, a direct sense of the reality of spiritual values, the desire to realise them in life, which is expressed by love for the high, beautiful and just. These three feelings contribute to emotional world impulses of selflessness. All good mental qualities are potentiated and serve as conductors of these impulses, grouped around the axis created by them.

All the negative qualities that do not correspond to the spiritual ideal, that is, egoistic emotions and material instincts, seem to stand out at first in a separate world, with which consciousness can no longer be firmly identified. If these negative qualities are manifested, then their manifestation causes reproaches of conscience and a feeling of dissatisfaction with oneself, Conscience is the voice of the ideal, and there can be no conscience without the ideal.

The measure of conscience is the highest stages of consciousness that a person is capable of. The higher these stages of consciousness, the greater the mental tension between zenith and nadir, the stronger the voice of conscience sounds and the stricter its lynching. This self-judgment of conscience causes the second stage of personality processing, in which materialistic instincts that can be processed are spiritualised by investing ideal value in them (for example, take the spiritualisation of the sexual instinct: instead of the brute animal passions are spiritualised love, in which mental, psychic, spiritual and spiritual components are introduced). Those materialistic instincts that cannot be spiritualised due to their perversion (vices) are overcome, and the forces accumulating on them are transferred to a more subtle plane of manifestation.

Thus, the tendency to drugs in a more subtle manifestation gives the search for more subtle mental planes. Negative egoistic emotions are overcome by self-forgetfulness in the name of serving the ideal. This self-forgetfulness is the result of understanding the true value of one's personality as an instrument for realising the ideal.

The psychic material of a person consists of planetary energies reflected in the earthly psychic sphere. Therefore, the sublimation of psychic material is the sublimation of these psychic energies, and the whole work is called purification - the sublimation of its planetary composition. The picture of planetary energies and influences presented in the seventh Arcana helps to understand its psychological composition, that is, its horizontal axis, and it makes it possible to clearly understand the psychic material that is subject to sublimation and harmonisation. In this work, it is necessary to observe commensurability. The human consciousness, located in the centre of its circle, should own its planetary composition, and not the planetary composition-consciousness. The over-development of one planet at the expense of another often creates intense, but monotonous manifestations of personality, which, despite the intensity of their manifestation, give up where the manifestations of the dominant planet are not necessary. Strong personalities who are able to manifest themselves fruitfully in all conditions and perform any tasks in the name of affirming the ideal are always versatile, that is, they have a balanced planetary composition and are commensurate in their parts. Therefore, it is good to put the Sun in the centre of its planetary composition and coordinate the other planets around their natural centre.

A highly developed planet does not need to be suppressed, on the contrary, the degree of its development shows the potential for similar development of other planets, which should be done. Knowing the nature of the planetary manifestations and applying the principle of self-discipline to yourself, you can arbitrarily change the nature of your personality and acquire talents and abilities that are absent at the beginning. Life itself helps those who have started such work by creating suitable conditions, because life is plastic and obeys the orders of a person's conscious initiative.

This work is postponed and marked around the right point of the horizontal axis, around the point of death (see the Seventh Arcanum). Death is a transition to another consciousness, and by such self-development, based on individual self-creative efforts, we transfer the personality to the next stage of development, to the next circle of its manifestation. The point of death coincides with the fire of the cross of the elements, just as the point of birth coincides with the water flowing into the nadir and thus determines the fulcrum, that is, the earth of this incarnation. The point of death-fire-directs us to the zenith, that is, to the realisation of the spiritual ideal - the air in the cross of the elements.

The realisation of the ideal in the personality and its manifestations expands the mental body, spiritualises the astral and refines the etheric body. This sublimation also changes the attitude to the ideal: consciousness rises and expands, that is, the central point shifts towards the zenith. The level of our stable, everyday consciousness increases, and the perception of the ideal expands. Accordingly, the formulation of the ideal, that is, the worldview, also changes. In short, having conditioned the growth of the personality, the ideal itself grows accordingly with its growth. In this case, the construction of a new personality corresponding to the new perception of the ideal begins according to the previous method.

If a person's consciousness is capable of such stresses, and the material and mental, is sufficiently plastic and the reserve of vital forces is sufficiently large, then the point of death of the physical body is transferred without changing the incarnation, and a new personality develops without wasting time on the inter-incarnation period.

In this way, it is actually possible to combine several incarnations during one earthly life, and there is no limit to their number.

This is the secret of earthly longevity, because only the insufficient plasticity of the conductors and the crystallisation of consciousness, which refuses further transformation and growth, cause death. What is said about the human personality applies in all details to all collective organisations.

Considering the circle of mental and psychic creativity of a person, we can note the reversibility of processes in it. After all, the stock that pours down from the point of birth and determines the instinctive life of the personality, that is, the nadir, is again refined, spiritualised and comprehended by a conscious transformation. By remaking himself, a person proves that there is nothing irrevocable, and asserts his power over the past. A person can overcome everything that life has made of him. Moreover, while working on the consequences, according to the law of the reverse effect of the consequences on the causes, he also makes changes in them, changing the past as well.

Nika Akasha, that is, the chain of causes deployed in the pictures of the Subtle World, is constantly changing by the conscious sublimation efforts of a person.

Nature confirms this process in the world of physical energies with its life. The reversibility of physical energy is established by the laws of physics, and in this process a part of the transformed energy remains irreversible, as if it is fixed by the result produced by it. This fact of irreversible residues would cause the so-called process of entropy in the earth's nature, that is, levelling and fading of the total energy reserve. But the Earth is not a closed system, and its total energy supply is constantly being replenished. Therefore, the entropy process does not actually occur, but instead there is a process of crystallisation of earthly forms, through which a flow of energies moving into each other in a forward and reverse direction circulates.

The same thing happens with the reversibility of psychic processes in the psychic world. The Akashic Record is not an established archive once and for all. Thanks to the ideological conscious work of forging personalities, the consequences of mental processes change, adjustements are made to the world of ideas. In the invisible world, details change the nature of the causes and the consequences that pull out of them, which are already reflected in the form of events. However, it is quite possible to modify the past, because the law of entropy crystallises the main stages of the past evolution. The principle of reversibility of processes makes only adjustements to these stages, obscuring negative and potentiating positive (or vice versa) forms of manifestation.

So, in his personal life, a person can correct his past, and this correction occurs in several stages:

1. Creating a picture of the future.
2. The realisation of this future.
3. Finding a connection with the past.
4. Creating a desirable picture in the past.

5. Identification of oneself with the entire arbitrarily constructed line of evolution.

6. Burning out undesireable cliches of the past with spiritual and mental stress, and the result of this is the destruction of the evil caused by the surroundings.

Thus, when a person remakes himself, he partially changes both his karma and the karma of those with whom he is connected or was connected.

Russian Icon of Guardian Angel, signed by V. Meshkov, 1904

The Devil

The Fifteenth Arcanum

" Astral light"

1. Logic
2. Psychic energy
3. Fate (Rock)
Numeric designation: 60
Astrological correspondence: Sagittarius

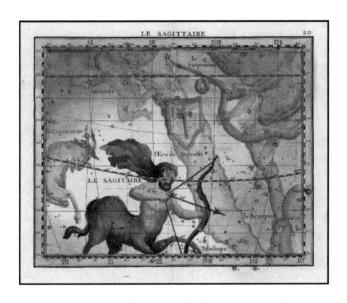

John Flamsteed, La Sagittaire (Sagittarius), 1776

The symbolic picture shows a creature with the figure of a half-man-half-woman and the head of a goat, sitting cross-legged on a cube that rests on an arc symbolising the surface of the Earth. The goat's head of the creature is an inverted pentagram, and a straight pentagram is inscribed on its forehead. There are three flames between the horns, in the form of a symbolic letter of the Hebrew alphabet - Shin. The chest of the creature is female, the hips are male, the legs are with goat hooves. Between the crossed legs is the sign of the Caduceus (a rod entwined with two snakes). The right hand is male and it says "dissolvo" ("dissolution"), the left hand, lowered down, is female, and it says "coagulo" ("coagulation").

In front of the creature are standing, connected by a chain, on the right - a man, on the left-a woman. The man's head is lowered down and the chain covers the burnt neck. The woman's head is raised up, and the chain covers her hips. This symbolic picture is so rich in content that meditation on it can reveal all the secrets of the ideomotor and psychomotor processes, the whole mechanism of action of Psychic energy and the whole mystery of the future title - astral light - refers to those subtle invisible worlds and the energy agent circulating in them, the power over which belongs to the human personality formed in the fourteenth principle.

The power over oneself, developed by the self-discipline mentioned in the fourteenth principle, the anchoring of consciousness in the spiritual realities of the ideal, gives power over the objective energy forces of the Subtle Worlds of the Earth. The development of the latter is the next task of the self-forging personality, for the transformation of the earthly material is the mission of humanity.

A man and a woman connected by a chain show the state of humanity in which it is in an unconscious blind submission to the psychic flow of the Earth, being only its enslaved conductor. The three fires between the horns of the goat's head show the state that can be achieved by a person for power over psychic energy, that is, in order, figuratively speaking, to sit between the horns of this goat and ride it along the planned conscious path. The whole androgynous character of the figure indicates the need to develop a psychic androgyne in order to be a complete person, because only a complete person can consciously own both streams of Psychic energy of the astral world of the Earth. So, in addition to being fixed in the Spiritual World and power over one's own mental-astral composition, it is necessary to psychically combine both sexes in oneself.

The picture symbolises the method of developing a similar androgyne in oneself, corresponding to the one that, in its synthesis, represented the mental-psychic essence of the Earth. The crossing of the legs of the figure, as well as the intertwining of the serpents of the Caduceus, indicate: the first is the intersection of the male and female lines in the general psychic construction of the Subtle Worlds, and the second, as if in the first, is the intersection of the psychic flow between the male and female incarnations. So, the right stream - positive - goes to the left, to the negative line, and the left negative is on the right positive (if you look from below up), and both pass through the neutral crossing point, but in different directions.

On the physical plane, we see the activity of men in cultural, state and other construction, that is, in all areas of the manifestation of male discipline. A woman is passive, remains in the shadows and is only an assistant to a man, besides bearing and materialising his seed. In the mental world, a man and a woman are both androgynous, that is, they have both passivity and activity, which means that their mental perception and activity in the emotional world are equally tense, but the directions in the mental-creative field are opposite. In a woman, in the active direction, in the direction of dissolving synthetic thought-creation ("dissolution"), in a man, in the direction of passively bearing thought-creation ("coagulation").

The psychic flow of a woman takes her to the upper floors of the mental region and develops in her especially strongly the upper parts of the mental body, that is, the carrier of ideas that have not yet been formed into a logical process and contain the overtone of spiritual energy. That is why a woman's mental consciousness is religious: in her consciousness, the thread between the spiritual and intellectual worlds is not completely broken.

The psychic flow directs the man to the lower layers of the mental Creative World, in the field of forming ideas into logical processes. But a man cannot draw these ideas from himself, because the separation of his intellectual consciousness from the Spiritual World is deeper than that of a woman, and his consciousness is not only not religious by nature, but is often anti-religious. Therefore, a man can only formalise, combine, systematise and develop spiritual and mental impulses and ideas that have fallen into his consciousness, the source of which is a woman. A man carries the mental seeds given by a woman and implements them in his cultural construction. Therefore, a man gets the strongest source of inspiration from a woman.

Inspiration is the moment of his mental conception, just as sensual ecstasy is the moment of the physical conception of a woman.

The general direction of the flow of "dissolution" determines the role of a woman in a universal task, as an inspirer, educator (for education is the sublimation of psychic material), a comforter, a natural mistress over the flow of Psychic energy, which she will dispose of much more easily than a man. Therefore, the establishment of order in the field of Psychic energy is a completely natural task for a woman. The orientation along the line of "coagulation" determines the role of men in the general cultural structure, as the bearer and the originator of ideological doctrines and systems and the realiser of spiritual values. This orientation defines him as the master on the material plane and the organiser of external forms of life, while the inner life with its subtle psychological relationships depends on the woman.

This is the dependence of the sexes on each other, which is symbolised by two chained figures. A man's head is chained to a woman, that is, the mental construction depends on the general level of female consciousness, Thus, the entire level of fate and the historical development of cultural construction depends on it. That is why during periods of declining consciousness and the loss of a woman's deep religious perception and spirituality, periods of stagnation occur in cultural construction, and men's creativity is expressed in such dark periods of stagnation only in materialistic forms of civilisation. Woman chained to a man by the area of material sources, her physical life depends on the level of consciousness of a man. That is why in the era of coarsening of male materialistic instincts, a woman loses her attachment to family and duty, natural material impulses freeze in her and the manifestation of her material instincts becomes chaotic.

A woman is by nature physically attached to only one man, just as a man can actually be mentally attached to only one woman. Impermanence in both cases is caused by defects in the responsibility of the parties: The spiritual responsibility lies with the woman and the material responsibility lies with the man. Both these principles, spiritual and material, are equally important and valuable, because in order to control the flow of Psychic energy, it is necessary to combine the psychic properties of both sexes in order to ensure the evolution of the construction and life of mankind. It is precisely the separation of these mental qualities and the sharp expression of the sexes that enslave humanity with a rough part of the psychic stream that floods consciousness with material instinct. Overcoming the material instinct frees a person from mental enslavement. This is the meaning of asceticism. But the path of asceticism, if it is violent, rarely leads to the desired results, while the development of complementary qualities refines consciousness, which, in turn, spiritualises the material instinct and frees it from it.

A man needs to acquire the contact with the Spiritual World that the best representatives of the female sex have. "In order to reach the Spiritual World, everyone must temporarily become a woman," says the ancient wisdom. This will reveal the principle of the Heart in a man, and this principle gives, in addition to spiritual contact, a wise knowledge of mental relationships.

To achieve the state of the whole, a woman must acquire the ability to formulate and develop her spiritual ideas into a religious and philosophical system, that is, to learn logic, as well as independence, responsibility, creative manifestations on the plane of material construction.

Of course, it is extremely difficult to achieve a complete androgyny, and when creating such a human type, the male and female traits will correspond to the physical sexes for a long time. But about the Initiates it is impossible to say whether it is a man or a woman, except for their physical shell, because they represent the type of a complete person - hence their poise and sensual calmness.

In this process, a person falls on the middle line between the streams of "dissolution" and "coagulation", and the flow of psychic energy itself pushes him into the Spiritual World. Thus, the sublimation of the personality in its parts of the mental, astral and etheric bodies, the expansion and growth of the ideal, respectively, with the growth of consciousness and the development of the psychic androgyne, transfers human consciousness to the Spiritual World, which is the source of all mental creativity and mental processes. There, a person will gain the opportunity to light a third fire in the mental plane, connecting the Mental World with the Spiritual.

The process of "coagulation" arises from the creative fire, that is, from the ability to strain thought-creation downwards when using differentiating deduction. The process of "dissolution" is born out of the dissolving fire, that is, the tension of synthesising thought-creation with the help of integrating induction.

The third fire is the fire that protects this tension, the gift of vision, synthetic target coverage with penetration into the essence of each particular. This is, as it were, the coverage of phenomena in their static form with the identification of their eternal essence, in which they are rooted.

The kindling of the guarding fire awakens a specific service to eternity and the ability to recognise eternal moments in the phenomena of life. Awareness lives neither in the past nor in the future, but as if in the eternally present. Of course, only such a consciousness is open to all the ways of the mental-creative world and the ways of the process of realising mental values in the world of the manifestation of psychic energies, that is, only such a consciousness can completely in its balance of the "three fires" master the ideomotor and psychomotor processes of earth construction. This is called "sitting on the head of Baphomet" (this is the name of the psychic flow formula given by the

Templars). The general flow of Psychic energy circulating around the Earth closes it into an energy circle, from which it is difficult for consciousness to break into the Spiritual World. Psychic energy is also called "Materia Lucida", that is, a luminous substance that is in constant spiral motion. Hence the general name of the principle that introduces us to the knowledge of the action of psychic energy - "Astral light". To private astral forces: a general order sent from the Spiritual World, introducing its own vibrations into it, is already distributed among its individual carriers. The most powerful orders are those given to the synthetic personifying essence of the psychic stream, that is, to Baphomet.

In its mental part, Psychic energy forms a world of ideological currents and this world of ideas obeys only a positive, that is, an idealistic pentagram order, which is indicated by a straight pentagram on the forehead of Baphomet. It is important to introduce a clearly outlined synthetic thought image of the ideal by creating an abstract representation of spiritual value. The ideomotor process then occurs by itself according to the logical law of deduction of mental currents of psychic energy. Mental consequences in the form of individual ideas are themselves generated in these intellectual currents and are captured by the correspondingly tuned human consciousnesses that develop and implement them. Of course, the giver of this new mental impulse should have an abstract overview over the actions performed, and specific performances should not be of interest to him, because they depend on individual karmas.

This Psychic energy is unconscious and does not have its own specific purposeful orientation, but acts only causally, according to the mental impulses given to it. This energy is subject only to the one who created a pentagram from his mental body, who came out of the sphere of its influence with his consciousness. The individualised forces, that is, the beings of the astral world, obey only orders, and all the energy in the aggregate can obey the powerful spiritual orders of the mental pentagram that has grown into the Spiritual World. Therefore, there is no need for a high consciousness to persuade astral beings and give orders With such an action, the account of the psychomotor process of realising the spiritual push given should not be missed. After all, this spiritual wave push is aimed at causing a new event, that is, to make a change in the direction of the currents of the psychic flow of the Earth. Therefore, it is necessary to know not only the law of the logic of the development of ideas, but also the law of the person who implements the energy process. This energy process is sharply polar, which means that every order given to Psychic energy causes flows of "dissolution" and "coagulation" in it. It is necessary to know where and how to direct these flows with your concentration. In addition, it is necessary to take into account the law of the intersection of these two streams, to understand that the mental part of the psychic energy in the emotional-psychic world is mirrored, and the processes of the psychic world are again mirrored on the physical plane.

As a hint of the mirroring of these reflections, we will say that changes in vibrations in the highest spiritual planes of the earth's atmosphere cause changes in the most condensed layers of Psychic energy, that is, in what we call negative astral currents or "hell". And that, in turn, strains the activity of the Higher Natural Spirits, which are sent to the etheric body of a person an impulse straining the earthly will, expressed by anxiety and a vague search for new ways. As a result, the overall effect of the highest impulse on coverage has a wide impact on the human masses. It is intense in action and appeals to the etheric body of the people, in which the germ of the will is enclosed, giving the astral and mental bodies the independence of searching for them. Less high spiritual impulses appeal to the astral and mental bodies of people, and the scope is more limited and the intensity of tension is less, but the ideals are more concrete.

This process gives a mirror image of the vertices of the creative triangles. The mirror reflection of the corners of their base is clear from the described crossing and reflection on different planes of the floors, because with the reflections of the line, the pluses go to the side of the minuses and back. This also explains why positive mental impulses cause a contradiction and tension of negative impulses in the environment, which must not only be taken into account, but also saddled, that is, be able to cope with them.

What has been explained here for a large action is also suitable for small private actions. The general rule of action of mastering the ideomotor and psychomotor processes is as follows: to be able to create a strong relief representation and image of the conditional and give a volitional order to the corresponding mental current that implements it. Of course, before giving such an order, it is necessary to get acquainted, up to the feeling of such, with the force that you subordinate to yourself.

The general picture is as follows: a person creates a representation inside his consciousness, imbued with the life of his mental energy, and objectifies this picture, that is, throws it from his mental body into the mental flow of the psychic earth stream. At the same time, he acts with his will on the Psychic Energy, which rushes to the created representation and spirals around it as if around its axis. In the upper parts of this spiral, an ideomotor process of differentiation of the general representation into the thought images arising from it occurs. Further, being saturated with the emotional vibrations of the environment, a picture of realisation is created. And then there is the realisation of the thought image in the minds of other people, if the representation related to human construction, or through an order to natural forces, if the representation related to the construction of nature.

The latter operation is more difficult, because in the final stage it deals with more extraneous consciousnesses for a person, with which it is necessary to first come into contact. But this last process can even create living material forms.

Such ideomotor and psychomotor processes are called the twisting of the astral vortex, because they create a new axis around which Psychic energy unfolds new spirals.

The totality of such astral vortices unfolds in the historical development of the planet and humanity, determining their common Fate.

Since the forces of nature act only on the basis of the orders of the pentagram from the Spiritual World, since most of humanity does not even have a glimpse of conscious spiritual mental creativity, the pentagram of the mental body and the full axis directed to the Spiritual World of the will, then the totality of karma humanity is certainly such a fate for a person, that is, the law of causality acting outside, and the dynamic cycles of this causality are connected not by conscious volitional efforts, but are connected:

- firstly, through chaotic emotions and fragments of thought spirals, somehow forming into mental and psychic power centres, then acting on human consciousness from the outside;
- secondly, by conscious thought-creation and conscious formation of astral vortices created by the leaders of humanity, which act on the human consciousness from the outside; - thirdly, by the conscious creation of distorted ideas, and therefore by the twisting of destructive psychic vortices directed to evil wills, again acting on the human mass from the outside.

Therefore, most people are the plaything of fate, that is, of all these active forces. And it is possible to overcome this fate only by searching for a way out to the Spirit.

Psychic energy is equally submissive to both positive and negative thought-creating impulses, because its mental currents are not pentagrammic and formless, and therefore do not have an individualised consciousness. This symbolically means the goat's head of Baphomet, that is, a pentagram turned down, only implementing other people's orders. But the evil will, brought up by discipline to the tension of black-magic power, to an independent it is not capable of thought-creation, because the consciousness that represents it does not penetrate into the Spiritual World and does not master the spiritual impulse of ideological creativity. Black magic thought-creation is reduced to the distortion of positive ideas by improper coordination of its component parts (and it creates itself).

The next part of the process takes place according to the same method as in white magic, but the motives of the will directed to evil, and therefore the created astral vortex, act corruptively on human consciousness and destructively on human natural construction. But the very will of the magician, directed at lies (misconceptions) and destruction, begins to have a destructive effect on the consciousness and personality of the black magician, and the destruction of consciousness and personality weakens the will and mentally subordinates the composition of the black magician to fate. This means that from being the master of psychic energy, the black magician gradually becomes its slave and an involuntary unconscious conductor of the destructive vortices caused by him. The same can be said about someone who partially masters the currents of Psychic energies, wrapping his egoistic desires in their small whirlwinds. In the end, he becomes only the conductor of these whirlwinds and the final slave of the passions and desires caused by him.

In conclusion, we will avenge the role of the historical involution of the fifteenth Principle in the human consciousness. The image of the fifteenth principle was located in the assembly hall of the Templar Order and was provided to the meditation of its members to study the law of ideomotor and psychomotor processes and the rules for twisting the astral vortex. At the trial of the Templars at the beginning of the thirteenth century, this fact was put forward as one of the main charges against the order and its members. The figure of Baphomet was interpreted as an image of the devil, and the fact of her presence in the assembly hall was interpreted as a substantial proof of devil-worship. Since the Templar trial was not conducted behind closed doors, the representation of the devil in the form of a goat spread and became popular. And the Templar expression "to ride on

Baphomet", that is, the ability to give orders and swirl vortices of Psychic energy, degraded in the mass consciousness into the idea of going to the sabbath to worship a goat-like Devil.

The fifteenth Principle corresponds to the sixth and speaks of the Will, shows the unfolding of the specific human will, enclosed in the etheric body and primarily manifested by passions and temperament as a measure of its tension. This will, when striving upward, grows into the psychic and mental world, grouping psychic and mental spirals around itself, and is carried out by them to the spiritual plane.

The human will directed to the Spiritual world is the so-called "axis of Baphomet", through which the human consciousness "sits on his head", having developed a pentagram from his mental body, the upper three rays of which relate to the spiritual Mind (Higher Manas), the lower two - to the earthly mind (small Manas), and the centre - to the subjective individual Ideal. The two horns of Baphomet symbolise the lesser Manas, separated from the Higher Manas and therefore involutive, and, consequently, led to the degradation of human thought-creation.

The mechanism of the created vortices is as follows: with each mental concentration, the human will is mentally transferred along the axis to the mental world and feeds the created representation with the "power of the lower", that is, the power drawn from the etheric body and strengthened by the vortex of Psychic energies directed upwards. This force, as it were, is rolled up in the mental body into a charge, which then, when the representation is thrown out of the mental body into the environment, is again deployed - it fits into the axis of volitional influence directed downward, that is, towards realisation.

Around this axis, the spiral of psychic energy is again twisted, turning into a materialisation energy. The stability of the axis of realisation and the force of action depends on the strength of the concentration of the will on the representation, that is, on the intensity of the mental will charge. This is the secret of creating psychic (astral) tornadoes. And the strength of the vortex depends on the strength of these tornadoes, which then, as a result, are created by the environment that has perceived the created thought image and the mental order contained in it.

The Tower

The Sixteenth Arcanum

"Coercion"

Logical exception
Mental tension
Physical destruction
Numeric designation: 70
Astrological correspondence: Capricorn

John Flamsteed, Le_Capricorne, et Le Verseau (Capricorn & Aquarius), 1776

The symbolic picture depicts a collapsing tower, which was struck by lightning. Two people fall from the top of the tower: one with a crown, and the other without it.

The sixteenth, seventeenth and eighteenth Principles are the consequences of the action of the fifteenth Principle and first the negative consequences are taken into account (the Sixteenth Principle), because these negative consequences are revealed in the spiritual life earlier than the positive consequences (the seventeenth Principle).

The general account of both, their synthesis and a general overview of the mental psychic evolution of the Earth are revealed by the eighteenth Principle (Earth Initiation).
The consequence of the breakdown of human consciousness, expressed in the self-interest of the earthly "I" was the

introduction of incorrect, distorted vibrations into the general psychic flow flowing down to Earth. The construction of incorrect representations about the relationship between the worlds about the forces acting in them, as well as about their tasks, filled the psychic world with distorted pictures, grimaces at reality, and individualised psychic forces into ugly formations.

Through the efforts of the Helpers of Humanity, the Guiding Spirits of its karma and the Spirits of Nature, these negative psychic formations were localised in the lower layers of the earthly astral, thus clearing its finer layers. These "basements of the astral world", inhabited by semi-conscious demonic beings, filled with ugly pictures and negative manifestations of the astral system, inevitably get excited by the use of the mechanism of the Fifteenth Principle and the creation of psychic tornadoes, which are consciously or unconsciously, that is, more or less intensively, used in every volitional manifestation of a person.

In these lower layers, all the negative karma of humanity is accumulated, all the burden that humanity drags behind it in its evolutionary development, as a result of its separation from the Spiritual World. These lower layers of the astral, located in the immediate vicinity of the material world, of course, are the first to resonate for the creation of new force fields and new evolutionary pushes. And they resonate hostility and negative to everything that surpasses the general human psyche to overcome them. The negative karma of humanity tries not to let it go to the next stage.

Thus, the volitional shocks created by the fifteenth Principle, first of all strain the negative karma of humanity, which pours out positively at first. Therefore, each volitional action first causes negative consequences in the environment, the elimination and overcoming of which clears the way for new opportunities. It is the existence and accumulation of this negative karma that prevents the smooth evolution of humanity. Each stage of its development leaves not only positive, but also negative remnants, which, straining and protesting against new opportunities, introduce an element of destruction. Thus, the principle of evolutionary development for external humanity is replaced by the principle of revolutionary leaps. This is also facilitated by the lack of plasticity of mental and physical materials.

Too dense materialisation of earthly matter inclines the human psyche to inertia, because human consciousness is tied to earthly forms. These forms, having lost their plasticity, instead of being transformed, are destroyed in order to arise in a new form. The human consciousness attached to them protests against this process, which is manifested in it by conservatism, which testifies to the inertia (Tamas) of the human psyche and forms a whole world of old habits in the lower astral plane. Therefore, each application of the fifteenth Principle is associated with a certain compulsion applied to the psychic world of the environment in the name of detaching it from old habits and dynamising new manifestations. This compulsion makes it necessary, in addition to creating positive ideas, to build a threatening idea of the real danger of stagnation, and consequently, decomposition, which will inevitably appear if a new mental-psychic vortex is not accepted. Every large or small psychic action on Earth to a greater or lesser extent has this character of compulsion, for which the operator assumes responsibility.

The general form of such coercion is as follows: "It will be as I find it necessary in my conscience and, if the environment resists, then I claim from experience and knowledge that there will be a threat of disaster." For more specific applications of the fifteenth Principle, the sixteenth Principle is formulated as follows: "Either the cliche I create is realised, or I perform actions that are unpleasant to the astral world." In most cases, the second part is reduced to a passive threat, that is, a refusal to produce something that is necessary in the complex of astral construction.

We must remember that the Psychic energy of the Earth obeys only an order and the commanding person must have a threatening weapon in his hands precisely because of the inertia of the earthly material, as well as due to the presence of "cellars" of the astral world. The operator can threaten these cellars of the astral world even more intensely, drawing pictures of all sorts of troubles and catastrophes.

It is because of the created earthly conditions that it is never possible to use all the material for new construction. The higher the operator's consciousness, the wider his dynamic coverage of this material, the more he can transform and use the created vortex. Of course, it is better if it transforms and sublimates the maximum of the recyclable material. But there will always be 'leftover'. The conservatism of human consciousness and the conservatism of earthly nature create those elements that cannot accept a new idea, a worldview resulting from it and new combinations of psychic forces. Therefore, the logical process that results in the mental world of the Earth and new ideological systems and worldviews that serve as the foundation for the milestones of the next evolutionary stages, always entail the logical exclusion of old ideological formations. These excluded ideological elements have their own psychic carriers in the image of human personalities committed to them. It is to these individuals that coercion is applied as threats to their sense of self-preservation, by creating pictures of dangers. If not out of conscience, then out of fear they become servants of the new construction. Among them, however, are also those who are not affected by threats. Their psyche is hostile to new formations. A common protest against the new unites them into opposition, and by collective efforts they unconsciously or consciously form a vortex of protest in the psychic atmosphere of the Earth. An astral tension is created between the old and new worlds. This astral struggle on the physical plane is poured out by wars, revolutions, cultural destruction, because by attacking a new cultural stage, the opposition destroys cultural achievements in general, that is, themselves. This struggle is necessary to clear the paths of human development from the old accumulations and remnants of those ideologies that the construction has outgrown.

Since man is the master of Psychic energies and the source of psychic nutrition of all earthly nature, the psychic struggle in the astral of the Earth also affects nature. The magnetic currents of the Earth change their direction: There is also a struggle in them. Changes in the direction of magnetic currents change the position of the earth's axis and a change in the position of the earth's axis entails geological disasters. Thus, astral tension also causes physical catastrophe. The lightning of a new mental thought-creation, striking the top of the ossified tower of the earthly world, shakes it to the ground, introducing new vibrations into the floors of the psychic world and into psychic nature itself. And the first to fall from the top of the tower is the "crowned one", that is, the old, outdated worldview that reigned over everyday life and, following it, the "uncrowned one", that is, the old forms and conditions of everyday life itself.

What applies to this broad picture of the new cultural construction applies to every private operation. Each time, by a concentrated representation of the desired goal, a person brings to life the manifestation of opposite ideas, which leads to resistance of the waves of the psychic flow. And a person should always take into account this resistance and find a way to influence or threaten. Therefore, if a person wants to achieve any realisations through the use of Psychic energy, then he must upset the resistance. At the same time, the awareness of the inevitability of defeat helps to set him up in a more balanced way and allows him to dominate his own emotions, which are easily strained with the intensity of desire to the point of enslaving the will of a person and shaking the pentagram of his mental body. The general development of human life, the development of the cognitive abilities of mankind and the corresponding cultural construction, taking into account the breakdown of human consciousness and the oblivion of the general evolutionary plan, goes according to the programme of the sixteenth Principle. The helpers of humanity and the guides of their construction, that is, the best consciousnesses among people, knowing the general plan of human evolution and its ultimate goal, force the flow of spiritual Psychic energy to perceive new stages of evolution and to the corresponding restructuring of the human psyche with their thought-work. This affects the consciousness of the masses, who - for the most part - reside only on the etheric plane. Compulsions to the application of new ideals exclude the possibility of horizontal sprawl, mental and psychic, from the roots of old ideals, leaving each time only their main trunk in the form of the law of continuity.

The human psyche is excessively crystallised and insufficiently flexible for evolutionary transformation, and therefore the cultural construction of each epoch is condemned to death and destruction, because the leaders of consciousness cannot completely pass into the next stage of development. It is conservatism, that is, attachment to the old forms, that causes the need for revolutions.

The common task of humanity is the knowledge of God and the development of its guides in the name of cultural creativity on Earth, that is, the realisation of the Common Good - an objective task - which accompanies the subjective one. Its general formula is: "transformation of the earth / of the material and its individualisation in its own vehicles around the axis directed to the Spirit of the will." Let us recall that the vital energy manifests on Earth on four planes or in four worlds, forming four stages of the development of human consciousness and therefore four earthly human bodies. There are seven forms of consciousness, taking into account the force directions flowing through these four planes of consciousness, and the lowest plane, the nadir point (the path of turning in the lower world), has only one form of consciousness.

The Evolutionary Cycle

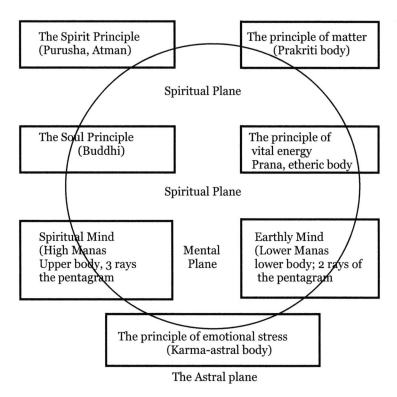

Figure 59

Humanity lives in potency on all four planes of consciousness and has potentially all seven forms of consciousness and the bodies that embody them. But these bodies and their associated cognitive construction tasks develop over time, and for the above reasons, these seven main stages of development are accompanied by mental and physical revolutions and geological upheavals during their shifts. These main seven tasks correspond to the main seven races that determine the history of human development, and each race in the epoch of its life and its construction will develop in humanity one form of consciousness corresponding to it and expresses it in the general tone of the culture of its epoch.

The construction begins with the spiritual plane and ends with the same spiritual plane, describing the circle of human evolution on Earth. Moreover, the first half of the circle refers to the objective construction of its earthly guides, that is, to the forging of the earthly human personality. The nadir point, as the end of the spiritual incarnation of immortal human individualities into the creation of the body, and the second half of the circle refer to the gradual subjective identification of the threefold human individuality of all forces in these created earthly vehicles.

It has already been mentioned in the seventh Principle that the spiritual core of human consciousness is reflected in its earthly composition by the physical body (according to the law of reverse reflections of the sixteenth Principle). This means that the matter of the Earth can be rebuilt and individualised only by spiritual consciousness, Therefore, power over matter is the most difficult achievement on the path of Initiation. The principle of Prana or Vital energy, which creates the human body, reflects the first shell of the Soul or the principle of Buddhi. Both of them establish a spiritual plane. The principle of Reason is reflected in the organ of its earthly manifestation (mind) and together with it forms a mental plane. The Kama principle, which unfolds into the world of emotional tensions or into what we call the psychic world, creates the astral body of a person, which is actually the ultimate point of his individualisation and the turning point of the circle of his development.

The first Race, highly spiritualised, whose consciousness was still in a potential state and not revealed in cognitive or creative activity, had the task of individualising the matter of the Earth into organs and tissues of the body. Possessing only spiritual consciousness, this race did not have a subjective inner gender. Reason, feeling and will were still merged in consciousness, which was like a blind conductor of the primary spiritual impulse. The matter of the Earth was at that time in a much finer state and the spirits of the people of the first race only touched it, leaving their imprints, which served as an impetus for the formation of physical bodies, which were henceforth connected by a power thread with these spirits. The bodies were precisely objective impressions and instruments of action on the matter of the Earth.

It should also be noted that in the era of the existence of the first, as well as the second race, there could be no question of a breakdown of consciousness, that is, of what we call the fall from grace, because consciousness was firmly rooted in the spiritual, and Reason was still absent in it. Thus, there was no self-activity of the world.

From this Spiritual World, the created earthly objects were perceived only as objective tools for future self-manifestation and construction on Earth. Therefore, the transition from the first to the second race was not accompanied by the phenomena described in the sixth Arcana, and the created shells were not plastic, capable of transformations and immortal.

The second Race arose directly from the first, that is, in the fulfilment of its first task - the creation of its earthly shells - humanity passed directly to the fulfilment of the second task - the creation of etheric bodies and the individualisation of the flow of the Life Force of the Earth and its embodiment in material forms. This made the principle of Buddhi tense up and manifest spiritual consciousness with the wisdom of direct perception of the laws operating in the Cosmos of vital forces and direct domination over them.

The second race created a closer contact of the earthly manifestation with the soul. At the same time, the second race individualised the etheric energy of the Earth, that is, it "gave a name" to the vegetable kingdom, just as the first "gave a name" to the mineral kingdom. Let's not forget that a word is a formula that groups the vibrations of creative power in a certain way. As long as the material of the Earth was thin, as long as it was under the jurisdiction of human consciousness and not subject to processing of the so-called spiritual nature, man directly reorganised it by creating and internally pronouncing such formulas-names. All creativity in the universe happens in this way. The second race has already become an androgynous race, that is, each representative of the race has already carried the beginnings of a sexual dual-command, which means that from the general synthesis of the Will, Mind and Heart, the Heart and Mind were rudimentally polarised, and the Will became their synthesis.

The will belongs to the first race, the Heart to the second, Mind to the development of the next task.

The second race, which, like the first, did not know Death, smoothly passed into the Third Race, that is, the spiritual consciousness of humanity strained its Higher Manas and created from it an earthly reflection of the lower Manas or the earthly mind, which is already able to orient itself in the surrounding environment and create a conscious worldview, world attitude and peace-building.

The abilities of the earthly mind are as follows: a clear understanding of earthly objects and the ability to combine them for a planned, expedient construction that reflects in the earthly materials the world of ideas contained in the Great Manas and created there.

In the third race, a type of complete man was created, who individualised the mental flow of the Earth in his consciousness and "gave a name" to its then carriers – the animals - thereby creating external forms for revealing the mental energy of the Earth. Thus, the mental plane was established and the mental body of a person was created. It remained only to individualise the Psychic Energy, that is, to create a dynamic focus of power tensions from each person and, by mastering the psychic flow of the Earth, to dynamise the general tension of the created conductors, that is, to create an emotional shell. Then, in the middle of the third race, tragedy occurred, the consequences of which are still affecting today. The reasons for it were stated, we will only note that the gap occurred between the Higher Manas and the earthly part of the human mental body and in the Formational World, that is, in the world where the lower Manas began to form earthly materials in its likeness. This break of consciousness or fall from grace can be called the loss of idealism and its replacement with materialism. Sex in the third race was already expressed in etheric bodies, and the exchange of sexes took place on the etheric and mental planes.

With the breakdown of consciousness the division of the sexes has already reached the material bodies, that is, something happened that should not have happened, because matter, reflecting the spirit, should remain one. This caused a coarsening: Impulses that arose during the division of material bodies into floors created chaos. During the separation in physical bodies, the sexes lost their additional halves in space and time. Identification with earthly personalities led to the oblivion of spiritual tasks. The intervention of the Spirits, who put the matter of the Earth in order, but condensed it, brought the phenomenon of the death of physical bodies. Attachment to material forms has deprived the mental and etheric bodies of plasticity. From this moment on, the sixteenth Principle comes into force in the cultural development of mankind, instead of the seventh Principle and the transition to the next race has all the characteristic features of its application.

The third race has already left material traces of itself that belonged to the second half of its existence, such as buildings and statues on Easter Island and giant statues in the Hindu Kush and its distant ancestors - the aborigines of Polynesia and Australia, the remnants of the Lemurian continent that died in the geological catastrophe that accompanied the change of the third race of the fourth - have also been preserved to this day.

The formation of the Fourth Race has already taken place with the help of the Higher Consciousnesses of the Helpers of humanity. Another third race was divided into alternating sub-races. From the fourth sub-race, which developed the reflection of the fourth Principle in the third Principle, the implementation of which was the task of the third race, the fourth was created with the help of spiritual leaders who synthesised the entire task of the second race in his consciousness. These spiritual leaders, as if laying the potential for their development and construction in the new races, are called "Manu" in Sanskrit - the symbolic name of a person who has preserved in integrity the pentagram of the mental body – Manas, that is - and therefore the Lord and Creator on Earth.

The task of the fourth race was the individualisation of Psychic energy by realising the emotional world and creating its power vortices around the axis of one's consciousness. The individualisation of the psychic flow and the creation of personal individual worlds is the limit of the process of individualisation of humanity, because it determines the world attitude of each person to the environment, as a Subject in the earthly manifestation to the Object.

It is the emotional world, consisting of power vortices, which protects the personality from the environment and creates its resistance, protecting it from dissolving into the general mental flow. The realisation of this task in the cognitive and construction aspects did not go smoothly, despite the spiritual help provided to humanity. The breakdown of human consciousness and its consequences prevented a smooth transition to the fifth race.

The fourth race has left many monuments about itself and many more nationalities belong to it, developing along with the peoples of the fifth race. The fourth race is known under the general name of the Atlanteans, and the then formation of the continents - under the name of Atlantis.

The third sub-race inhabits the African continent.

The fourth sub-race of the fourth race died relatively recently - in the era of the conquest of America by the Spaniards.

The sixth and seventh sub-races of the fourth race, as reflecting those principles, the full realisation of which has not yet come in time, developed further along with the fifth race (China-Tibet).

The fifth Race, after the catastrophe of Atlantis, was formed from the fifth sub-race of the fourth race, called "the sons of Yoga and Will" and in the historical aspect - the Celts, under the leadership of Manu, known as Rama or Yanma. The fifth race travelled from west to east and finally settled in Hindustan, which became a hotbed for spiritual forging, building from the basic ideals, and its further expansion. From here, it began to move west again, settling South Asia (Iran), Europe, and then America.

Like the fourth race, the fifth race is divided into seven sub-races, each sub-race into seven nationalities. The first subrace is the Hindus, the second is the Iranians, the third is the Greeks and Romans, the fourth is the Romance peoples, the fifth is the Germanic, the sixth is developing in Russia and in North America, the seventh is in South America.

The task of the fifth race is the individualisation of the Higher Manas, that is, the Mind. This task is especially expressed in the fifth sub-race, which is the centre of the fifth race. The slogan of the fifth race is Everything by measure, number and weight; its method is the creation of independent worldviews and an individual attitude to the main ideal of humanity - the search for Truth. Therefore, the Helpers of humanity only invisibly help people of the fifth race, leaving each of them to develop their own world of ideas and concepts about God, the Universe and themselves, and only occasionally remind them of the need for spiritual memory.

The breakdown of human consciousness is most pronounced in the sixth race, because it happened by breaking the connection between the Higher and lower Manas. This breakdown of consciousness is illustrated by all the images, the ugly philosophical stories that the fifth sub-race of the fifth race gave birth to. Misconceptions, which are the postulates of philosophical teachings, were expressed in all sorts of shades of materialistic and political schools and poisoned the consciousness of Europeans, closing them with scepticism and doubt from the perception of the values of the higher spiritual mind, that is, ideals. Therefore, the main task of the fifth race is to restore the connection between the spiritual mind and the earthly mind, that is, to eliminate the breakdown of consciousness. This task should be performed by the fifth sub-race, the carrier of the reflections of the beginning of Buddhi in Manas, which makes it possible for direct spiritual perception. From the sixth sub-race, the next sixth race will develop, eliminating the material division into gender through changing and improving the differentiation of the sexes.

The seventh subrace of the fifth race is still in an embryonic state and will develop along with the subraces of the sixth race.

Each race develops under the particularly strong influence of one of the planets of our system, because it develops on Earth some of the seven principles, the representative of which in the Solar system is one of the planets.

Thus, the first race, according to its task, developed under the sign of Saturn - the carrier of the principle of matter in the system. The second race is under the sign of Jupiter, the carrier of the etheric principle of Prana. The third is under the sign of the now-disappeared broken planet, whose functions are partly taken by the Moon, partly by Mars and which was the carrier of the small Manas, the carrier tasks that have now passed to the Earth. The fourth race developed under the sign of Mars - the carrier of the emotional principle. The fifth race will develop under the sign of Venus, and in the Initiatory Schools of the fifth race it is said that the planet Venus is now adapted to the Earth and the High Consciousnesses developing on it are especially actively helping humanity, sometimes incarnating on the planet Earth. The White Brotherhood of the Himalayas counts among its members - Adepts of the Highest Initiations - a considerable number of these Venusians who have come to us. The sixth race will be under the protection of Mercury, the bearer of the principle of Buddhi. The seventh race is directly under the protection of the Sun, the carrier of the Atman principle.

Thus, the planets have tasks and missions in relation to the Earth. The minds inhabiting them help earthlings in building the next cultural epochs of their development.

The earth in its historical development also already has several phases of existence, recorded in the four kingdoms of nature. The listed human races historically develop only in one of its phases, namely in the fourth phase. The first phase, or the first circle, of the Earth refers to the stage of forging the mineral kingdom, that is, the strongholds of the material foundations of its existence. This circle of the Earth passed through the path of Saturn and the consciousnesses inhabiting it were mineral consciousnesses. In the further phase, the etheric body of the Earth was developed under the sign of Jupiter, that is, the Earth passed the stage of Jupiter. The consciousnesses of that period were vegetable consciousnesses. Then the Earth passed through the stage of Mars and the dominant consciousnesses on it, which developed the astral principle, were animal consciousnesses. Then the Earth entered the phase of lunar existence, that is, the development of a mental body, a task that lay on humanity. In

the general evolutionary circle performed by the Earth, humanity in the fourth race and in the fourth sub-race was at the point of the extreme nadir. Just then there was the coming of Christ, who gave an impetus to all. In this way, he overcame the nadir point and gave humanity the opportunity to move from involution to evolution. By the appearance of the fifth race, this nadir was crossed and the ascending line of the second semicircle began, that is, the line of striving from form to spirit. Now the Earth and humanity are following the line of spiritual evolution.
Let us note a small but significant fact: The appearance on Earth during the life of the fifth race of Radium, which introduced mobility and plasticity into the atomic compositions of the Earth's elements.

The Star

The Seventeenth Arcanum

Natural peace

Hope
Intuition
Signs of Nature
Numerical designation: 80
Astrological correspondence: Mercury

Mercurius Planetenmaskers

The symbolic picture of the Arcanum depicts a naked girl surrounded by stars, bending over the Earth, which she waters from a jug. In front of her is a desert, behind her is a blooming plain, over which butterflies flutter.

The Seventeenth Principle establishes and takes into account the positive consequences of the application of the fifteenth Principle. The Seventeenth Principle describes the era of the deployment of the new world after the collapse of the old one, the development of new opportunities after overcoming the resistance of the old ones. The general process of the emergence of new opportunities is as follows: Conservatism, attachment to old forms and the world of created habitual manifestations form a stage of consciousness called tamas or inertia. The application of the fifteenth Principle sets this world in motion and replaces the property (guna) of tamas with the property (guna) of rajas, that is, the dynamics of incessant transformation. From the struggle of Tamas and Rajas a new stable world is being developed, and the elements of the new construction are fixed again by the property of tamas, which binds consciousness to new forms, which ensures their detailed development. The result of this struggle is a new property of consciousness that forces it to stand above this struggle and gives it the opportunity to supervise both forces. Consciousness acquires the property of "sattva", or rest in motion. This peace is in motion and the result is the achievement of wisdom each time at the next level of knowledge, because wisdom is the ability to monitor phenomena and acting forces and the ability to regulate them. After the turbulent sixteenth Principle, the epoch of the seventeenth Principle begins and the new construction, after overcoming the revolutionary stage, enters the evolutionary stage, that is, transforms its dynamics into the general process of natural development.

The same applies to special cases of the application of the fifteenth and sixteenth Principles. It is in them that the changes that a person makes to his personal destiny or to the close circle of his personal relationships occur after the stage of struggle, fixing his victory with the natural development of the created new opportunities. The axis of this development becomes a special experience of a calmed and wise will, called Hope. Hope is knowledge of the goal and confidence in the correct application of the law of expediency, steadily leading to the realisation of the intended goal. Without hope, no building of knowledge is possible, because the absence of hope also shows the absence of the will, the expression of which it is.

After the breakdown of consciousness and the acquisition of a fulcrum (instead of a suspension point), the will of a person curled up in the etheric body and from there directed the axis of his personality to the Higher Worlds. Hope - the very spring of this will - is at the same time a memory of the past stages passed, before the breakdown of consciousness, when the will was rolled up in the spiritual core of a person and directed down to the unfolding in new forms of his potential possibilities. That is why the hope of modern humanity always flares up with an objective reminder of possible achievements and sets the spiral of the coiled will in motion with an internal push, which awakens in her memories of the stages she passed earlier (before the fall) and directs the will along the power line of the past, which will turn out to be the future of this will, now directed in the opposite direction. After all, every person, being one of the individual foci. Before his fall, man had already fulfilled volitional tasks, that is, he radiated his potential for individual initiative, but after the fall, this power potential curled up in his etheric body, bearing the imprints of his previous manifestations. These former manifestations of a person flare up in him from objective impulses caused by Hope. That is why Hope is so individualistic and in different individuals different objective impulses awaken it and strain the will. These objective impulses in a person striving for Initiation, of course, come from the World of the Spirit and have the character of illumination of the entire consciousness. Basically, the aspirations of humanity are always illuminated by the Hope for the best, although this best is often understood in a distorted and reduced form.

The hope that guides humanity's will to evolve is the illumination of its consciousness by spiritual impulses given to initiates. It is also in vague memories of the "golden age", that is, of the former lost Paradise, which must be reached again. This Hope, which sees the future and recalls the past, is guided in its construction by every cultural epoch, as well as every individual building a private life, looking for better conditions. In the picture, this hope is symbolised by a naked girl, because the virgin will to the spirit, when it awakens, throws off all the shells and growths of earthly desires. The stars surrounding the girl indicate the direction of this will to the ideal, and she also waters the barren sands of the future with her desire for self-manifestation and for the expansion of her achievements in building a new world.

Hope, illuminating the entire human consciousness, opens it up to the perception of new opportunities for self-development and creativity, according to the ideal. This direct perception of the possibilities or spiritual forces that move humanity is called Intuition in the broad sense of the word.

Intuition has two aspects. The first of which is sensory awareness or what is called Faith, because Faith is the direct perception of spiritual values and forces. The organ of this perception is

The heart, or rather, the two corresponding centres in our astral body, expressed by two centres of the nervous system, which are little developed in modern man.

The first of these centres - plexus cardiac - is located in the middle of the chest near the heart itself. It is an organ that catches the spiritual impulses of the future, and through it there is an insight into the future, as well as an insight into Other Worlds, that is, into the area of our future experience. With the help of this centre, we come into contact with We will recognise their powers and correspondences with the lower worlds. Thus, the gift of prophecy appears under the condition of a sensitive and developed plexus cardiac.

The second centre is located in the upper right part of the brain and is connected to the centre of the bell. This is the centre of the cup, accumulating our previous spiritual experience. The degree of insight depends on its development, and consequently, the ability to read the Akasha chronicle in the Subtle World. Readings of those imprints were left in the waves of Psychic energy by the law of entropy by past events and guiding forces that acted at previous stages of human development.

These two centres (the heart and the cup) are closely connected with each other. Insight into the future also directs insight into the past, and the development of the spiritual consciousness of the heart centre depends on the accumulations in the bowl and the heart.

The second aspect of Intuition is creative intuition, called Inspiration, which manifests itself in different areas of human creativity. All the great and valuable works of the human spirit in the fields of scientific, artistic or social construction have always been created thanks to the impulse of creative intuition or inspiration. The centre of this creative intuition is the centre of the bell. Straining, one opens the perception of creativity, the sources of the force, from the cosmic environment, perceives spiritual possibilities waiting for realisation, and then transmits them for registration in earthly conditions to the mental centre corresponding to the throat centre in the nervous system.

And this creativity has two directions with a predominance of orientation to the future. But the introduction of new cliches into this future under the influence of cosmic spiritual impulses modifies the Akashic chronicle along the line of reverse influence in its correspondences. Unused impulses are reawakened from the past to life and begin to influence the present.

Every spiritual creative impulse given to the construction of the future stirs up waves of Psychic energy and the Akashic chronicle imprinted in it, which thanks to these waves comes to life, begins to create new combinations in particulars from the cliches of the past, striving to survive in the present and the future of humanity. Thus, a person, straining spiritual creativity with his thought-creating process, is the ruler not only over the future, but also over the past.

Intuition is the key to all knowledge and to all creativity. A person can find this key by cultivating Hope in himself, as a real spring of his will. That is why hopelessness is death in the spiritual sense, because it cuts off the possibility of connecting with the Spiritual World. That is why hopelessness is the very spring on which forces that are most often hostile to human evolution play.

All knowledge has already been given to humanity and is rolled up in the language of its concepts. But because of the allowed abuses of them, these concepts were crushed and profaned. To ponder these concepts, to find their source and the forces corresponding to them, means to resurrect them and acquire through them the wisdom of the knowledge contained in their formulas. Each concept hides a long history of the thought-creating process of its development and the power spirals of psychic associations associated with it. This is the basis of the magic of words, because when we pronounce a word, we bring ideomotor and psychomotor forces into motion.

Since the concepts expressed in words have changed with each epoch of humanity, the forces contained in words belong to the general synthetic force formation of the corresponding epoch, that is, some kind of egregore of humanity. Egregores in each epoch are not an amorphous formation, but a hierarchical ladder of collective consciousnesses. These collective consciousnesses are created from individual consciousnesses united by one idea and its embodied carrier, which is the centre of the egregore. Such egregores are formed in the higher layers of the Subtle World, around the centre of the spiritual ideal, clothed in a mental form, that is, living on the mental plane.

After the physical death of the main carrier of the ideal and its closest collaborators and contemporaries, the egregore is firmly rooted in the subtle psychic layers and its earthly members are the physical vehicles of its ideal and power life. With the death of the earth chain united by him, the egregore grows and strengthens, but the darkening of consciousness in the earth chain, spiritual blindness only in name of those who are its carriers, but in fact ideologically alien to it, that is, is as treason to the egregore and will deprive it of the possibility of contact with people. This weakens the power of his action and will not give him "nourishment from below". Without receiving a new psychic and etheric force due to the lack of volitional aspiration of people, the egregore leaves the Earth, its shells become thinner, pass into a fiery state that characterises the mental plane, and disappear into the Cosmic Spiritual World. This means the end of the mission of the egregore and its central consciousness and the need for a new spiritual impulse. The egregores are arranged hierarchically, according to a system of peripheries with a central point, depending on the spiritual level and volume of the ideals they are the bearer of, and the central egregore seems to control all the others.

The word, saturated with the spiritual power of the revealed living concept, sets in motion the forces of those egregores, the idea of which this word particularly vividly embodies. The speaker of the word comes into contact with the egregore, and the forces of the latter flow to his aid. All ceremonial magic is based on this fact, using symbolic words and characters associated with the ideals and psychic vortices of the egregore. The magician in his astral operations relies on the mental and psychic forces of the egregore through the utterance of sacramental, that is, symbolic words, and the drawing of symbols and circles.

Such operations are not recommended now, because they limit the operating individual's world attitude and worldview, that is, the Covenant and the task of the fifth race (the techniques of ceremonial magic corresponded to the task and mission of the fourth race). With the development of the Higher Mind, each person himself must resurrect concepts in himself, build representations from them, master the power hidden in the symbol of the concept and, without outside help, at least relying only on the spiritual essence of the Sun, create an ideomotor-psychomotor process. And, of course, at the same time, to be aware of yourself as a person, as a conductor of the spirit and the divine creative force. This means that the intuition of modern humanity should be directed directly to the Search for God, and with the help of Teachers, this intuition should recognise the milestones of such a search.

Reading the Akasha Chronicle, as well as awakening insight into the future at its first stages, requires a fulcrum. It is necessary to focus your attention on some object implemented on the physical in the plan, in order to have a starting point for the development of this ability. After all, every physical object is a link in a long chain of energy or life changes.

The first stage of the awakening of clairvoyance is clairaudience, that is, the ability to perceive objects not statically, as is usually done, but dynamically, restoring with thought the entire process of life development associated with these objects. So, each individual stone can tell us about the process of formation of the Earth and about the chain of geological upheavals. So, each antique item can restore before us is a picture of some historical mission of humanity. After all, the Akashic record is imprinted everywhere in the physical world around us.

The second stage will be a special feeling of this past when coming into contact with objects. This is called clairvoyance. When this stage is reached, the ability to create a passive state in oneself that excludes the personal "I" and its incarnational experience is sufficient to turn into clairvoyance, the ability to perceive pictures of the Akasha-chronicle department associated with physical objects or furniture. And only after reaching this stage is it possible to penetrate into the Akashic chronicle and read its archives in addition to physical objects. But often even experienced consciousnesses in this regard take only a physical object corresponding to their need as a fulcrum and a key that opens the door.

Reading future cliches is also easier, especially at first, with the assistance of physical objects. The fact is that the future is created from the causes generated in the past, but these causes are divided into four planes corresponding to the four worlds. Each of them has its own flow of causalities acting on physical events. While these flows are being realised in human life, they are already imprinted as invisible pictures in the three kingdoms of nature, directing their life. Spiritual causality is imprinted first of all in the Mineral Kingdom. The group consciousnesses of minerals that live on the spiritual plane of the Earth are called angels who create the planet. In relation to them, the mineral composition of the Earth is their final expression and generation, spiritualised by their power.

Therefore, the events of the future, as well as new spiritual impulses entering this future, are imprinted first of all in events and incidents concerning the Mineral Kingdom, and therefore geological processes. The appearance of radium and the increasingly frequent earthquakes over the past century are signs of the beginning of a new era in the life of humanity and the Earth, while humanity itself is still in a state of using the results of past construction. The consciousness of the prophet can determine by these signs the strength of the spiritual impulse, its nature, the general picture of the new era and the timing of its onset.

The impulse of spiritual causalities, penetrating the mental plane, strains the mental causality in it, accelerating its processes. This is imprinted in the Plant Kingdom, whose group consciousnesses live on the mental plane, organising, nourishing and purifying the general stock of mental energy (chitta).

The priests and priestesses of antiquity determined the future within the life of their peoples, as carriers of ideas, by the state of sacred trees and flowers. Divination by animals, especially by their entrails, refers to reading already existing astral cliches. The group souls of animals are on the astral plane and they are already affected by the development, in particular, of the pictures of future events, making their changes and imprints in the animal world. Note here that astral cliches are always more private and differentiated in character than the mental ones, which form a spiritual impulse, as it were, break it into parts. Therefore, the general picture perceived by the prophet is always correct in its general applications.

The mental picture perceived by mental intuition is correct from the point of view of the people or the egregore to which the clairvoyant belongs. The astral picture is correct from the point of view of the soothsayer himself, moreover, his personal relations to events are also imprinted on his divination. So, one soothsayer can consider happiness that another does not consider happiness at all. And besides, the personal interpretation of events often mistakes the plane on which this event should be interpreted. Thus, the prediction is always the more correct, the higher the level of consciousness of the soothsayer. It is possible only from the spiritual plane by the process of creative deduction to establish a correct picture of the future, and a special sense of future correspondences protects from the interference of one's own imagination. But sometimes the psychic waves are already so tense and the events are so close that their pictures penetrate into the undeveloped consciousness, for some reason, harmoniously tuned to these waves. But such predictions are always fragmentary, it is just as easy to make a mistake in the timing of events, because it is difficult to grasp and take into account all karma (because of its many lines).

The events in personal lives are most easily captured with the help of mental contact with the client. But let us note that the signs of the future are like shadows falling into the physical world from approaching events that have already been determined in other worlds, and these shadows are imprinted everywhere on the objects of the physical world. Their discernment and reading depends on the sensitivity of people's intuition.

Astrology also belongs to the same category of reading the signs of nature. The basis of astrology is seen not in the physical world, but in the mental world. That is why attempts to explain the influence of the luminaries by physical relations with the Earth do not lead to anything. By a planet, we must understand not only the materialised world, but the entire sphere of its power influence with all the imprints of its Akasha-chronicle in the Ocean of the Psychic Energy of the Solar System.

The life of the planet with all the events taking place on it occurs during its rotation around the Sun and is imprinted in the psychic waves of the solar system in its orbit. So, by a planet we should understand the sphere of force that it outlines by its rotation around the Sun. Each time she passes by some cliches printed in this sphere, she crunches the forces contained in them to life, and thus their physical vibrations sent into space change. That's why the position of the planet in relation to the Earth always generates other combinations of psychic waves that unfold on the Earth into corresponding facts. In the psychic Earth's atmosphere there are receivers and resonators corresponding to individual planets. They reflect, refract and adapt to the earthly conditions the vibrations of psychic energies coming from the planetary spheres, and these reflected vibrations determine the character and fate of peoples, but also the fate of individual people.

The horoscopes also take into account the movement of the planets, and not only their position at the time of birth, that is, the influence of those planetary parts of the Akasha chronicles, past which these planets will pass, from the moment of a person's birth to his death, will be taken into account. Therefore, according to the fates and characters of people, it is possible to draw up a picture of the planetary Akashic chronicles, if they have sufficient experience and review in this regard and are able to take into account and subtract from the sum of such an earth experience the transformations that the planetary radiation was subjected to in Earth receivers.

Let us also say that the fulfilment by a person of this specific human mission, based on his individualised will, makes a person the master of these planetary influences, which he adapts to the best performance of his tasks and coordinates according to his creative understanding. Therefore, the motto of astrology is:

"The stars incline, but do not compel"

The Moon

The Eighteenth Arcanum

Reflected light

The Occult hierarchy
Occult obstacles
Occult enemies
Numeric designation: 90
Astrological correspondence: Aquarius

Bonatti, Aquarius

The symbolic picture depicts the road. On either side of the road are sitting a dog on the right, a wolf on the left, both howling at the moon. This road begins with a pool of blood, to which Cancer the crab is backing away. And at the end of the road, on both sides of it, you can see truncated pyramids, through which light streams from above.

The Hieroglyph of this principle is also interesting, depicting a roof that symbolises the really existing roof under which the life of the Earth passes. This is the crystal layer of the stratosphere, which does not allow cosmic vibrations and energy layers, or partitions, in the etheric, astral and mental worlds of the Earth to pass to the Earth of a certain order, which separated these worlds and therefore divided into layers a single stream of earthly creative force. The numerical value of this Principle with this roof gives an idea of what Initiation has become for earthly humanity in its current state.

Cognition (actions) of the creative force and mastering it is given with great difficulties because of the partitions created between the worlds. The purpose of the Initiation has changed accordingly. The expansion of consciousness to a cosmic volume and the rooting of the ego core in the Absolute is still only a theoretical, separate ideal, the realisation of which is possible only by superhumans, such as Buddha, Ramakrishna and others. Therefore, the goal of the earthly Initiatory school of earthly esotericism was to create unique personalities of this type from a person who aspired to the Truth. Thus, the goal of modern Initiatory schools is to erase the seal of the fall in people's minds, that is, to restore the continuity of consciousness, restore the connection between the earthly worlds that follows from it, master the continuity of the creative force and return to man the knowledge that he naturally possessed before the breakdown of his consciousness.

In the initiatory language of the Western schools, the three states of consciousness - Tamas, Rajas and Sattva - when applied to a person, define three types: the flow person, the aspiration person and the new person. The flow is a mass of people who do not think about anything except satisfying their earthly selves. A person of aspiration is an idealist who fulfils himself in accordance with an ideal and implements this ideal in life. A new person is a person whose consciousness stands above all ideals, because it is directly connected to the Spiritual World, and owns the continuity of ideomotor and psychomotor processes in the name of building the Common Good.

The living life of the Spiritual World, the living values created by
this life, are not directly accessible to the human consciousness,
which has cut itself off from the Spirit and created a fulcrum in
the earthly material world instead of a suspension point to it. The
values of this world are presented to us as living realities, and the
values of the Spirit are an inanimate abstraction. The human
consciousness cannot perceive spiritual vibrations, because they
do not correspond to its own vibrations. Therefore, spiritual food
for a person should correspond to his consciousness. This is what
the Higher Powers took up, agreeing to help humanity.

The Earth is, as it were, at the bottom of an ocean of etheric
energy, on the surface of which the Moon floats. She is in the
depths of the lunar sphere, which refracts for her the sunlight of
the life-giving Spirit, the direct influence of which she would not
bear. Figuratively speaking, human consciousnesses on Earth are
fish that swim in great depths and are invisible to those living on
the surface. The sun's rays penetrating these depths, just enough

for the vision of these fish, and a brighter light would blind them, threaten their existence. The initiation gradually teaches these fish to live in the higher layers of the lunar water and develop the embryos of wings, which will then open to carry them, having floated to the surface, into the air of the Spiritual World, of which they will become birds. The path of Initiation begins when the fish begins to suffocate in the deep layers, unable to bear their high pressure further, and yearn for the great light of knowledge and the vastness of activity.

This conclusion of us into the lunar sphere, which transmits to us only the reflected, refracted light of solar spirit-making, is symbolised by the main title of the principle, and the degree of refraction and the force of action of this reflected light in the layers of the lunar strata determine the level of the occult hierarchy and the level of consciousness living in different layers in this ocean. The dedication is located above its water, and therefore the pyramids are lost in the picture. The peak is available to those who have become a bird from fish, that is, from the Son of the Earth - the Son of the Sun, a New Person whom the human consciousness perceives as something different from itself in essence and deifies. That is why all the Sons of the Sun, that is, the consciousnesses directly connected with the World of Spirit, with the solar hearth of spirit-making, anchored in it and having found their point of suspension, are ascended by people to the altar to the great sadness of these consciousnesses, who only want to show people by their example that they are not fish, but birds, and can grow your wings.

Two paths lead from the depths of the Earth to its surface, one path is outlined by exoteric religions, the other by esoteric schools. The exoteric path is for those who, having managed to grasp the guiding hand of the Teachers and Helpers of Humanity, refuse in their name from individual efforts to climb out of the depths of the sea and subordinate their consciousness to the ideal and the paths indicated by the guiding high consciousness. It is not important for these people to get acquainted with Earth. They close their minds, they focus their feelings only on the desire to swim to the surface, clinging to an outstretched hand, regardless of what is happening around them. This is the meaning of the religious path and the churches that represent it. Those who swam out this way will have the task to plunge into the ocean again, but with a suspension thread, so that, after getting acquainted with the living conditions of its floors, they can provide the inhabitants of these floors with the help that was once provided to them themselves.

Those who follow the exoteric path have shown egoism in their desire for salvation, which they then redeem by helping others. Besides, they always cling to one hand, and there are many of them outstretched. And since it is this hand that helps them, they do not see and deny the others. Therefore, when they come to the surface, they enter only one spiritual light vortex and only when they return to Earth will they be convinced of the existence of other spiritual forces and they will acquire the synthetics of consciousness. Those who follow this path seek salvation in objective life and objective ideals, dissolving the subjective core of consciousness in them. Therefore, this path is objective.

The esoteric path is for those who, despite their helplessness, retain in their consciousness the intuition of a person's spiritual self-worth. They do not cling to the outstretched hand, but firmly stand on the created fulcrum of the material world and only try to distinguish the light signs and milestones flashing in the waves of the ocean, from the outstretched "driving hand". For them, the great consciousnesses of the Teachers are not gods erected on altars, but signs and examples of leaders offered for recognition, study and achievement.

Those who follow the esoteric path open their minds to the widest perceptions and strain their creative abilities to achieve the ideals, that is, the values of the next lunar layer. They study spiritual teachings, strive further and further along the milestones of consciousness, breaking through the partitions between the individual layers with the power of striving for Truth. And at the same time, their feeling is strained by the desire to help those whose layers of existence they have left. Such souls on Earth swim to the surface, following only the steps placed by the Leaders, and gradually acquire the synthesis of consciousness, because in the upper layers the milestones of various paths merge. Floating from layer to layer, they get acquainted with the world of the Earth and, having floated to the surface, they do not need either a repetition of the experience or the redemption of egoism, because during the journey they have already provided all possible help. This path is subjective, because the support is inside a person. Strengthening and developing, this inner support becomes a subjective Knowledge of God.

These paths are constantly in opposition in the spiritual life of mankind. Their representatives tend to blame each other for the wrong orientation, for a fundamental mistake in their foundations, and so on. But we must remember that it is not a person who chooses his own path, but the intrinsic path of an individual, that is, their inner nature, in addition to his conscious will, determines his belonging to one of these paths. The path of religion, that is, the exoteric path, with its stages and with its hierarchical stages, is accessible to everyone who tries to think about it.

The esoteric path is hidden, because few consciousnesses can follow it, and exposing the knowledge gained on it would only confuse those who are not destined to follow it. But at the same time, only those who follow the esoteric path can help their exoteric brethren by carefully sharing their achievements with them, adapting their formulations to their consciousness and directing the general human construction to the next stage of evolution. Those who follow the esoteric path, as it were, from the very beginning, become an servant of the Helpers of humanity, and therefore the demand for selflessness on the widest possible scale is presented to him from the first steps along the path.

The occult Hierarchy corresponds with its degrees of dedication to different layers of earthly Psychic energy. There are three main worlds. Human consciousness gradually develops on three planes. There are, therefore, basically three degrees of Initiation. In modern Initiatory Schools, they are coloured by the terminology of freemasonry and establish the degrees of apprentice, journeyman and master. These three stages correspond to the three planes of consciousness or the three worlds: etheric-physical (student), astral (apprentice) and mental (master). Moreover, the top, that is, the spiritual plane, is already above the surface of the earthly world and unites both truncated pyramids, because in fact this bifurcation is illusory and is only an incorrect reflection of the Single Path in the earthly world. We can say that the idea of two roads arose only in the minds of people, because in fact, the esoteric path begins where the exoteric path ends, and is a path for those souls who have returned to the Earthly world for a second time to study it and provide assistance to others who need help, after being taken out of there for the moment to obtain a suspension point. That is why it is necessary for the leaders of the esoteric path to gauge, when accepting a student, whether he has a memory of the suspension point.

According to the law of specularity of reflections, the first stage corresponds to Initiation (theoretical) into the mental world. The student is given an overview of the principles and ideas manifested in the Universe and guiding life earth people. He comes into contact with the greatest spiritual ideals of the human race. He is given the opportunity to get acquainted with the spiritual foundations and principles manifested in all religious and exoteric schools, and he is required to develop a synthetic consciousness. He is also given the basics of knowledge of the laws and forces operating in the psychic or astral world.

At the second stage, a person practically gets acquainted with the psychic world, transferring his consciousness to this plane with appropriate exercises and developing the corresponding organs of perception and influence in the astral body. At this stage, he needs to get acquainted not only with the forces of good, but also with the forces of evil, that is, involution. At the third stage, the initiate gets acquainted with the apparatus of action of the physical plane, that is, he learns to master the ideomotor and psychomotor process for controlling events on the physical plane, as well as the processes of nature. At the same stage, his consciousness becomes anchored in the Spiritual World.

The further stages of Initiation already relate to the ascent to the top of the pyramid and are deeply subjective experiences and changes of consciousness, the milestones of which are carefully outlined for him. Since the planes of Other Worlds are refracted and reflected in each plane of consciousness and in the world enclosed in it, these degrees, of course, have their own divisions. Thus, an Occult Hierarchy of consciousnesses that have reached different levels of their development will be established.

On his way up the ladder of Initiation, a person meets subjective and objective resistances that make this ascent difficult and even dangerous. The dangers of the exoteric path in their total sum are reduced to the following: consciousness, loaded with a ballast of incorrect concepts and materialised ideas, is attached to the spiritual to the leader, deifying the latter and relying on his spiritual help. From the wrong concept of this help, theories of grace arise that deprive a person of the manifestation of personal initiative. A distorted image of the Spiritual Assistant is formed from incorrect ideas, and this image gradually obscures his real spiritual face. An illusory picture is created in the psychic atmosphere, to which human consciousnesses are drawn from the lower strata, thus leaving their true Saviour. The astral world of the Earth is filled with similar images of gods created by people and imbued with their Psychic energy. These images grow stronger and grow, absorbing the psychic and etheric bodies of people who are directed to them by the axis of the will. The consciousness attached to these images, as it were, goes blind and is incapable of further evolution. And since nothing stands still, instead of evolution, there is an involution of consciousness, expressed in fanaticism, intolerance and hostility to everything that is not directed at the astral picture of his deity equips him to pass a real, big and dangerous transition.

The dangers on the esoteric path are reduced to the following: Penetrating into Other Worlds and studying their structure horizontally, consciousness can easily lose the spiritual axis passing through them vertically. It can cling to only one plane or sub-plane for a long time, multiplying the terms of its incarnations and delaying the execution of the main task. This danger is especially great for types with a predominance of Water or Earth.

Another danger is the possibility of damage to their conductors by the desire to prematurely penetrate into an unfamiliar area. After all, all the layers of the worlds are separated from each other by partitions, and without sufficient training of the guides, passing through these partitions hurts them. The wounds of the mental body are expressed by the loss of the correct scale and the correct assessment of the relationship between the worlds. This brings an element of fantasy into the worldview, which can be expressed in madness.

The defeat of the psychic shell causes a loss of a sense of commensurability and easily turns into a sense of isolation from the surrounding, which can also be expressed in mental oddities and abnormalities. And the injury of the etheric body causes a disorder in the system. These dangers threaten most of all the types with a predominance of Air and Fire. In the esoteric path, it is important to maintain a balance between the vertical aspiration of consciousness and the horizontal development of the vehicles. Therefore, the element of cooperation between initiates is important in it, because through psychic exchange they can balance each other and avoid these dangers.

Such dangers exist not only in the field of theory, they are constantly exposed to the one who goes through the path of Initiation and many consciousnesses have been torn from him. These dangers caused the need for tests, which the leaders, that is, the hierarchically senior ones, put to the leader. For passing through a dangerous transition in a small form (test) hardens the consciousness and the consciousnesses of those who have broken down on these dangerous transitions either remain at these stages (in the first case), or are repelled by the reflection of their own power down (in the second case). These consciousnesses become the occult enemies with which the Initiate comes to encounter. They either want to use the latter for their further advancement and are waiting for the moment of its weakness to stick to it, that is, for possession. Or these consciousnesses, full of bitterness because of failure, try to hinder the Initiate in his achievements.

The method of their attack is reduced to the so-called "envolt", that is, to sending, figuratively speaking, an astral bomb filled with poisonous "gases" of their anger and frustration, into one of the vehicles of the Initiate. These bombs are created in different ways, but for their creation, a fulcrum is always needed, that is, in the hands of the envolting person, there must be something connected with the envolted person, because this will create a psychic contact between both. Any witchcraft on traces, on blood, on objects belonging to the envolted, on a doll depicting him, refers to the choice of such a fulcrum. Similarly, disembodied beings take possession of some lack of the envolted and inflate it. To protect yourself from these envolts, you can do this:

1) strengthen the axis of your consciousness and your will directed to the spirit;

2) subjectify and strengthen your guides;

3) learn to protect yourself with a magic circle or, rather, a cylinder created from your own Psychic energy;

4) in case of a strong attack, to call for help a ray from the Spiritual World - by focusing on one of its Inhabitants who is currently karmically closer to consciousness (the Teacher's Call).

Those who are attacked by occult enemies should not send them a return bomb of hostility and hatred and must instead remember that this would be to attack the unfortunate, wrecked and drowning. Often, their desperate clinging to those going up is taken as an attack. Therefore, it is best to send a good thought and a good feeling of compassion in response to the clinging incarnate and non-incarnate; you can not push them away from you, but give them a helping hand and become their leaders. And then their anger and resentment often turn into fervent devotion, which can help the consciousness going forward.

On the exoteric path, people also meet occult enemies. These are those who once suffered a crash and, with wounded pride, turned away from any spiritual search in general, began to imperiously hinder the seekers. These worst enemies of human evolution have already lost all contact with the Spiritual World and only a vortex of ossified anger around the axis of their prevents the envolts from mental collapse: since feeding this vortex from incarnation to incarnation with evil deeds, the power of their malice grows. These are the most dangerous of all larvae, because they arose on the axis of the once aspiring human will. They are only individualised power conglomerates of people's negative thoughts. These larvae, whether embodied or not, take advantage of the weakness or stupidity of people, strengthening them in the creation of false ideas and replacing spiritual realities with illusory pictures created in the Subtle World. These include the statements:

"the devil can take beautiful images"

"the wolf walks in sheep's clothing"

"those who have ears, let them hear"

We will not understand the representatives of the world of larvae and their activities, we will only note that it is now that humanity is teeming with them, it is now that they sometimes master even the best consciousnesses, using the "dog heads" (the tenth Principle) of their weaknesses, and they make them their servants by the ways of possession. Let us only note that in total, their activities are reduced to turning people's attention away from the true steps of ascent to the World of the Spirit, replacing them with fantastic and often beautiful pictures of the Subtle World, behind which the mask for the devil, who does not let people to the true values of the spirit, has shifted for the seer. The method of this, at first a little subtle, gradual deviation of people from the truly spiritual paths is the interspersing of distorted ideas in their worldview, which at first are visible only to a very sharp mind in recognition and experienced in its development. But gradually growing to gigantic proportions, these distortions lead people to irrevocable dead ends (from where it is very difficult to get them out, because the consciousness does not want to put up with the need to erase the illusory experience obtained and the time spent on it).
The Eighteenth Principle outlines to us the ways of man in his present state. He mercilessly reveals to our consciousness that everything is cognisable, you will see the reflection of true values on the waves of the Psychic energy of the Earth. He tells us that no matter how much we struggle in these waves in pursuit of truth, we will not catch the slightest pure ray of it. He tells us that all our earthly constructions testify only to these dreams and self-

deceptions, when we take reflections for real value. Everything that we comprehend with the organs of our physical, astral and mental bodies refers only to those ideas about the truth that humanity itself has created in the waves of the ocean of Psychic energy of the Earth, since its fall being at the bottom of this ocean. A fish that has swum even into the upper layers of water is still a fish and is doomed to descend again to the lower layers for new ascents.

This is the wheel from the symbolic picture of the tenth Arcanum. Thus, the circle from the tenth to the eighteenth Principle is completed. We ascend in it, preserving even in the highest achievements of consciousness the "dog's head" of our earthly origin, and in the lowest falls we preserve the human head of the desire to get out of the earthly waters. But no objective knowledge obtained through the organs of our guides in all the worlds of the Earth, and no construction of an objective Common Good will help us get out of these waters.

Therefore, the main goal of spiritual paths is not to know the earthly worlds and their structure, not to creatively expand one's achievements in them, but, speaking in symbols , to grow those rudiments of wings that every fish has and which turn it into a bird capable of flying above the waters of the Earth.

This cultivation of wings is a subjective work on the gradual change of one's own consciousness. To find in all its changes the core belonging to the unearthly world, to find your immortal soul, which contains the Cosmic Infinity, to develop the ability of acute recognition between eternal values and illusory ideas - this means to grow wings for flight.

The Sun

The Nineteenth Arcanum

Sunlight

Synthetic philosophy
The Great Work (Ethical Hermeticism)
The Philosophers ' Gold (the Philosopher's Stone)

Numeric designation: 100
Astrological correspondence: Pisces

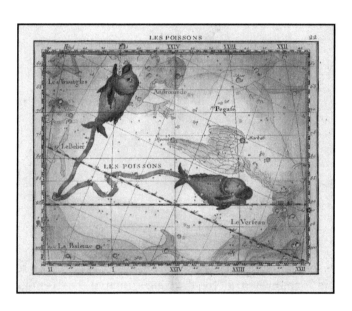

John Flamsteed, Les Poissons (Pisces), 1776

This symbolic picture depicts a low wall, in front of which there are two naked children. Bright sunlight falls, showering them with gold coins.

Having gone through all the Principles, up to the sixteenth, we return to the first and we are again faced with the task: To know and find ourselves. But thanks to the stages already passed, consciousness has acquired the ability of recognition, of having felt the grace of the Spiritual World and its aspiration to it. In addition, the consciousness has determined what it does not need. And objective knowledge has lost its value for the seeker, especially since all the combinations in the three worlds are still not covered. But the knowledge of the process of their formation led to the knowledge of their internal springs, that is, their essence, and interest in them disappeared. Consciousness will now have to either break through the roof, or again descend into the lower layers under the power of illusory ideas created by humanity. To break through the roof means to detach from the Earth, from a fish to become a bird and direct your flight into the unknown, having support only in yourself. Of course, this transition marks a completely different stage of consciousness. This is a different attitude to the world, a different worldview, based not on a fulcrum, but on a point of suspension to the Sun, the spiritual rays of which are each consciousness.

The hieroglyph of the Arcanum is interesting, the occult meaning of which is an axe. It symbolises the mental effort that we ourselves must make to cut through the roof of the eighteenth Principle. The Nineteenth Principle is a way out of the hopeless conditions created by the sixteenth Arcana. This is the Principle of growing wings for flying to the Above ground spheres. The wings grew imperceptibly for the seeking consciousness during its work and wanderings through the earth's movements. The spiritual axis of consciousness was strengthened by subjective work, overcoming obstacles, fighting for one's path. If only glimpses of the Spirit World can be found in the conditions of earthly existence, if all the knowledge formulated by the mental body of a person and received from the objects of the earthly worlds does not satisfy the thirst for truth, if the direct knowledge of spiritual values has not been obtained and if the result of the search was a disappointment in the possibility of spiritual achievement, then the real achievement of these searches is the following: The separation of consciousness from the earthly spheres with the reflections contained in them, the readiness to find a way out of them at all costs and the acquisition of extreme tension of will and spiritual aspiration to the spirit.

Thus, moments of despair cause extreme tension of the Heart, Mind and Will, change the entire consciousness at once, elevate it to another level, from where a way out of the situation is observed. This state is symbolised by the hieroglyph of the axe. In it, all the forces of a person and all his subjective tension are directed to the desire to get out. If this exit from under the roof of the eighteenth Principle occurs instantly or almost instantly, it means that it was prepared for a long time by the previous work. The state of consciousness of a person who has found such a guide by means of vehicles, that is, by a mental, astral and etheric-physical body cannot be identified with the imprints of knowledge and abilities received in these bodies. It cannot even identify itself with the axis of the will on which these bodies are built. His entire earthly personality, ennobled and developed by previous work, becomes an objective weapon in relation to man and the acquired knowledge and power, rolled up in this tool, can be redeployed if circumstances require it. He himself is no longer interested in all this.

The move is symbolised by the image of two naked children. The subjective "I" of a human being is, as it were, thrown out of the earth waves in this tension. It is naked because it has thrown off the veils of all the achievements of the earthly guides. It is in the state of a child who has no experience in the world where it took off its clothes. It is sexless (both children are asexual), because the core of consciousness, the spiritual "I", is the same in both men and women. This spiritual "I" is thrown to the surface of the earth's ocean at the moment of a desperate cry for the spirit.

The human "I" stands naked in the face of the Spiritual World as it is from the beginning and will be until the end. And the only thing it knows about itself can be expressed by the phrase: "Here I am, what I am and as I am." At this moment, the human "I" is fixed in the World of the Spirit and changes the point of support to the point of suspension. The one who experienced this moment will never forget it and from that moment on his entire worldview and his entire attitude to the world change. He is no longer a fish swimming in the water, but a bird flying in the sunlight. The sunlight is the whistle of spiritual insight, the light that flashes in the depths of the subjective consciousness, which knows its immortality, its eternity.

Then, after this moment, a person must again return to the conditions of earthly existence, because his past karma binds him to the Earth. But his consciousness is no longer immersed in the Earth's waters, but hovers over nothing. It can no longer be identified with the earthly vehicles, that is, the mental, astral and etheric-physical body. It cannot be identified with the imprints of knowledge and abilities acquired in these bodies. It cannot be identified with the axis of the will on which these bodies are built. His whole earthly personality, enobled and developed by previous work, becomes an objective tool in relation to a person, and the acquired knowledge and power, which are stored in this tool, can be deployed again if circumstances require it. All this is no longer his interest.

It is when consciousness is detached from its earthly personality that the centres in which the spiritual self is reflected are designated in its various bodies. In the mental body, the centre of the bell flashes, in the astral, the centre of the heart, in the etheric, the solar plexus shines with an even light. This kindling of the centres signifies the acquisition by the bodies of special abilities reflecting the spiritual "I". The flashing Bell centre in the mental body makes it possible to establish a synthetic worldview expressed in synthetic philosophy.

This synthetic worldview is deeply different from all previous attempts in the same direction. The latter were all reduced to a more or less successful eclecticism, but a truly synthetic worldview based on the direct conduct of the Spirit through all forms of its expression could not be established without a Spiritual core. The synthetic worldview cannot be formulated, because in each formula the dependence on space and time, that is, on the stagnant conditions of education, is limited, and can only express a part of the general synthesis. The synthetic worldview is subjective, because it expresses the subjective connection of the "I" with the Spiritual World and, at the same time, it is common to all who have found their point of suspension, because it reflects Spiritual Unity in itself.

A synthetic worldview cannot be expressed in any teaching or any mental language, but at the same time it can partially result in any formula, depending on the circumstances, adapting to the environment. The syntactic worldview resides in the subjective core of consciousness and can adapt to any circumstances. All religious philosophical teachings are only separate facets of this diamond, in the centre of which is the sunlight of Spiritual Truth. Thus, the nineteenth Principle, igniting this spiritual core, sums up the last synthetic result of the work done in the mental body and replaces the ideomotor processes of the mental plane with direct radiations on the surface of the Spirit. Then these radiations are developed by the minds of the inhabitants of the Earth in theory and teaching.

That is why it is impossible to demand from the consciousness that has emerged from the earthly waters and is fixed in the Spirit, the development of a system and a doctrine. This would mean to occupy our forces with what people themselves can perform and interfere with the activity of consciousness by sending spiritual charges and establishing spiritual paths. This explains why the Teachers of Humanity have never been philosophers and taxonomists in our concept. It was as if they were throwing mental gold in order for people to melt it into coins themselves.

The flashing of the Heart centre in the astral body gives one the opportunity to manifest the divine power – Love - because the Spiritual ray reflected in the Heart is unselfish Love. This is the centre of all ethical Hermeticism, but this centre flares up only when the astral body is put in order by all the previous work and the consciousness brought out into the Solar Spiritual Light can be reflected in it. All the previous work was needed only for this purpose. Methods of creating astral vortices of the fifteenth Principle, methods of coercion of the sixteenth, intuition of the seventeenth, ways of overcoming obstacles and fighting enemies of the eighteenth, straining various centres of the human psyche - all this disappears and is replaced by a powerful radiation of Love. This Love is the most powerful tool of psychic influence, giving everyone the best for him according to his capabilities and understanding. At the same time, Love is the most powerful tool for fighting enemies and protecting against them.

The love that flares up in the Heart centre is no longer a refracted, but a true sunbeam in the psychic world, not an aspect of the earthly resonator of the sun, but the presence of the Sun itself. In the personality itself, in its psyche, the presence of the Sun harmoniously groups the entire planetary composition around itself, replacing the reflections of the planets with true penetrations of their rays into the psychic world of the personality. In this way, an especially intense astral body will be created, which is a magnet of intense action in the environment. Such personalities do not need to go to people, people come to them freely, because the reflections contained in their psychic planetary composition are powerfully attracted by the real vibrations of the planets. This replacement of the reflected planetary composition with a real harmonious world of planets around the Solar Centre is the Hermetic Great Work.

In the etheric body, the Solar plexus has the ability to capture pure Solar Power. This concentrated pure Solar Life Force is the philosopher's Stone that has the property of turning all metals into gold, cultivating plants at a rapid pace, curing all diseases, renewing the supply of vital energy, ensuring immortality. The Philosopher's Stone and the elixir of life are the same.

This philosopher's stone is enclosed in the Solar plexus of the etheric body of the one who came out into the Sunlight. Therefore, alchemy can be practiced only by those whose consciousness has found a point of suspension to the spiritual essence of the Sun, whose mental body is connected with the Solar Mind, the astral body with the Solar Heart and the etheric body with the Solar Life Force. The same applies to those who are engaged in the treatment of magnetism and to those who are trying to gain power over the phenomena of nature.

Thanks to the help provided to those who are going to the Spiritual World, this ascent is often completed before the earthly guides are put in final order. The bottom line is that with the establishment of centres, it is easier and faster to complete Hermetic Work in all three planes. Therefore, finding the suspension point does not at all mean the mental emergence of a perfect human being. It is only after this ascent that the most serious part of Hermetic Work begins, but this work already takes place confidently, without tragedies and sufferings, because the Illumination of the Spirit accompanies it.

From now on, the joy of construction accompanies every step, because man in his subjective depth is aware of the illusory nature of all the troubles, doubts, sufferings, obstacles and enemies in the earthly world. The human consciousness lives in the eternal, it is connected with the Spiritual World and is in contact with the Divine Spirit and the Creative consciousnesses of our system, who are always ready to provide active assistance, both in building themselves and their neighbours, who are also going to the Spiritual World.

Judgement

The Twentieth Arcanum

New Man

Attraction to God
Astral Rebirth
Development over time
Numeric designation: 200
Astrological correspondence: Saturn

Saturnus, Planetenmaskers

The symbolic picture of the Arcanum depicts a grave with a fallen tombstone. A man, a woman and a child rise from this grave. Their heads are raised up, and they look into the sky at the trumpeting angel.

Let us pay attention to the astrological correspondence of the last four Arcana. The zodiac constellation of Pisces (the nineteenth Arcanum) refers to the development of the Subjective principle, to the withdrawal into oneself and overcoming the interface with the objective world and the extreme obstacles in that. The twentieth Arcana corresponds to Saturn, the twenty-second to the Sun, the twenty-first, or zero, to Orion.

The correspondence between Saturn and the Sun is especially interesting: Saturn is the sphere of the extreme hierarchy of Solar influence, that is, as it were, the outer shell of our system; the Sun is both its centre and the doors to Space and Eternity.

After leaving the earthly world, consciousness will not come into direct contact with the Sun. It should still undergo a number of changes - starting with the influence of Saturn - and gradually adapt to the influences in their pure, rather than reflected, form, which will make the consciousness able to reach the twenty-second Principle, that is, under the direct influence of the Sun, but without the danger of burning in its rays.

The entrance to the sphere of influence of Saturn is marked by a meeting with the so-called Guardian of the Threshold. This meeting takes place after the suspension point of the nineteenth Arcanum is found, but before the entry of consciousness into the reality of the Spiritual World. finding this point of suspension, therefore, can be characterised as such an instant illumination of the entire consciousness, after which there remains confidence in the reality of the Spiritual World and the consciousness of one's belonging to it.

The degree of accommodation of the received spiritual ray depends on the creative work done on one's earthly personality, on the purity and transparency of the conductors and the degree of self-control acquired, also the fortress of the created spiritual connection. Without preliminary subjective work, therefore, it is premature to break into the Spiritual World; and a meeting with the Guardian of the Threshold, inevitably following a spiritual insight, is dangerous for the consciousness whose conductors are not purified, because this may threaten a new break in the newly established connection and throw consciousness far back. Thus, the creation of a new spiritual connection with the Higher World will be more difficult for the practitioner. The meeting with the Guardian of the Threshold is known to all Initiatory schools and the leaders who prepare students for this moment, the upbringing of the personality and the establishment of the volitional axis in it, put special emphasis on the development of the Pentagram of the mental body.

The Guardian of the Threshold is the totality of all the incarnational karma accumulated by the initiate, which is synthesised at the moment of his exit from the waters of the Earth into a personified being. In the Guardian of the Threshold, it meets with itself, or rather, with the synthesis of all its earthly personalities formed in the chain of its incarnations and merged into one entity. If the initiate has not subjected his personality to the process of purification and transformation or has not completed this process, then karma with an inexorable sequence draws him back to those cliches that require transformation. And since he meets with his objectified personality, at the moment of the karmic demand, the consciousness is, as it were, reabsorbed by the karmic flow in the most negative parts of the ego and becomes what is called in the Initiatory schools a "Defeated Guardian of the Threshold". If the main karmic lines are transformed by the purification of the vehicles, that is, the spirituality of the mental body, the enlightenment of the astral body and the discipline of the etheric body, then the meeting with the Guardian of the Threshold is reduced to a revision of all past incarnations.

During this revision, the need for some corrections and alterations in the composition of its conductors comes to consciousness and this work temporarily binds it to the Earth, along with great efforts to replace it in its own incarnation of planar reflections with real planar radiations as part of its earthly bodies. This calm revision testifies to the victory over the Guardian of the Threshold, that is, about the complete non-identification of consciousness with its earthly personality and its karma. Thus, from Saturn, consciousness gets the mastery over karma.

After this victory, consciousness passes psychically through the spheres of subsequent planetary influences, acquiring from Jupiter a special invincible cheerfulness; from Mars a special intensity of experience that is not characteristic of earthly people; from the Moon, a small Manas and the vibrations of motherhood and guardianship; from Venus, the ability of ideation; from Mercury, the general plasticity of the soul without loss in the adaptations of its spiritual person. And finally, when he comes into contact with the Sun, the spiritual core flashes up in him, that is, a full awareness of his divine origin and unity with God.

This voice of the spiritual core, the "voice of silence" or "the voice that sounds in the desert" is precisely the divine attraction - the first subtitle of the twentieth Principle, the desire for spiritual help received from the Redemptive Cliche. This voice, drowned out by the agitations of the conductors of the earthly personality, now sounds in the consciousness like the trumpet of an Archangel, no longer allowing him to attach himself to the states through which he passes in the planetary circles. This is the Voice of Eternity. Only after leaving the sphere of influence of the Earth can consciousness survive this Voice of Eternity as an irrefutable reality and then his whole worldview turns upside down. Then his Initiation into the Spiritual World begins.

The values of this world cease to be abstractions and their reality is perceived with a thousand times greater persuasiveness and intensity than material realities were once perceived, when instead of a point of spiritual suspension, all cognitive and creative possibilities were based on a material point of support. Everything that is lived in the world of the Earth seems to be a dream. Immersion in the earthly conditions of the continuing incarnation of such a consciousness is ghostly and, through these ghosts, it sees the manifestation of spiritual rays. The paths of earthly searches and dreams are ahead of him with mathematical clarity, the illusions of earthly life cannot capture him and his task is to restore values in their original purity in the conditions of earthly existence, among these illusions created by the play of countless refractions and reflections of spiritual truths in the energy flows of the Earth.

For this work, he needs to start for himself a new cycle of existences on Earth in new vehicles. He creates a new, truly astral, that is, stellar, body for his earthly manifestations, replacing the earthly mental body with the Mind, the three rays of the Higher Manas, in which knowledge and creativity merge into one. His astral body, created from pure planetary vibrations, which include distant cosmic vibrations, is only a shining veil of an immortal soul, the shining centre of which is the Sun.

Of course, such a transformation also transforms the etheric body, merging it with the astral body, and the physical body becomes what is symbolised by the words "The Temple of God". As a result, it is the only one belonging to the Earth in the organisation of the Initiate's guides. This is symbolised by the subtitle "Astral Rebirth" and the picture of the family coming out of the coffin as a new cycle of existence (according to the 336th symbolism, the application of the Law of Dynamics is depicted by the family).

The consciousness of Eternity is the perception of the Divine essence with all the potential of possibilities. The consciousness of Eternity is the restoration in one's own consciousness of connection with the Absolute through the Divine centre of consciousness. In the earthly life, the consciousness of Eternity can be achieved only in the state of Samadhi, characterised by the inaction of all vehicles, including Buddhi, because every action is a flow of changes, which is incompatible with Eternity. Therefore, the ideal of "non-doing" in all spiritual schools is considered the highest, but it cannot be understood as constant doing nothing.

The ideal of "non-doing" is the complete detachment of consciousness from any state, and it is clothed in shells only in the case of manifestation. These shells are perceived as something to the consciousness of an outsider by their nature and the investment in them is associated with the concept of sacrifice. The natural state of consciousness is immersion in Eternity, in the Absolute, it is life in the Ever-Present, before which time is an illusion.

The past and the future exist only when consciousness puts on shells and they are needed by it only to carry out actions for the sake of helping the environment. As long as the world exists, that is, as long as there are consciousnesses, identified with the shells, there are actions, there is time. For the creation of the Initiate, time is the unfolding of Eternity, so time is infinite. Infinity is an expanded Eternity. Time is not an abstract concept, but a real flow of changes that unfolds into the Infinity of possibilities, the potential of the Absolute.

There is no present in time, because the moment of transition from the past to the future is elusive and indefinable for a consciousness immersed in the flow of time. The present exists only where the flow of time stops with its flow from the past to the future, where the Eternal comes into its own. Every time we have spiritual insights of consciousness, we catch this moment standing, that is, Eternal, and time then unfolds the captured spiritual ray into a series of experiences, actions and changes that occur under the influence of the perception of this spiritual ray.

Rare is the person who has not had at least one "eternal moment" in his or her life, that is, an instantaneous insight, even if the reason for this was some kind of external push. This "eternal moment" changed the direction of their way of thinking, their emotional life, their manifested actions and, in this changed flow, their life unfolded in events and facts the eternal value that had entered their consciousness.

The relation of Eternity and Infinity is the relation of basis and function and in the human psyche these two principles determine two spiritual and psychological types: Mysticism and spiritual esotericism. These two types can be determined only after leaving the sphere of influence of the Earth. The type of mystic strives for Eternity, for the direct immersion of consciousness in the Absolute. His natural state is "non-doing", and every act for him is associated with an element of spiritual suffering. The type of spiritual esotericist knows about the anchoring of his consciousness in the Absolute and can at any time bring it into a state of Samadhi, that is, immerse his vehicles in inaction, going into the Eternal. But at the same time, he joyfully accepts Infinity and putting on shells is not associated with the element of suffering, but with creative joy, the creation of new opportunities in the flow of time, reflecting eternal values. The esoteric goes to the Eternal through the Infinite, to God through the Universe, while the mystic wants to pass through the Universe, immersing himself in God.

The path to achieving the state of a perfect person, which involves merging with Infinity and the Beginning of Eternity, is impossible without deep inner work, liberation from one's own shortcomings and negative qualities and this, in turn, requires efforts aimed at self-knowledge. Without awareness of one's own advantages and disadvantages, it is impossible to approach perfection. Self-knowledge involves self-observation and self-study.

To an unenlightened and spiritually undeveloped person, it may seem that he only does what he observes himself and knows himself in the process of life. However, everyday self-observation and self-study is significantly different from the process of genuine spiritual and esoteric self-knowledge. If a person begins to observe himself seriously, then from a certain moment he comes to the conclusion that he does not know himself enough, especially if he begins to observe himself from a spiritual point of view. The oppressive feeling described here is already the beginning of true self-knowledge.

The painfulness of such a feeling when knowing oneself is inherent in the very nature of the human soul emphasises how strong the desire to consider oneself is in a full-fledged and true person. No matter how ugly a person looks, he must have the courage to soberly look at his own ugliness. Until now, man has not perceived his inner ugliness for the reason that he has not yet sufficiently immersed his consciousness in his own essence. It is only in such moments of complete honesty to oneself that a person begins to understand the full power of his self-love in all its inflated magnitude. At the same time, he is amazed at how little desire there is in him to throw off this self-love.

All these spiritual qualities are especially noticeable in a person's relationships with other people. With true self-knowledge, a person suddenly learns, for example, that his goodwill to a friend in the unexplored depths of the subconscious has the appearance of envy or even open hatred; when trying to cope with these negative feelings, they break out of the subconscious with a downright spontaneous force and manifest themselves in his external relations. There are many more examples of such an external disguise of a person's hidden subconscious feelings, when he himself is sincerely confident in his goodwill and conscientiousness. Such an in-depth kind of self-knowledge occurs when observing oneself outside the physical body, when no self-justifications are able to obscure the true images of the Spiritual World. This kind of self-knowledge has a depressing effect on the soul at first, but no soul who wants to get closer to the Spiritual World can avoid it, because it inevitably arises due to the special relations that a person enters into before his soul. He observes himself from a completely different point of view and comes to the conviction that such as he is, he is not acceptable for the light world, and that there is something in him that must be thrown off in order to get the right to consciously cross the threshold of the Spiritual World.

Difficulties in fulfilling these requirements can cause different reactions in a person. Or he will begin to criticise spiritual truths that make it difficult for him to enter the invisible world and explain them with empty fantasies, hiding behind this criticism a subconscious fear of truths, that is, the habit of living in what is perceived by the senses and the mind. This is a special universal form of self-love, seeking justification for its a habitual existence and worldview that has no place in the Spiritual World. Many, having reached the threshold, are afraid of their own unadorned appearance, which is the Guardian of the Threshold, which does not let unprepared souls into the Spiritual World. And many retreat, not having the courage to step over it.

A person who has experienced such an experience at the very threshold of the Spiritual World becomes convinced that it is a blessing for the ordinary human soul if it is not allowed to be unprepared for the threshold. This benefit is impossible to imagine otherwise as some Higher Power that protects a person from the dangers and horrors that await him at the threshold of the Spiritual World and caused by his own disgusting appearance.

Before the threshold of the Spiritual World there is a strict guard who vigilantly watches that an immature person does not penetrate through it. It is easier to bear all the doubts and ignorance of the Spiritual World than the sight of that appearance, which must be thrown off in order to obtain the right to enter the Spiritual World. In no case can a person be allowed real insight in spiritual areas until he has acquired the necessary abilities for this. Therefore, when entering the invisible world after death, if he is not yet ready to work in it, a veil is thrown over the phenomena of this world. He will see them only when he is quite ready for this.

The Lesser Guardian of the Threshold is an independent being that a person can perceive only at the appropriate stage of development. His appearance is terrible and, therefore, it is necessary to have all the presence of mind and trust in his path in order to courageously meet him with his own appearance, which protects him from premature entry into the Spiritual World. The Guardian of the Threshold is the outstanding karma of a person, his moral balance, acting in the form of a sensually living being generated by the person himself.

The meaning of the Guardian is perceived by the student approximately in the following words: "Until now, you were dominated by forces that remained invisible to you. Thanks to them, each of your good deeds has received his reward and every bad act entailed bad consequences. Thanks to their influence, your character was created from your life experience and thoughts. They determined your fate: They determined the measure of joy and suffering assigned to you in each of your incarnations in accordance with your behaviour in previous incarnations. They dominated you as a comprehensive Law of karma. From now on, you yourself will carry out part of the work that they did upon you.

"Before, you have suffered one or another heavy blow of fate and you did not know why? It was a consequence of some harmful act in one of your previous lives. Have you met happiness and joy, which were also the consequences of previous actions? There are beautiful features in your character, but there are also ugly spots. Both are created by yourself thanks to your previous experiences and thoughts. Until now, you didn't know them, only the consequences were revealed to you. But the karmic forces have seen your previous actions, your innermost thoughts and feelings and they used them to determine what you should be and live now. But now all the good and all the bad sides of your past lives should be revealed to you yourself.

"Until now, they were in you, but you couldn't see them. Now they come out of your personality and take on an independent image that you can see. And here I am myself - a being who has woven a body for myself out of my own noble and your evil deeds. My ghostly image is woven from the pages of the account book of your own life. Until now, you have carried me invisibly within yourself and it was a blessing for you, because the wisdom of your hitherto hidden fate continued to work invisibly in you to extinguish the dark spots in your image. Now, when I have learned from you, this hidden wisdom has also departed from you and is transferring its work into your own hands.

I must become perfect in myself, a beautiful being, or else perish. If the latter had happened, I would have dragged you down with me into the dark world. In order to prevent this, your own wisdom must now be so great as to take on the task of that hidden wisdom that has departed from you. After you cross my threshold, my visible image will not depart from you one step. And if in the future you do or think wrongly, you will immediately recognise your guilt by the disgusting, demonic distortion on this image of me. Only when you correct all your past untruths and purify yourself so that further evil becomes completely impossible for you, then will my being turn into a radiant beauty. Then I will be able to connect with you again for the benefit of my future activities.

"My threshold is built from all the feelings of fear that you have, from all the fear of the possibility of taking responsibility for all your deeds and thoughts. As long as you still have some fear of self-management of your destiny, this threshold has not yet been completed in all its parts. And until you get at least one single stone in it, you will be forced to fatally stop in front of it or stumble over it. Do not try to cross this threshold until you feel completely free from fear and ready for the highest responsibility.

"Until now, I have come out of your own personality only when death has withdrawn you from your earthly life, but even then my image remained closed to you. Only the forces of fate that ruled over you saw me and could, according to my appearance, develop your powers and abilities in the intervals between death and a new birth, so that in your new earthly life you could work on the beauty of your appearance for the benefit of your further development. And I, myself, was the one whose imperfection invariably forced the forces of fate to bring you to new incarnations on Earth again and again. Because of me, the Leaders of Karma assigned to you a new birth. And only by unconsciously transforming me in this way, thanks to the renewed lives, into complete perfection, would you be freed from the Lords of Death and completely united with me. And in merging with me, he would have passed into immortality. Here I stand now before you, visible, as I stood beside you, invisible, in the hour of your death. Having crossed the threshold, you enter the realms that you previously entered after physical death. You will enter them with full consciousness and from now on, while continuing to wander around the Earth outwardly, you will, at the same time, wander in the kingdom of death or, what is the same, in the Kingdom of Eternal Life.

"Verily, I am also the angel of death, but at the same time I am the giver of an inexhaustible Higher Life. Thanks to me, you will die at the life of the body to survive the rebirth to an indestructible existence. The realm into which you are now entering will introduce you to beings of a supersensible order. But your first acquaintance in this world is destined to be myself, who is your own consciousness. I used to live my own life, but now you have awakened me to my own being and I stand before you as a visible measure of your future actions and as your own reproach. You were able to create me, but at the same time you took on the responsibility to create me."

The above appeal should be submitted not as something symbolic, but as a real experience of a spiritual disciple in the highest degree.
The guard should warn him not to go further if he does not feel the strength to meet the requirements contained in this appeal. No matter how terrible the image of the Guardian is, it is only the result of the student's past life, only his own character, awakened to an independent life outside of him. The training of the student should be aimed at enduring this spectacle without any fear and at the moment of meeting, feeling his strength so increased that he can quite consciously take on the transformation of the Guardian.
The Guardian of the Threshold has expressed his demands and a whirlwind rises in the place where he stood, which extinguishes all the spiritual lights that have hitherto illuminated the path of life. Complete darkness spreads out before the student and out of the darkness comes a further exhortation: "Do not cross my threshold until it becomes clear to you that from now on, you will illuminate the darkness in front of you. And do not take a single step further until you have gained confidence that there is enough combustible substance in your own lamp." And only then does the Guardian of the Threshold pull back the veil that has hidden the Deep Secrets of Life until now.

The Fool

The Twenty-first Arcanum

Love

Radiation
Illusion
Sign (Symbol)
Numerical designation: 300 or 0
Astrological correspondence: Orion (if we take the value 300)

A print of the copperplate engraving for Johann Bayer's Uranometria showing the constellation Orion. This image is courtesy of the United States Naval Observatory Library.

313

The symbolic picture depicts a mountainous area. A man in a stupid hat is walking along the path. Over his left shoulder, he holds a bundle on a stick. In front of a person is a chasm in which the mouth of a crocodile is visible. A dog runs after the man, who tries to keep him from falling into the abyss, clinging to his clothes with his teeth. A person does not look in front of him, but to where the clouds are formed in various combinations.

The picture depicts the person in a negative aspect, that is, it says how not to act. Its purpose is to disguise the twenty-first Principle, the construction of which can give dangerous keys to the path-walking person if they are handed over prematurely. The secret of this principle is revealed after Initiation into Hermeticism, that is, after mastering the apparatus of the earthly Baphomet. And only when the consciousness is completely and firmly closed in the Spiritual World can the mystery be perceived without the danger of decomposition of one's own consciousness and breakdown into black magic. This mystery relates to the construction of the apparatus of the Universal Creative Mind, of which we are a part and, thus, giving the keys to man's own self-creation and creativity, at the same time threatens to cause scepticism in him that os much more hopeless and deep than ordinary human scepticism, if the human consciousness has not outgrown itself. Those areas that lie above the principle of Reason can no longer be called areas of manifestation of consciousness, because they go to the very depths of the subjective spirit and open only with the fading of consciousness, that is, the ability to distinguish between Subject and Object. These areas are reached not by the exertion of reason or consciousness, but by the exertion of a mystical-religious feeling and can be marked by the meaningless word "super-consciousness".

This area is marked by a meeting with the Second Guardian of the Threshold and is characterised by an element of Godliness, if by God we mean the Creative Logos of the Universe.

The twenty-first Principle, if we assume a zero value, runs like a red thread through the twenty-second Principle and it is not for nothing that it also marks the upper ray of the redemptive cliche. What is zero? This is the source of all numbers and it is not for nothing that it is designated by a circle, it is the limit of infinitely small and infinitely large quantities. Even visionary mathematicians have long ceased to attribute the value of emptiness to zero. Zero is the self-closing circle of the world. Zero is a potential that has undergone differentiation since then, that is, the incomprehensible material of all the magnitudes of the world. It denotes the completeness of absolute Unity, and therefore the main title of the principle Love.

The science of love is unknown to people, and, perhaps, it is impossible to formulate it in earthly existence. To do this, we need other instruments of perception of thought-creation than our earthly guides and even than our Higher Manas. Only the full development of the Buddhi principle with all the organs of perception and creativity enclosed in this thinnest shell of our Spirit creates the conditions that are necessary for studying Love. But Love is the only force of the Universe - creating, dissolving and protecting. Its root nature and unity are incomprehensible and elusive for consciousness, but these three aspects are manifested in all world processes. Thinking about the experiences of love, even in our earthly state, listening deeply and subtly to its strings, a person can take revenge on the most contradictory shades. These contradictions arose from the inability to understand the primary source of all our manifestations on all planes of consciousness.

As the root of power, creative love seems to contradict its own nature: After all, to create the means to isolate something out of itself, that is, to violate unity. At the same time, if we think more deeply into the meaning of creativity, we will see that every manifestation of it establishes a unity between the subjective and objective world, imprinting the Subject in the Object and, as it were, drawing the Object into the Subject. We cannot explain in words or even mentally formulate the primary process of dividing Unity into Subject and Object, or the last process of restoring their Unity. But those who have reached the deepest heights of these subjective-spiritual states are unanimously confirmed that in both cases the first and last mystery of Love is manifested.

We can observe a distant and closed reflection of these processes in man-woman love. And here love tends to Unity, then to separation, in order to have a subject and an object of its manifestation. We can find the same thing among mystics - bhakti-yogis - precisely at the stage in which God appears as a beloved or beloved; love appears either in the form of ecstasy of complete surrender, or in the form of rapture of separation for the contemplation of the beloved.

In the aspect of polar separation, Love is a single creative force, because all forms of the world on all its planes are born from the tension and interaction of the poles. Love in this aspect is Life in all the dynamic processes of the Universe. Love in the aspect of unity is the Dissolving force of the Universe. This is a process that subjectively expands consciousness and transfers it to a higher level. This is a process that dissolves forms in their synthetic source and, again, an example can be taken of androgynous love, where both poles, being lost and dissolved in each other, pass into a more perfect state that includes both poles of the world. Thus, love in a dissolving aspect, even in a narrow manifestation, will save you from egoism and increases the level of consciousness.

In its third aspect, as a Single Protecting Force, Love is expressed by Universal Motherhood, which keeps both of these processes in balance, and in the purest form asserts a fundamental Unity.

There are many aspects of Love and love in the forms of human existence, but the basis of it is always based on polarisations in some plane of consciousness. These polarisations should not be understood only as manifestations of the physical sex, there are much more subtle polarisations, which in relation to some planes put us in the aspect of one sex, and in relation to others - in the aspect of the other sex. Physical polarisation only emphasises the predominance of one sex in the psyche. Therefore, the incarnations do not follow the line of gender, but in this respect they change depending on the psychic stress. On this polarisation all relationships of consciousnesses in the Cosmos are based.

All the psychic influences on each other, not only of people, but also of people on the forces of nature, are based on knowledge and conscious operation of polarisation. Those who say that all magic is based on the interaction of the sexes are right, but those who understand it in a rough sense are wrong. After all, in a very subtle sense, a bhakti yogi is either a man or a woman in relation to God, who changes his aspects accordingly and this is the secret of his spiritual growth, because Love in the manifested world is always polarised and seeks to restore unity. This is the evolutionary power. Therefore, without Love, no achievements are possible - neither knowledge, nor realisational power.

In Sanskrit, Love has three names: Manifested psychically, as an aspiration, it is called **Kama**; manifested mentally, as a search, it is called **Bhakti**; and in its external spiritual aspect, it is called **Prema**. The first in human life is expressed by falling in love, often even regardless of gender; such a subtle love is a very frequent phenomenon on the part of a student to a teacher.

The second is expressed in human relations by friendship, that is, by mental mutual attraction. The third love in human relations is expressed by the feeling of a universal spiritual connection: 1) between a student and a teacher, 2) between friends who deeply understand each other, and 3) between a man and a woman, if they are sister souls.

The mechanism of the power manifestation of Love was already outlined in the eighteenth Principle. The first subtitle of the twenty-first Principle refers to love as the primary radiation of the Spirit. To realise your emotional origin means to realise yourself as a manifestation and conductor of Love. This means that the essence of all your searches and actions is to create Love. Only with such a closeness of the spiritual core in the world of Love, it is possible to get acquainted with the apparatus of its manifestation without harm.

In the mental body, the main accumulator of the forces of love and the main centre of its manifestation is the centre of the Bell. In the astral body, such an organ is the centre of the Heart. And in the etheric body there is the sexual centre, in which all our will for evolution is coiled up. The ability to connect these centres and the ability to subtly use the forces of the etheric sexual centre give the key to any power over Psychic energy in its mental and astral manifestations. In this ability to connect their bodies and use the concentrated power of the etheric body lies the possibility of creating living representations that guide the chain of realised facts.

And so, when a person seizes this opportunity, the fatal question arises before him: "Since I can create ideas and fool other people with them, even if for their benefit, then am I not the same myself? I was fooled by external consciousnesses, which entangled me in the mouth of much more powerful ideas created by them. Since I can build illusions and, if I know the apparatus of their creation, then the personified World Mind-Logos, of which I am a part, according to the known Law of analogy, also builds illusions-representations realised in the Universe, and therefore created the illusion that is called myself? Or am I an illusion, that is, belonging entirely to the objective world in relation to another Subject, of which I am a representation, or am I myself this Subject, and then the whole objective world without an end to all representations?"

Since consciousness was created on the plane of the Higher Mind, as a product of the relationship between the Subject and the Object, the statement of such a question means the end of conscious life. This moment is the moment of meeting with the Second Guardian of the Threshold. This meeting is fraught with two dangers:

1) if the consciousness is insufficiently fixed in the subjective depth, complete agnosticism threatens with the destruction of consciousness, which in this incarnation will end in madness, and in other worlds it will destroy the mental body and the individual monad;

2) with insufficient purification of consciousness from subtle forms of egoism, a psychological substitution of the spiritual core of consciousness with some aspect of it with which it is identified, mainly with our mental principle. In this case, there is a separation of the individual from the spiritual core and the assertion of his highest mental principle as the centre of the Universe, there is a feeling of omnipotent power along with the darkest scepticism and isolation. And since the upward moves are closed in this state, the downward move remains and again, the Higher Manas is replaced by the earthly mind, while preserving one acquired mental experience and knowledge of the

secret of the Sephira "shin". This is how the most terrible and powerful larvae are formed, having an hermetic Initiation that gives power over the psychic energy of the Earth. These creatures fall into the right small triangle of the descending triangle of the hexagram (see Figure 44). Their consciousness is higher than the consciousness of people, but it is directed towards involution.

To successfully pass through the test by meeting the Second Guardian of the Threshold, it is necessary to strengthen the axis of consciousness in the deepest recesses of the soul, that is, Love is necessary. Spiritual Love is the root of religion. You can reach all the levels of Initiation available on our planet and still be defeated by the Second Guardian of the Threshold, if you do not have Love in your Heart and religion in the Bell. But religion is no longer in the sense of connection with the Spiritual World and finding its point of suspension in it, but in the sense of feeling something indefinable in oneself, that it lies behind consciousness in whatever form, which is the background and the true homeland of the "I", where every Subject and Object disappears in the unity we call God. The development of the ability to be a witness of oneself and the world saves one from identifying the spiritual core with consciousness.

Immediately after the victory over the Second Guardian of the Threshold, the whole world appears to be unreal and your own consciousness only a dream in which dreams are created. But on the other hand, another reality is acquired, namely, the reality of living connections between consciousnesses, which establishes their unity in addition to all historical conventions, ethical standards and laws, that is, an eternal Essence is perceived in each phenomenon and not a manifested form.

In this world of true realities, all the scales of the Mind are collapsing and other scales, the scales of the Soul, are applied. The intensity of Love and the intensity of Life determine the value of phenomena. The twentieth Principle already introduces us to this area, and the twenty-first Principle precedes it. If we consider that in the system of twenty-two major Principles, the last four, briefly denoting the four minor areas, are given in reverse order, then this explains:

1) the law of the reverse reflection of the fifteenth Principle.

2) the caution of the Initiator, who first seeks to strengthen the suspension point created in the disciple to the Spiritual World

and make the spiritual core of his consciousness fall down before meeting with the Second Guardian of the threshold.

After all, after a brief experience of Eternal Reality, a trace of it remains in the immortal soul of a person, which will become a guiding star in the difficult process of detaching the spiritual core from consciousness. The main thing is that during this separation, the true Spiritual Core is found, that is, one's own Divine Essence and the potential of individual consciousness would not be destroyed and could - in the future - be used "from top to bottom", that is, as an instrument of manifestation. This process is similar to the meeting with the First Guardian of the Threshold, when it is important to preserve the integrity of the earthly vehicles. Having detached from the Higher Manas, the Soul is freed from self-hypnosis and hypnosis of ideas generated either by its own consciousness or by the collective consciousness, into which its individual consciousness was an integral part. And it is important, first of all, to perform the second part of the work aimed at strengthening the self-hypnosis of one's own ideas in order to free consciousness from the hypnosis of collective ideas.

The mystery of "Shin" will give this opportunity to consciousness: To voluntarily identify with the ideas created by itself. True, instead of one "stupid [fool's] cap" it puts on another, but this other is created by itself and therefore it is easier to get rid of it. These representations make sense when they overcome the dependence on collective representations and therefore should be the reverse of the latter. For example, let's take the hypnosis of the collective idea of humanity about old age and death, which does not exist anywhere in the universe, except for human consciousness. To get out of the hypnosis of these ideas, it is not enough to deny them, but it is necessary to build an idea of constantly renewing youth and continuous birth.

Let's give another example: We know that high Initiates can absorb the most powerful poisons without harm. Again, all the dangers and ideas about harm are only representations of human consciousness, but it is not enough to ignore them or simply not know them, because the subconscious will still perceive the usual hypnosis. It is necessary to create in it an idea of the usefulness of everything that our body absorbs, and the idea of the body itself as a powerful alchemical furnace that processes everything for its own good.

Or here is another example: High Initiates can go without food for a very long time, they saturate the tissues of their body with prana, which in their view takes the form of nutrients, and therefore really nourishes the body. Let us not forget that there is a product of thought-creation in the world, but it is possible to fully master the apparatus of thought-creation only by breaking out your consciousness from the power of any hypnosis, even divine.

The experienced cognition of the above has led the brave consciousnesses that persisted before this experience to understand the world as , as a network of illusions - representations from which the core of consciousness can only escape, but it should also be released. The first stage of this liberation is associated with a titanic struggle taking place inside one's own consciousness and this struggle will cause at first a negative attitude towards Maya. But then when they go out into the world of pure perception of Love and Life, they also acquire the Love of Life. After all, all these illusions are manifestations of Love and its creative power. The world, which was first subjected to denial, is accepted back by a transformed attitude towards it. And the winner of the Second Guardian of the Threshold cannot be otherwise. The difference between spirit and matter is erased, the last dualism of God and the World," I "and" not-I", disappears. Consciousness can voluntarily fade away from complete non-identification and be identified voluntarily with any consciousness. This is Freedom, where there is no Law, but there is the Joy of creative play.

For a person free from illusions, from Mukti, as it is called in India, the world, though Maya, is not a meaningless illusion. Meaning will be acquired when causality and expediency disappear. Only then does a thing acquire its own value and the true right of its existence exactly in the form in which it is, because every phenomenon is an imprint of some aspect of Love manifested in Life.

Each phenomenon is a sign that speaks about the Gods, a symbol of one of its creative possibilities and each phenomenon, at the same time, is also a sign of itself, that is, of the Initiate himself, and tells him about himself, because we can only include in our consciousness what has been in us for centuries. The providence of this state inspired Dostoevsky to the words that he put into the mouth of the elder Zosima: "Every person is responsible for the whole world", because what enters into the consciousness of a person has always been contained in it and is one of its constituent parts. Thus, everything in the world speaks about ourselves, and we hide in the world exactly what we ourselves are made of.

Since each thing has the value of its own inner meaning, then the evaluation of phenomena changes, because it occurs not according to conditional measures, but according to the inner essence of the phenomenon itself. Thus, the ethical difference between good and evil is erased and every moment of existence has meaning. The reality of this state of affairs is confirmed by the rarest, but real facts in our life. Let us remember the robbers who became saints, let us remember the sinners who became carriers of the spirit.

The secret of the Sephira "shin", which ignites three fires in our three vehicles of creative power, will give us the key to transferring creative power to any plane of all manifestations and this connects the worlds of these manifestations in ourselves. The most vivid expression of the creative power of our etheric body is the production of our own kind. Rolled up in the sexual centre, this creative force determines the reserve of sensuality, which itself indicates the degree of wealth of creative power. But saving in this regard is wastefulness in relation to the reserve of forces. The observance of economy, that is, self-control in the field of the manifestation of the sexual instinct, transfers the creative force to another plane of manifestation. But it is not enough to expose yourself to asceticism, which alone can only shake the nervous system and bring more harm than good. It is necessary to ignite the Heart centre in the astral body, and then the reserve of sensuality becomes the temperament of the manifestation of love and potentiates its intensity.

The creative force transferred to the astral body is directed to the service of one's neighbour and in the presence of talents due to the planetary composition, it strains these talents with a thirst for creativity, expressed on the astral plane by art. The same creative force transferred to the centre of the Bell ignites the mental body with the search for Truth and, again, in the presence of talents determined by the planetary composition, is revealed by mental creativity - a philosophical, scientific or ideological desire for the realisation of Truth. Finally, translated into the Spiritual World, this force strengthens our religion, that is, our connection with this world and ignites us with intense God-seeking and mystical religious creativity. Of course, the forms in which this creativity manifests itself depend on the planetary composition of the mental or astral bodies. This is how religious philosophies and mystical art are born.

The process of transferring the creative force from the etheric body to the higher planes of its manifestation often occurs unconsciously in life. A strong sensual love, a passion that embraces the person, for not having the opportunity to be realised and live out life in the etheric plane, sublimates into intense Love. It also potentiates creative manifestations in other areas and since the Heart, in addition to the Bell, is connected with the World of the Spirit, the more intense such Love is, the more mystical religious connotations it receives and the more valuable and spiritualising the creativity it excites. Let us recall a the example of Dante and Beatrice. If this love had lived out on the ethereal plane, there would have been no "Divine Comedy". This transfer of creative power to other levels of manifestation can also be done consciously. Anyone who knows the secret of the Sephira "shin" can use it in both directions - both in the sense of the subjective work of transferring the creative force up from matter to Spirit and in the sense of building descriptive representations.

So, let nobody complain about their sensuality, for they will be able to transfer it, by igniting the Kundalini current, to the astral and mental plane and from there transform it into a powerful spiritual current. The key to this flow is the construction of appropriate ideas, the ability to merge consciousness with them, self-discipline of the will and the development of creative talents in oneself.

The Great Guardian of the Threshold

The appearance of the Small Guardian of the Threshold clearly shows what it is still missing in order to achieve that bright image that can once again inhabit the pure Spiritual world. Unconsciously, a person stands every night before a Small Guardian of the Threshold, which, upon awakening, prevents him from consciously entering into his own inner essence, since now a person would not be able to transfer his own appearance in all its unsightly appearance.

Having entered the supersensible world, the disciple becomes convinced that this world was already there when there was no mention of the sensory world and that the entire external world developed from the invisible world. He begins to understand, that he himself, before he first came to this sensory world, first belonged to the supersensible but this former, supersensible, world needed to pass through the sensory one. Its further development would have been impossible without this passage, without people who developed the corresponding abilities on Earth. In the supersensible world, the fruits grown in the sense world ripen, which will be defeated as such, but the results of which will become part of the Higher.

This gives us the key to understanding illness and death in the sensory world. Death is nothing but an expression of the fact that the former supersensible world has come to a point beyond which it can develop further by itself. He must receive a new influx of life, which will become a struggle against common death. From the remnants of a dying, frozen world in itself, the beginnings of a new one have blossomed. That is why we have death and life in the world and one thing slowly turns into another. The dying parts of the old world continue to cling to the rudiments of new life that have come out of them.

This is most clearly expressed in man, as he carries his shell on himself, what has been preserved from the former, ancient world. And inside this shell, the germ of a being is formed, which is destined to live in the future. Thus, he is a dual being, both mortal and immortal.

The mortal is in its finite state and the immortal is in its initial state, but only within this dual world, which finds its expression in the physical-sensory, does a person learn the abilities necessary to lead the world to immortality. His task is to extract fruits from the mortal himself for the immortal. Thus, a person carries within himself the elements of a dying world that work in him and whose power he can break with the help of newly reviving immortal forces. This is how a person's path goes from death to life. A person should admit to himself in his dying hour that the dying beginning was burned by the teacher and that it is a consequence of the past, with which he is closely connected. The burden of earthly life is only an expression of how much the new life was able to take away from the dying past and the disease is only the continuing action of the dying parts of the past.

From all of the above, we get an answer to the question: "Why does a person only gradually make his way out of error and imperfection to Truth and Goodness?"

His actions, feelings and thoughts are at first under the power of the transitory and the dying. Out of the transitory, the sensory-physical organs are formed, which are therefore doomed to share a perishable fate and with them everything that is the result of the activity of these organs, that man had to develop in himself for his further development. Thus, the Small Guardian of the Threshold is a semblance of humanity in its dual nature, consisting of the transitory and the imperishable. A person cannot achieve a luminous image, because he is still entangled in the physical-sensual nature. The process of human liberation also includes his reincarnation in increasingly highly developed and advanced human forms, as well as passing through all the more pure forms of moral and religious views.

But the Little Guardian of the Threshold is only the result of past times, containing the germs of the future. A person must bring with him to the future supersensible world everything that he can extract from the sensory world. If he had brought with him only what was woven into his double from past times, then he would have fulfilled his earthly task only partially. After some time, therefore, a second, Great Guardian of the Threshold, joins the Small Guardian of the Threshold. Let's imagine again in the form of an appeal what happens when we meet this Second Guardian of the Threshold.

After a person has learned what to get rid of, an exalted, luminous image appears on his path. It is difficult to describe this beauty. Towards this soul, freed from all sensual ties, comes the second Guardian of the Threshold and says approximately the following:

"You have freed yourself from the world of feelings and won your right to a Homeland in the Spiritual World. You don't need your physical form anymore. But look at me. Look how immeasurably high I stand above everything that you have made of yourself so far. You have reached the present stage of perfection thanks to the abilities that you could develop in the sensory world, but now the time must come when your liberated forces will begin to work on this sensory world themselves. Until now, you have only freed yourself. Now, liberated, you can free all your companions in the sense world with you. Until now, you have moved forward as an individual. Merge now with the whole in order to bring with you into the supersensible world not only yourself, but also everything else that exists in the sense world. Someday you will be able to connect with my image, but I cannot be blissful while there is misery. As a single liberated person, you could already enter the realm of the supersensible right now. But then you would be forced to look at the sensuous being that is not yet liberated of the world. And you would separate your fate from theirs. But you are all connected to each other. You all had to descend into the sensory world in order to bring out the forces for the Higher from it. The forces that you have entangled in the sense world with them, you must now share with them. Therefore, I am blocking your access to the Higher Regions until you turn all the powers you have acquired to liberate the world you are involved in.

"With what you have already achieved, you can remain in the lower regions of the Spiritual World, but I stand before the gate to the Higher One, like a '*cherub with a fiery sword before the gates of Paradise*' and I block your access, while you still have the strength left without use in the sensitive world. And if you don't want to use them yourself, others will come who use them. And then the high Spiritual World will perceive all the fruits of the sensual. The soil with which you have grown together will disappear from under your feet. The development of the purified world will leave you behind, you will be excluded from it. Thus, your path will be "black". Those from whom you have separated go the "white way".

So the All-Faced Guardian of the Threshold announces itself shortly after the meeting of the Initiate with the First Guardian. But the Initiate knows exactly what lies ahead if he succumbs to the temptations of a premature stay in the supersensible world. An indescribable brilliance comes from the Second Guardian, but the connection with him stands before the contemplating soul as a distant goal. He knows that this union will be possible only when the Initiate turns to the cause of liberation and salvation of the world all the forces flowing to him from this world. If he decides to follow the requirements of the higher light vision, he will be able to contribute to the liberation of the human race. He will bring his gifts to the sacrificial altar of humanity. If he prefers his own premature ascent into the supersensible world, then the flow of humanity will pass by him. After his liberation, he will no longer be able to draw any new forces for himself from the sensory world. If he still devotes his work to him, it will only be if he refuses to extract any benefit for himself from the very field of this further activity.

This choice of the white path depends entirely on whether a person at the moment of this choice is already so purified that no egoistic motives will make the temptations of bliss tempting for him. For these temptations are the greatest that can be imagined. There are no temptations on the white path, that is, nothing here echoes egoism. What a person receives in the higher regions of the Spiritual World is not something emanating from him - his love for the world around him. On the black path, a person's egoism does not lack for anything and if someone is looking for bliss only for himself, then he will probably go the back way.

Therefore, no one should expect from the occultists of the white way any instructions that contribute to the development of his own egoistic "I". The bliss of an individual person does not at all intersect them, it is exclusively concerned with the development and liberation of all beings - both humans and all human companions in this world. Therefore, they only give instructions on how to develop their forces for general work in this direction. For the same reason, above all other abilities, they put selfless self-giving, readiness for sacrifice. Therefore, whoever really follows the instructions of the good teachers of occult science, he will meet the requirements of the Great Guardian.

The student is kept away from the Aboveground World until he enters it with a willingness to give himself and to participate in the General Work. The natural omnipotence of the Sun is immersed in the very depths of the Divine Spirit and is directly in contact with the Absolute. It can be said that the Sun consciousness constantly contemplates God within itself. The Sun itself can be symbolically defined as an open door to the Eternity of the Absolute, and the being living in it can be defined as the guardian of the Threshold of this door.

Arthur Bowen Davies, Dweller on the Threshold

The World

The Twenty-second Arcanum

The Realisation of the Great Work

The Absolute
The Magician's Crown
Natural Omnipotence
Numeric designation: 400
Astrological correspondence: The sun

Il Sole, dettaglio da una miniatura del codice De Sphaera

In the Symbolic picture is drawn an oval formed by a snake biting its own tail. In the centre is the figure of a dancing girl, in whose hands two sticks are on the same level. In the four corners of the picture there are images of four hermetic animals, with a taurus in the lower right corner and a man in the upper left.

The astrological correspondence - the Sun - denotes the highest stage of consciousness that it needs to reach in order to connect with the Absolute. The centres of Life and the Creativity flowing out of them are scattered throughout the universe and, in our system, such a centre is the Sun. Having reached the solar consciousness, the soul will finally throw off the illusions of representations and will be freed from the self-hypnosis of its own consciousness, that is, the principle of the Great Manas, which is rolled up into the organ of idolatry.

The solar consciousness seems to cover the entire universe, although it is enclosed in the framework of the physical body. This physical body is only a conductor of the golden radiance on Earth. Having reached this state, the soul no longer needs any guides and will pass directly through the physical body, borrowing each time for its manifestation the necessary vibrations directly from the external environment, because it is the mistress of all these vibrations.

There is no need for any more space travel for God-knowledge and God-worship because the spiritual essence is the essence of the Sun and is immersed in the very depths of the Divine Spirit, directly in contact with the Absolute. It can be said that the Sun's consciousness constantly contemplates God within itself. The Sun itself can be symbolically defined as an open door to the Eternity of the Absolute and the being living within it can be defined as The guardian of the Threshold of this door.

The meeting with this Third Guardian of the Threshold is already devoid of a dramatic shade and is a joyful meeting between your own spiritual self and with God. The Solar Religion, therefore, was considered the highest religion of antiquity, the natural symbolism of which is fixed on our sky. But this religion is so high that the consciousness of modern humanity cannot perceive it in all its purity, perceiving it only in a Redemptive Cliche of its reflection, divided into aspects and sectors of actions.

It is difficult to define a state that is independent of these conductors using the symbols of the lesser Manas and even the fixing formulas of the Greater Manas. Therefore, the Buddha speaks of a Great Silence coming at the threshold of Nirvana. The transition to this state can be symbolically expressed by the following representation: The Soul, the principle of Buddhi, embraces the entire circle of the Universe, both in space and in time, while the Spirit is immersed in its eternal essence and thereby establishes the Unity of the essence of all phenomena in the Universe embraced by the soul. The individual consciousness, like a funnel, absorbs the reality of this state and transmits its ray to the earth's conductors. There are countless such individuals in the universe and there are even more guides associated with the conditions of existence of individual luminaries, because individuality changes them over time on each luminary. But the soul is one, there is only a Universal Soul, it is boundless. The Spirit is eternal.

Circle of Life: Buddhi-Life, Spirit Atman (doors to Eternity) - the transition to the Absolute.

Circle of Antiquity: The Funnel of the Great Manas (Mind), Individuality, the Great Manas in a person.

These states are achieved in complete silence but, at the same time, not only the earthly conductors of the personality are turned off but also the individual consciousness itself, which does not belong to the Earth, but to the planetary system. Of course, these states slip away with any manifestation, remaining a background of manifestations, to which you can always return. In its essence, the "I" feels like an Absolute, abiding everywhere. In its manifestation, the "I" feels like a thread of the Absolute, manifesting as an individual through personal vehicles. In fact, each being is such a thread of the Absolute, conscious or unconscious, that is, it has grown or has not grown to this self-knowledge. In such a state, horizontal planes disappear, because the divinity of phenomena, as expressions of the threads of the Absolute, is quite clear. The horizontal planes are illusory, since they arose due to the work of Manas and illusory self-identification with the states of consciousness created by them. The realisation of oneself as the divine thread of the Absolute is the realisation of the Great Work within oneself. The realisation of All outward Doing is the transformation of the world into a divine manifestation. Thus, the rejected Maya becomes the veil of the Mother of the World, that is, the World Soul. To find the Philosopher's Stone means to find the divine essence of each phenomenon, to be able to evoke it and, thus, transform phenomena. This gives a natural Omnipotence, not burdened with any taste of power, but connected only with the manifestation of Love. Who will not joyfully and voluntarily submit to the influence of the soul, which will be able to make valuable gems of the divine manifestation from the surrounding environment?

Not only people but also angels recognise this spiritual, gentle Omnipotence. The actions, therefore, are also about the phenomena of such an "I", which appeals to the divine essence of every phenomenon, not only do not pose a test, but are a magnet of the highest intensity for everyone in whom the spark of Atman is alive. It is only in the shadows with a faded consciousness that they cause death spasms of anger.

This natural omnipotence is shown to us by the examples of great teachers such as the Buddha and Ramakrishna, whose actions were always aimed at revealing the divine essence of everything that their consciousness touched.

The process of such actions is the radiation of the Spiritual Core, acting directly on the Spiritual core of another consciousness, which is one for everyone. Already this Spiritual core instantly changes the vibrations of individual consciousness with its radiation and through it changes the vibrations of the mental psyche and the etheric energy of the conductors. This is the basis for the miracles of instant conversions of sinners into saints, as well as the healing of diseases, accompanied by the words: "Your sins are forgiven." This spiritual formula speaks of an instantaneous change of consciousness in the direction of spiritualisation, burning the karma of the past at this last stage of physical manifestation.

By the direct radiation of the Buddhi principle, which embraces all the phenomena of universal life, changes are made in the waves of karma, which change the relations between the elements. The Spirits of Nature perceive the order of these changes, leading them to the processes of nature. This explains the miracles that are being done in the natural world.

As for the second subtitle "The Crown of the Magician" or, rather, the Crown of the Initiate, it is expressed by listing the qualities of the manifestation of solar consciousness, called the Twenty-two advantages of the magician:

1. The Magician sees God without dying (without losing the individual "I").
2. The Magician remains unchanged in all changes. He hears the song of life and owns all the poles.
3. The Magician is born and dies voluntarily and is free in his thought-creation.
4. The Magician is the lord of every form, all the laws of the world are in him.
5. The Magician reigns together with heaven and hell serves the magician.
6. The Magician is omniscient: All paths under the Sun and Moon are open to him, and he knows the remedy for all diseases.
7. The Magician does not know the longing of the soul for his sister, since he carries her and the elements in himself.
8. The Magician does not depend on karma, but Creates Karma on Earth.
9. The magician possesses creative power in the three planes of manifestation and possesses the secret of romantic youth.
10. The Magician is the bearer of the Common Good, and his words are the Covenant.
11. All the forces of the world help the magician.
12. The magician rests his feet on the sky, giving light to the Earth.

13. The Magician knows his reincarnations.
14. The Magician overcomes space with its deduction.
15. The Magician possesses the ability to dispose of all types of Psychic energy.
16. The Magician does not know compulsion and is not afraid of death.
17. The Book of nature is open to the magician - he has all kinds of clairvoyance.
18. The Magician does not know obstacles or dangers and does not have enemies.
19. The Magician owns the Philosopher's Stone and has the ability to transform even garbage into gold.
20. The Magician has power over the past and the future, living in the eternal.
21. The Magician does not know disappointments and is able to create illusions of the world.
22. The Magician is immortal even with the physical body, he is able to dissect his consciousness and split the shells.
Peace, Glory and Joy are his lot.

To these advantages, we can add twenty-two aspects of mastering Psychic Energy which, according to analogies, depending on the growth of consciousness, can be applied on a planetary, and then on a cosmic scale:

1. When gathering everything inside yourself, close yourself off from the surrounding influences. Go into your subjective depth and from there distribute your mental, astral and etheric capabilities. Pull yourself together and remember that you are the centre.
2. Do not tell anyone about your plan. The departure of the word is the departure of energy, so do not relax your tension. The environment should not know what you are planning, but it should hear about what you want to do: The expectation and tension of its elements will reveal your friends and enemies.
3. Hiding behind a secret, build representations using the methods necessary for your task - concentration, meditation, contemplation. With the latter, let go of the idea of an emotional-volitional attitude, but continue to carry it calmly in your mind so it will develop and stand out as an independent force, without losing contact with you, so the force will result in a fact.
4. Rely mentally on the creative cycles that you have previously implemented. Do not try to create something that lies outside of your experience and expand the line you started from small to

great. Previous achievements are your foundation. Do not be distracted by other thoughts - they will come to you when it is necessary.

5. Be able to handle the dark and light forces - creation and destruction. Do not forget that the dark forces are the dark guardians of the boundaries of your work. Do not create a counter-pole of repulsion from them but attract them as a measure of doing. So you will master the two poles, remembering that the tension of one causes the tension of the other and the thinning of one is the thinning of the other. So, use the threat of enemies as advice.

6. Be able to spiritualise and materialise. For the first, having a suspension point – religion - develop and strengthen it with spiritual exercises and the stay of consciousness in the Spiritual Sun. For the second - preserve, develop and strengthen the nervous system in the body, using the life force of the Sun. So you will build an axis between the spiritual will and the earthly will, along which Psychic energy will flow upward in a spiral. Remember that only the combination of these two generates a real action. Only those of your actions are successful which coincide with the general plan of the Universe and the deadline for completing the task. Everything else is doomed to failure.

7. Be able to attract the planetary currents to cooperation. Prepare yourself with the planetary breath - with it you will strengthen your dominance over the earthly battles of the planets, and having acquired it, you will enter into relations with the planetary Entities. Remember that each action must have the entire planetary spectrum in order to capture all the elements in the environment.

8. Take into account the strength of the resistance of the environment and the danger of a return blow of the psychic charge. Therefore, let your messages be positive. Be able to master the counteraction - the construction of a mental image of the second possibility, designed to use the strength of the latter.

9. Every action must pass through three stages of the manifestation of Psychic energy, through: The mental plane, where a representation is built by concentration; the astral plane - a picture of the unfolding desired future; and the etheric plane - the volitional tension of sending this picture to the environment. The created load on the etheric plane itself already puts pressure on the consciousness of the surrounding and causes the desired event. Caution will help prevent emotional investment in the action - in the name of maintaining dominance over the environment.

10. Be able to pronounce words. The word is the final formula of action, containing a mental scheme, an astral picture and etheric power of the latter. The Word defines and creates events and phenomena. Be able to reveal the content of the sacred magic words and apply the power contained in them to your action. The word is the centre and the facts are its periphery. Having mastered the power of the word you will be able to expand the centre point into a circle and bring the circle to a point.

11. If you are weak, summon the forces of the egregore, whose sacred words you use. Summon harmoniously attuned helpers and make a mental chain of them. Remember that two people neutralise each other, three are three times stronger than one, seven are seven times seven times and with fifteen you, yourself, are able to move the whole parade. Be able to attract the Spirits of Nature, that is, the Spirits of the Elements, to your work. Be able to make a complete chain.

12. Be able to make a sacrifice in time and use it. The victim is a pillar of power, necessary for Creativity. Be able to use the Subtle Forces activated by the victim. Measure the victim with the result. Do not mention it yourself either by thought or by word - but let it be seen in a Thin and Dense layer.

13. Separate the mental body from the astral, the astral from the etheric and then the etheric from the physical. Lay out the composition of your personality and send your bodies into space and time, accurately determining the picture of their preliminary concentration. The solar plexus is the spring of the allocation and sending of your bodies.

14. Feed the Dense bodies with the energy of the Subtle bodies, strengthening the consciousness in the Spirit, its energy flow is exhausted. To work in the Subtle conductors, feed them with the power of dense bodies, the power of the Earth, for which your action is assigned. Strengthen the point of suspension and contact with the source of the Spirit and do not get off the ground but strengthen the fulcrum. Between these points, create an axis of waves by which the earthly will of the etheric body tends upwards, and the spiritual will-downwards. At the points of their contact, a vortex is created that captures the environment.

15. So you will master the secret of the birth of vortices of Psychic energy and the ability to create and direct its spinning spirals. Do not leave the suspension point, let your "I" be above the vortices. Create them by the order of the spirit, not by the request of desire. Do not take into account the details of the mechanism, because they depend on the environment and taking them into account will break the unity of action. Be able to create the right

mental gender in yourself, according to the nature of the vortex. Be able to wait for the" departure to the ground " sent by you a vortex, that is, an implementation. Repeat the actions if necessary, but do not interrupt his forces by creating other vortices.

16. Be able to threaten with the construction of frightening representations in case of resistance. The magician holds a cup of patience in his right hand but a sword of intimidation in his left. Be able to use coercion.

17. Draw life force from nature to replenish the reserves of the lower conductors. Draw on the Psychic energy of the Sun - it awakens intuition. Be able to sensitively catch the signs of nature in order to dominate the latter. The charges of the Solar Psychic energy of a person are similar to natural electricity, but more complicated than it. So you will be able to command the grass, rain and clouds. But when dominating, remember the Love and respect for nature and its forces - do not abuse the domination.

18. You are not alone. You are a link in a hierarchical chain that goes into Infinity, and you fulfil its task. Find your own hierarchical line and use wisely the creative power flowing through it. Do not change the egregore line, do not go from step to step. Remember that your karma falls on the egregore and its tasks are yours. By the power of the egregore, defend yourself from enemies, weave an impenetrable network from it against envolts. The circle and your aura, imbued with the power of the egregore, are your shield. Apply his mantras and symbols. Know the nature of the forces and the qualities of the vibrations flowing out of them. Sensitively distinguish friends from enemies by the quality of their thinking and vibrations. Do not attack yourself but protect yourself. The best protection is the powerful radiation of the heart.

19. Attract to action all your forces - large and small, contained in your qualities - group them around the axis of action. In the same way, use all the vibrations in the environment. You are the centre of action and remember that the magic of personal example is the strongest. The more perfect you are during the action, the more perfect the result of the action.

20. Be able to take into account the timing of the entry into force of the thought images created by you. Use the mental calm of the environment to throw them into the energy waves. The ability to take into account deadlines is the wisdom of action.

21. By the centre of the Bell, seek contact along the hierarchical line with spiritual cosmic radiations. Seek contact with the

environment with your heart. Create mental images in your
mental body, the top of which is in the nervous system
the system is the throat centre. Create an emotional picture in
the lotus of the Solar Plexus and with a volitional push collected
in the sexual centre, push the formed living thought form into an
individual or collective environment - for independent life in it.
This is the apparatus of creativity.
22. Build yourself an egg of the mental body by the circulation of
mental energy, an egg of the astral body by the circulation of
cosmic Psychic energy, an egg of the etheric body by the
circulation of the Kundalini current. Connect the glowing eggs
with the spiritual axis. By feeding each other, the bodies remain
plastic and transform the tissues of the physical body. So you will
gain immortality.

The dancing girl in the symbolic picture speaks about the "Great
Planet of the Mother of the World", that is, about the state of
freedom that the "I" reaches, living in the shell of Buddhi with its
roots immersed in the Absolute. In this state there is no
Hierarchy, no laws, nor any regularity. It is true that the universe
was created by the "unreasonable (super-intelligent) will of God"
or "the game of the Mother of the World". But such is the nature
of the part of our Mind that it perceives every manifestation of
the "Will of God" as a law. And now, by his own thought-
creation, he establishes the cycles of the great dynamic law in the
directions of causality and expediency - these two sticks,
which the dancing girl holds at the same level. And only the one
who, having got used to the ideation of the Mind, begins to see
and (understand) the incomprehensible free will, is already able
to juggle both sticks independently and arbitrarily.

Mantras to the Arcana

1. I am
2. Not I, but You-I adjure you by your God
3. Nothing happens, everything is born. I am a child of God
4. The weight of the comprehended - I realise
5. Everything that is light helps me, everything that is dark helps me
6. I am free - nothing will take me prisoner.
7. The Spirit always overcomes the flesh in me.
8. Peace, peace, peace - in me, and peace to all, I live for the future.
9. My mind is as bright as the sun. The heart is as pure as a crystal. The soul is as big as the universe. The Spirit is as powerful as God - and is one with Him.
10. Neither to the right nor to the left nor to God, I will create God in myself.
11. I am strong, I am brave, I am fearless, for I am pure in spirit, heart and flesh.
12. I do not condemn anyone and do not reject anyone, but I accept and understand everyone.
13. I am immortal, and nothing in the worlds can destroy me.
14. I control myself and measure my manifestations.
15. I am the creator of my karma, and therefore I am the lord. All responsibility is on me and in me.
16. I die and am reborn like a phoenix from the ashes.
17. Distant worlds attract me to infinity.
18. Let the past die, at least to extinguish it when it was the blood of his Heart.
19. I have all the Wisdom of the World in me.
20. I live in the eternal: the past and the future are mine.
21. Every moment is the present, in which I create in the image and likeness of God.
22. God is in me, and I am God in the flesh.

A General Conclusion of the

Twenty-Two Principles

The application of the Great Work consists in the complete restoration of the continuity of consciousness in all the vehicles of the Adept's earthly personality, in the acquisition of shells, the result of which is the plasticity of the vehicles capable of endless smooth changes and the immortality of the physical body.
In the Mental body of the Adept, the creative Mind and the earthly mind are merged, the earthly mind is absorbed by the creative Mind and represents the recognition organ of the latter. The earthly astral body connects with the soul (Buddhi) and represents only the light shell of the latter, woven from cosmic rays. The etheric body is a stream of the purest life force (Prana), which constantly renews the physical body and thins it until the entire dense composition is replaced by a new one. This process should be completed by the age of 120, that is, by the maximum age of human life, after which his body becomes immortal and unfadingly young.
The adept, living with consciousness in the Eternal, is the Master of his shells. He can manifest in his different bodies, thickening them in different places at the same time. It easily exteriorises one shell from another, splitting and interlocking them arbitrarily. Signs of transformation of the Adept's physical body are as follows:

1. Reduction of specific gravity.
2. Non-susceptibility to diseases, infections and poisoning.
3. Slowing down the aging process and stopping it, rejuvenation.
4. Ease of exteriorisation.
5. Incombustibility, deflection of bullets, arrows, and so on by vibrations of the etheric body.

The old physical body of the Adept is gradually dying, due to the cycle of the Kundalini current, its materials are burned, being gradually replaced by new, more perfect ones. By the age of 180, this process ends: By this time, the former body finally dies and a new Adept body is finally formed.
The general conclusion from the twenty-two Principles: The first Principle was fully realised in the twenty-second: the snake bites

its tail. But the figure described by the snake is not a circle, but an ellipse, that is, the potential opportunity, having been realised, has changed. It includes new opportunities from the cosmic environment embraced by it, which, as it were, stretched the potential and by this stretching cause it to a new circle of manifestation, to the creation of a new Universe. This temporal process is reflected in every moment of time. The construction of the universe is thus never finished.

Since the construction of the universe is never finished, there is no end point at which we could get out of it; however, this end point is everywhere.

The first Principle was fully realised at the twenty-second: The snake bites its tail. But the figure described by the snake is not a circle but an ellipse, that is, the potential opportunity, having been realised, has changed. It includes new opportunities from the cosmic environment embraced by it, which, as it were, stretched the potential and by this stretching bring it to a new circle of manifestation, to the creation of a new Universe. This timeless process is reflected in every moment of time. The construction of the universe is thus never finished. Since the construction of the universe is never finished, there is no single end point at which we could get out of it; rather, this end point is everywhere.

The twenty-first Principle, with its zero value, already outlines an ellipse, because a snake biting its tail is the zero of the first Principle. And the apparatus of the twenty-first Principle, which entangled consciousness in Maya, and again freeing him from Maya, passes through each of the twenty-two Principles in his different aspects. Thus, Maya is hidden in each of the twenty-two Principles and by understanding any Principle and implementing it, you can get rid of this Maya and master the apparatus of the twenty-first Principle.

Each consciousness must determine for itself which Principle is closest to it, that is, the embodiment of which Principle it itself is. This determines the individual path, and all other Princeps will enter this path under the aspect of the main Principle. But it is possible to determine this main Principle only after a thorough acquaintance with all twenty-two Principles.

Thus, according to twenty-two Principles, thoughtful consciousness can arrange all esoteric and exoteric teachings and related disciplinary schools of communities or churches that lead consciousness from the world to God, from Maya to the Absolute. Note that the esoteric schools are built primarily under the sign of the nine first Principles, the exoteric ones - under the sign from the tenth to the eighteenth, and the last four Principles merge these directions into a common achievement. So, every consciousness that aspires to join the world of spiritual realities, can find a way out in its own specific aspect, there is a way out everywhere, because the twenty-two Principles are reflected in all the manifestations of the Universe. Each consciousness must determine for itself which Principle is closest to it, that is, the embodiment of which Principle it itself is. This determines the individual path and all other Principles will enter this path under the aspect of the main Principle, but it is possible to determine this main Principle only after a thorough acquaintance with all twenty-two Principles.

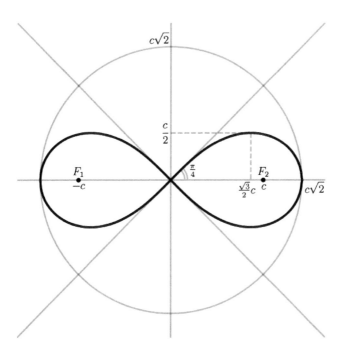

Arcana titles expressed by phrases

All twenty-two Arcs together are the Wheel of Life, in which the beginning, meeting the end, begins a new circle of the spiral.

1 -- 10 Arcana are the principle of the Universe.
10 -- 19 Arcana are power and psychic energies.
19 -- 22 Arcana are the manifestation of psychic energies in the four planes of consciousness.

The First Arcanum

The general title is "The Divine Essence, the Archetype".
Potential opportunity (primary source) is realised, he wants to manifest himself and wants to manifest himself. The motive of the manifestation of Love.

Subheadings:

1. The manifested Subject (Spirit) is always divine in its essence, taken in general or particular aspects, and is always identical with itself.
2. Self-affirmation is the basis of self-manifestation.
3. Self-affirmation is a potential force that transforms the environment of manifestation in its likeness.

The world is the Self in all stages of manifestation.

The Second Arcanum

The general title is " Divine manifestation (Wisdom)". The environment, embraced by the Love of the Primary Source (Subject), is brought into the first movement (Life).

Subheadings:

1. The manifestation of the possibility of the Subject, that is, the object of the first matter (hence the word "mother"). In essence there is a part of the Absolute where matter and Spirit are one.
2. Self-denial is the basis of perception and readiness for change.
3. The flow of change in its synthesis is manifested in a life inspired by self-consciousness.
The world is not Me, forever changing.

The Third Arcanum

General title: The World Mind. The mind - the product of the Spirit (subject) and the First Matter (Object) - reflects the unchanging self-consciousness and the flow of Life changes the stages of consciousness.

Subheadings:

1. The Divine Nature. The Universal Mind or the Law - the One Creator of the Universe - expresses the potential possibilities of the Subject with Ideas: therefore, the nature of all things is Divine.
2. The principle of birth. Nothing is created, everything is created from the Logos or the Mind by the process of its thought creation.
3. Separation of parts. Generated is a part of the whole in a narrowed form, and it itself becomes a process of polarisation by the producer.
Streams of consciousness.

The Fourth Arcanum

General title: "Cosmic Law".
The nature of the Subject, that is, the manifested "I", is connected with the nature of the Object, that is, the developer. The principle of the thought process and the establishment of stages (the allocation of a part) is expressed by the Quaternary Law of Global Dynamics.

Subheadings:

1. Form. All phenomena are created by the manifestation of this regularity to different planes of consciousness, which consists of different relationships between the subject and the object. There are four such planes.
2. Authority. Any subsequent manifestation is based on the previous one and relies on it.
3. Application. The form is a selection from a separate cycle of phenomena, the internal structure of which is expressed by a cross of elements.
A materialising process or causality.

The Fifth Arcanum

The general title: "The Manifestation of Life or Universal Magnetism".

The reflection of the subject in each cycle individualises it into a focus of manifestation of conscious initiative. This is how the individualisation of the initiative is established.

Subheadings:

1. Quintessence (Will). In the cycles, individual consciousnesses are developed that dominate their form. Their sign is the Will to show initiative according to the law of expediency, that is, in the reverse direction of the dynamic flow.
2. The knowledge of good and evil. The continuity of the dynamic cycles of the world spiral unites individual centres in cooperation.
3. Natural religion. Such individualisation presupposes a natural connection (religion) of the centres of individual cycles with the Divine Subject of the All -common "I".
Spiritualising individualisation.

The Sixth Arcanum

The general title is "Choosing paths".

The flow of centrifugal (psychic) energy differentiates the potential capabilities of the subject in the circle of creation. The flow of centripetal force (mental energy), individualised into centres of co-knowledge, integrates the cycles of manifestation in the primary sources.

Subheadings:

1. The method of analogy. In both directions, there are cycles, not equal, but similar to each other.
2. Pentagrammic freedom. Initiative will. He can choose between directions, but the continuity of transitions according to the law of analogy connects the will with either causality or expediency.
3. The space environment. Both power flows are interwoven - they move into the universe and into each part of it with two power triangles of thought-creation "up" and "down", conducting

the forces of the top and bottom into cycles, that is, spiritual and material energy.
The magnetic field of space.

The Seventh Arcanum

General title: "The Victor". The centre of consciousness initiative plus created in the sixth Arcanum, the energy shells from living beings located on a hierarchical ladder and are the causes of world construction.

Subheadings:

1. The spiritual energy of the Subject with his thought-creation dominates the psychic and material energy of objective forms or shells. Domination of the Spirit over form.
2. The victory of the subtle over the dense. The victory of conscious expediency over unconscious necessity establishes the evolution and enriches consciousness with the energies of the newly formed environment.
3. The rights of ownership. Everyone has something over than it works.
The establishment of the principle of hierarchy.

The Eighth Arcanum

General title is "Justice".

The stability of the created is ensured by the equality of causal and expedient forces.

Subheadings:

1. Balance and movement. The excess of evolutionary forces translates the phenomenon into the following states, where it again acquires stability, thanks to the force of the environment's resistance.
2. Regularity. Justice is the equality of expediency and causality: it creates the necessary conditions for the life and manifestation of beings.
3. Karma (causality). Karma is the realisation of balance and justice at the beginning of any historical development.
Construction Conditions

The Ninth Arcanum

General title is "Dedication".

The creative force consists of the equilibrium co-creating and dissolving forces and transforms forms, proceeding from the original source and returning to it.

Subheadings:

1. Dedication. Creative power is transmitted along the ladder of the Universal Hierarchy, establishing the principle of leadership.
2. Managers (patrons). Each knows the mechanics of the creative force and knows its applications in the size of the post occupied.
3. Caution is taking into account the actions of creative forces. Dedication to the field of manifestation of spiritual, mental and psychic forces.

The Tenth Arcanum

General heading: "Implementation".

Realisation - full deployment of a potential opportunity into a creative force that gives an impetus for an action.

Subheadings:

1. The covenant is the unfolding of a potential opportunity into the sphere of the Spiritual World.
2. The world view is the deployment of the mental world in ideas.
2. The wheel of life. The world mill is the unfolding of opportunities into the cycle of phenomena.
The realisation of the plan from the spiritual to the material.

The Eleventh Arcanum

General title: "Purity".

Unselfishness is a condition for mastering creativity.

Subheadings:

1. The divine power is manifested by spiritual energy (spiritual impulses).

2. Human power is manifested by the creativity of mental energy.
3. The force of Nature is manifested by etheric and physical phenomena.
The manifestation of power on all planes depends on the purity of the conductors.

The Twelfth Arcanum

General Title: "Sacrifice".

Sacrifice is the bestowal of the conditions for the manifestation of creative forces.

Subheadings:

1. Charity is the result of the manifestation of spiritual power.
2. The Soul of the Messiah will set an example of the ideal application of mental-psychic energy.
3. The zodiac is a set of causes of the manifestation of natural forces.
The universe is based on the law of mutual sacrifice of the lower to the higher and the service of the higher to the lower.

Thirteenth Arcanum

The general title: "changing stages of life".

Subheadings:

1. Immortality is essentially the "I", the subject of change is unchangeable
2. Death and reincarnation. Shells are borrowed from the objective environment. They are born and die according to subjective karma.
3. Transmutation of energies. In nature, nothing changes, but only changes its appearance. The primary energy of life takes various energy forms.
Death is the converter of the mother's life in the field of the diversity of its forms.
by natural phenomena.

The Fourteenth Arcanum

General title: "Personality".

Every organisation, including a human personality, is a product of mental and mental structure.

Subheadings:

1. Deduction (from general to particular). Any mental education, including human the human personality is a powerful product of deduction and spiritual postulates.
2. Comparability. The law of commensurability of the whole and the parts and comparability of the main coordinates ensure the viability of such formations.
3. Reversibility of processes. There is no irrevocable past. Any force process can be reversed to the previous state, although with a leak. The construction of personality is based on harmony between active and passive elements and the law of co-measurability of parts and the whole.

The Fifteenth Arcanum

General title: "Astral light".

The energy materials of the Earth are a field are a field of applications of the human creative will by combining force vortices in it.

Subheadings:

1. Logic. The ideomotor process of deduction is determined by the logic of the historical development of things.
2. Psychic energy. The psychomotor process implements the plans, and the psychic energy is similar to the human will in two directions (good and evil).
3. Fate (Rock). The consequences of the manifestation of the ideomotor and psychomotor process determine the overall picture of the historical paths of humanity and man that is, fate. The ability to apply yourself to the environment in the secondary and the environment to yourself in the main.

The Sixteenth Arcanum

The general title is "Coercion".

The domination of the human will over the energy potential of the Earth and the imprinting of its thoughts in it will force the object of this domination to new formations, introducing the principle of revolutionism into them.

Subheadings:

1. Logical exception. Materials that cannot be processed according to the design of the picture are subject to a logical exception.
2. Mental tension. It causes a mental tension in the environment, that is, the opposition of the eliminated elements.
3. Physical destruction is actually manifested by the collapse of old formations.

The assertion of one thesis or impulse acts through coercion and leads to the destruction of another thesis or impulse.

The Seventeenth Arcanum

General title: "Natural peace".

The necessary conditions for conscious construction are a mental balance and peace achieved by relying on the order introduced into the earthly conditions.

Subheadings:

1. Hope. Knowledge of the Will of the general picture is more achievable-
2. Intuition. Knowledge of the Will opens the consciousness to the general Plan and the ways of its implementation, which makes it possible to read the Akashic Chronicle.
3. Signs of nature. Reading the laws of nature-mind-the ability to find the prints of the Akashic Chronicle in natural combinations. The deployment of a new world is possible after the collapse of the previous one and after overcoming the resistance of the former elements.

The Eighteenth Arcanum

General title: "Reflected light".

Reflects the light of the guiding systems and the earthly teachers. It is a direct contact with the spiritual core of humanity.

Subheadings:

1. Occult Hierarchy. The occult hierarchy of the Priests stands between man and the divine consciousness.
2. Occult Obstacles. Discharges of psychic bombs, oppositional elements form occult dangers and obstacles to the implementation of the Hierarchical Will.
3. Occult enemies. Individualised images and invisible oppositional forces constitute a contingent of occult enemies that must be defeated.

The purpose of initiation - the expansion of consciousness to a cosmic volume is possible only when it is subordinated to hierarchies.

The Nineteenth Arcanum

General title: "Sunlight."

The thirst for direct contact with the spiritual world will direct the human consciousness to the solar light, that is, to find oneself as a creative spirit who does not resort to the support of his past helpers.

Subheadings:

1. Synthetic philosophy. Creating an invisible synthetic worldview, philosophy, which can, depending on the requirements of life, be expressed in any mental language.
2. The Great Work (Ethical Hermeticism). Finding a personal task of Doing Everything, bringing the Divine Principle into oneself.
3. The gold of the Philosophers (The Philosopher's Stone). Finding its objective task of searching for a mental philosopher's stone that turns the materials of the earth's nature into gold, that is, into a sublimated state.
The light of the spirit flashes only when the astral body is put in order by the previous work.

The Twentieth Arcanum

General title: "A new person".

The creation of a new person out of oneself implies a genuine responsibility.

Subheadings:

1. A person becomes God - like being radiating light.
2. Astral Resurrection. Resurrection, as an entry into a new cycle of consciousness of Cosmic citizenship and cooperation.
3. The acquisition of power over time as a tool of implementation of space tasks.
Development over time.

The Twenty-first Arcanum

The general title is "Love".

Getting out of Maya, that is, out of the old habitual representations and images created by humanity and shaking off self-hypnosis with facts.

Subheadings:

1. Radiation. Perception of the world as a process of one's own thought-creation.
2. Illusion. An understanding of the illusory nature of phenomena and the ability, if necessary, to identify with illusions, while remaining at the same time free from their effects.
3. The sign. The perception of facts as symbols, the growth of-experiencing spiritual changes.
Liberation.

The Twenty-second Arcanum

The general title is "The Realisation of the Great Work".

Merging of one's consciousness with the Divine Subject-volume, that is, with the original source.

Subheadings:

1. The Absolute. The rooting of consciousness in the Absolute, achieved by gradual stages of immersion.

2. The Magician's Crown. The knowledge of one's mission, that is, the potential possibility of the Absolute, which forms the core of consciousness.
3. Natural Omnipotence. Knowledge of the ways of creating illusions and methods of their implementation gives a natural omnipotence over the manifested world.

God is in me, and I am God in the flesh.

Odilon Redon, The Muse on Pegasus

	General title	1st subtitle	2nd subtitle	3rd subtitle
	Spiritual Plane	**Mental Plane**	**Astral Plane**	**Etheric Plane**
1	Self-consciousness Love	Divine Essence	Masculine origin	Nature Defining
2	Primary energy Life	Substance	Female Beginning	Nature Definable
3	Lotus-Miro-Divine Howl Mind The Creator	Nature	Principle Releases	Highlighting parts
4	Regularity	Development of xxx Dimension – causality	Authority	Form
5	Individualisation of life/construction/mental bodies	Religion	Individual initiative	Worldwide Connection
6	Two streams	Method of analogy	Freedom of choice, voli-tion	Broker
7	Secondary dominion Of the spirit of causality over the form	The principle hierarchies	Victory	Right owner-ship
8	Balances	The Justice Movement Libra		Karma
9	Subjective orientation, sublimation	Initiation		Caution, dedi-cation to world of facts
10	Objective Testament of the General Worldview Sublimation Benefits			Wheel of Life
11	Purity	Power Divine Hu-man	Power	Power Nature
12	Sacrifice	Mercy	Soul of the Messiah	Zodiac
13	Transitions	Immortality in Essence	Death and reincarnated	Transmutation Energy
14	Personality	Deduction, Commensurability, Reversibility Positive		
15	Astral (starlight)	Logic	Mental Energy	Rock
16	Coercion or necessity	Logical ex-ception	Psychological Tension	Physical Destruction
17	Honour	Hope	Intuition	Signs

				Nature
18	Limit	Occult Hierarchy		
19	Breaking the Limit	Vital Synthetic Philosophy	The Great Making	Philosophical Gold
20	Voice of Eternity, Divine Rebirth, changes in attraction or resurrection			Time
21	Love	Radiation	Illusion	Sign
22	Implementation The Great One Doing	Absolute	Crown, Mara	Divine Incarnation

Hymn to the Dream

Nina Roudnikova

A dream is stronger and brighter than a thought,
A dream will eclipse reality,
A dream will disperse the gloomy darkness
And it will illuminate you with a bright light.
The dream reigns. The mind only rules
Her impetuous horse;
He puts arches out of roses and laurels
And lays a carpet of flowers on the path.
And the strict mind pales before her
Labour will disappear in its rays.
She will dispel the swarm of doubts,
And the whole world falls into the dust.
Everything is available to her, everything is possible,
He breaks down obstacles with triumph,
Before her, everything is small, everything is insignificant,
How small is the idol before the Deity.
Her all-powerful carelessness,
Its flight height is...

Oh, vast as eternity,
Oh, radiant dream!

Index

Astrology, Parmigianino

Printed in France by Amazon
Brétigny-sur-Orge, FR

17791637R00208